EAT THIS NOT THAT!® 2013

The No-Diet Weight Loss Solution
Completely Updated and Expanded

BY DAVID ZINCZENKO
WITH MATT GOULDING

RODALE

This book is intended as a reference volume only, not as a medical manual. The information given here is designed to help you make informed decisions about your health. It is not intended as a substitute for any treatment that may have been prescribed by your doctor. If you suspect that you have a medical problem, we urge you to seek competent medical help.

Mention of specific companies, organizations, or authorities in this book does not imply endorsement by the author or publisher, nor does mention of specific companies, organizations, or authorities imply that they endorse this book, its author, or the publisher.

Internet addresses and telephone numbers given in this book were accurate at the time it went to press.

Eat This, Not That! is a registered trademark of Rodale Inc.

Rodale books may be purchased for business or promotional use or for special sales. For information, please write to: Special Markets Department, Rodale, Inc., 733 Third Avenue, New York, NY 10017

Printed in the United States of America

Rodale Inc. makes every effort to use acid-free ♾, recycled paper ♻.

Book design by George Karabotsos

Cover photos by Jeff Harris / Cover food styling by Roscoe Betsill
Hand modeling by Ashly Covington
Interior photo direction by Tara Long
All interior photos by Mitch Mandel and Thomas McDonald / Rodale Images
Food styling by Melissa Reiss with the exception of pages 291–309 by Diane Vezza.

Illustrations by R. Kikuo Johnson

Library of Congress Cataloging-in-Publication Data is on file with the publisher

ISBN-13: 978-1-60961-824-7 trade paperback
ISBN-13: 978-1-60961-567-3 direct-mail hardcover

Trade paperback and exclusive direct mail edition published simultaneously in September 2012.

Distributed to the trade by Macmillan
2 4 6 8 10 9 7 5 3 1 paperback
2 4 6 8 10 9 7 5 3 1 direct-mail hardcover

We inspire and enable people to improve their lives and the world around them.

rodalebooks.com

DEDICATION

To the 8 million men and women who have made ***EAT THIS, NOT THAT!*** a publishing phenomenon and who have spread the word to friends and relatives about the importance of knowing what's really in our food. Because of your passionate efforts, food manufacturers and restaurant chains are waking up to the fact that more and more of us demand good, solid information about our food, and healthy choices that will let us drop pounds and stay lean for life.

And to the men and women working in America's fields, farms, and supermarkets, waiting tables, and toiling in kitchens everywhere: It is because of your hard work that Americans have so many options. This book is designed to help us choose the best of what you've created.

—Dave and Matt

ACKNOWLEDGMENTS

This book is the product of thousands of meals, hundreds of conversations with nutritionists and industry experts, and the collective smarts, dedication, and raw talent of dozens of individuals. Our undying thanks to all of you who have inspired this project in any way. In particular:

To Maria Rodale and the Rodale family, whose dedication to improving the lives of their readers is apparent in every book and magazine they put their name on.

To George Karabotsos and his crew of immensely talented designers, including Mark Michaelson, Elizabeth Neal, Laura White, and Courtney Eltringham. You're the reason why each book looks better than the last.

To Clint Carter, Cathryne Keller, and Hannah McWilliams: Your tireless efforts behind the scenes makes these books what they are. Thanks for everything you do.

To Tara Long, who spends more time in the drive-thru and the supermarket aisles than anyone on the planet, all in the name of making us look good.

To Debbie McHugh, whose ability to keep us sane and focused under the most impossible circumstances cannot be overstated.

To Erin Williams: Your hard work ensures these books are as polished as possible. Thanks for dotting our i's and crossing our t's.

To Allison Keane, Kate Bittman, and Kateri Benjamin: Thanks for helping us get the word out.

To the Rodale book team: Steve Perrine, Chris Krogermeier, Sara Cox, Mitch Mandel, Tom MacDonald, Troy Schnyder, Melissa Reiss, Nikki Weber, Jennifer Giandomenico, Wendy Gable, Keith Biery, Liz Krenos, Brooke Myers, Nancy Elgin, Sonya Maynard, and Sean Sabo. You continue to do whatever it takes to get these books done. As always, we appreciate your heroic efforts. —Dave and Matt

Check out the other informative books in the ***EAT THIS, NOT THAT!***® and ***COOK THIS, NOT THAT!***™ series:

***Eat This, Not That! for Kids!* (2008)**

***Drink This, Not That!* (2010)**

***Cook This, Not That! Kitchen Survival Guide* (2010)**

***Grill This, Not That! Backyard Survival Guide* (2012)**

***Eat This, Not That! Supermarket Survival Guide* (2012)**

CONTENTS

It's Time to Make Friends with Food Again.

IF YOU'VE STRUGGLED with your weight, like two out of every three Americans today, then you've probably come to view food less like a friend and more like a frenemy. It's always around, and sure, it's fun to be with. And yet, you can't help but suspect that your favorite foods have an ulterior motive and a plan for stabbing you in the backside.

And you're not being paranoid. With all the news about "pink slime" in our hamburgers, all the confusion about gluten in our bread, and all the fuss over New York City's attempts to ban the Big Gulp, it's no wonder we've begun eyeing our favorite foods and beverages the way Eli Manning eyes a defensive lineman. Look out, it's cholesterol! No, it's saturated fat! No, wait, it's high-fructose corn syrup! Ahhh!

Well, it's time to pull the gravy train out of Food Dysfunction Junction. *Eat This, Not That!* is your guide to eating all of your favorite foods while effortlessly shedding 10, 20, 30 pounds or more. There's no magic diet plan, no deprivation period, no giving up the things you love. Instead, by making simple food swaps, you'll learn how to indulge to your belly's content—while making your belly shrink at the same time.

How is this possible? It's simply a matter of knowing a few secrets—secrets the food industry doesn't want you to know.

For example, let's say you want to go out

for a beer and some chicken wings. Order the Wings Any 3 Ways appetizer at Uno Chicago Grill and you've just downed 1,340 calories, 108 grams of fat, and more than 2 days' worth of sodium.

I know what you're thinking—oh, great, this guy's telling me I can't go out for wings anymore? Exactly wrong. With the nutritional guided missile that is *Eat This, Not That!*, you'll know that an order of Classic Buffalo Classic Wings at Applebee's has about half the fat and calories—and they're still decadent. Make that simple swap twice a week and you'll drop 19 pounds this year—without changing anything else about your diet. (You'll also lower your risk of high blood pressure significantly!)

Does that kind of weight loss sound too easy to be true? Well, don't take it from me. In the following pages, you'll meet men and women who have dropped 25, 50, 75 pounds or more. And they did it not by dieting, not by sacrificing, but by eating their favorite foods, whenever and wherever they liked. All that these successfully slimmed-down folks needed was to make a few smart swaps that helped them strip away hundreds of calories a day, like magic.

Maybe the idea of losing weight rapidly, and keeping it off permanently, seems about as plausible as Al Sharpton and Rush Limbaugh opening up a potpourri shop together. (Warning: Don't try to imagine what that would smell like.) Well, it isn't. But losing weight quickly and easily does require having a bit of knowledge and making some smart decisions—and that's what this book is designed to help you do. Whether you're whipping up breakfast at home, popping into the drive-thru for lunch, ordering up delivery for dinner, or swinging by the ice cream shop for dessert, you'll know instantly how to indulge your cravings, satisfy your taste buds, and still strip away hundreds of calories a day—without ever feeling hungry or deprived.

Is it really that simple? Yes. But before you move on and discover the thousands of amazing, indulgent, and delicious foods, from fast-food burgers to supermarket desserts, that are going to help you strip away fat fast, I want to share some eye-opening—and, literally, life-altering—information with you.

See, as the editor-in-chief of *Men's Health*, I've spent the past 2 decades interviewing leading experts, poring over groundbreaking studies, and grilling top athletes, trainers, and celebrities for their health and fitness advice. And over and over again, I've been shocked by how the traditional wisdom about nutrition that we all take for granted—nutrition myths, actually—have been proven untrue. Indeed,

"I shed a small person!"

Charlie Barzilla was in 3rd grade when he realized that he was bigger than other kids. Throughout grade school, he continued to outpace the growth of his peers, packing on 10 to 20 pounds every year. By the time he graduated high school, he had leveled off at 285. He was no longer gaining weight, but he wasn't losing it either. He was just a big guy. After a few false starts with diets and exercises he began to question whether he had a medical condition, perhaps something hormonal, that was making it impossible for him to lose weight. He didn't imagine it was his diet. He just ate what any big guy would eat. That couldn't be the problem, could it?

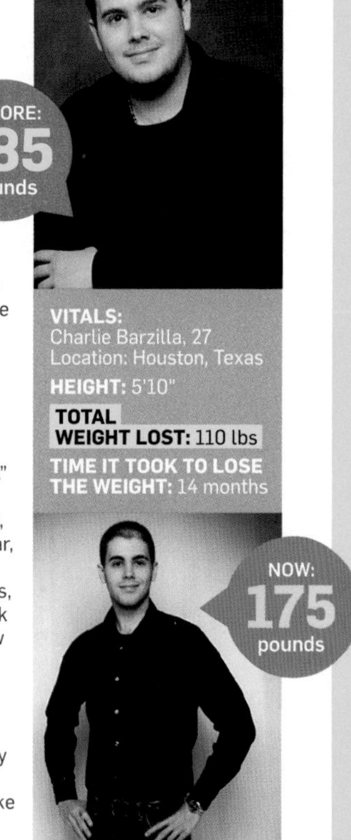

BEFORE:
285
pounds
VITALS:
Charlie Barzilla, 27
Location: Houston, Texas
HEIGHT: 5'10"
TOTAL WEIGHT LOST: 110 lbs
TIME IT TOOK TO LOSE THE WEIGHT: 14 months
NOW:
175
pounds

THE HARD TRUTH

Charlie scheduled an appointment with his doctor to investigate, and he discovered that he didn't suffer from any metabolic disorders. What he did suffer, however, was a high risk of insulin resistance and cardiovascular disease. "My doctor was blunt," says Charlie. "He told me, 'You are looking at diabetes and very likely a heart attack before age 30 if something doesn't change.'"

Diabetes and heart disease run in Charlie's family, but he wants a better life for himself. The doctor's warning convinced him that he needed to double down on his effort to lose weight.

Shortly after, Charlie discovered *Eat This, Not That!*, and he immediately recognized that it was different from the other weight-loss plans he'd seen. It was practical, something he could use without overhauling his lifestyle. He began carrying the book with him when he went out to eat, and he quickly identified his problem. "I had a habit of picking the worst thing on the menu, whether it was a bowl of fettuccine Alfredo with garlic bread or some double-meat, double-cheese burger slathered in mayonnaise," he says. Once he discovered how many calories he could save by making smart swaps, the weight started peeling off.

WHO'S THE NEW SKINNY GUY?

Charlie lost weight quickly, but he didn't realize the extent of his transformation until one day while shopping at the mall. Charlie ran into his uncle, whom he hadn't seen for months, but when he walked past, rather than saying hello, he gave Charlie a cursory glance and kept on moving. "He didn't even know who I was!" Charlie recalls. "That's when I realized that the mental image my whole family had of me didn't apply anymore." He kept using the book to shave calories from his diet, and in little more than a year, he had shed more than a third of his entire body mass, significantly reduced his risk of disease, and begun a new chapter in his life. "When I was overweight, I was always so self-conscious about what other people thought of me that I'd rarely go out of my way to talk to people," he says. "Now I take every chance I can to meet people, to go places, and to enjoy being young!"

when it comes to eating well, Americans' nutritional understanding is about as confused and unfair as the country's tax code. While 99 percent of us are overpaying in terms of calories eaten and belt holes loosened, the 1 percent—those who know the secrets—are padding their Swiss cheese bank accounts and partying it up on their private nutritional islands. We're on a diet; they're laughing up a riot!

Well, it's time to bust those myths. Let's democratize dessert, liberate libations, and let freedom Ring Ding. Knowing myth from reality is what separates the fit from the fat, the slim from the sloppy, the toned from the torpid. Here's a whole lot of eye-opening good news, starting with:

Nutrition News Flash #1: FAT WILL NOT MAKE YOU FAT!

→ In fact, not eating enough fat can make you fat. A 2008 study published in the *New England Journal of Medicine* found that a diet high in healthy fats proved to be superior to a low-fat diet, both in terms of weight loss and overall health benefits. Saturated and trans fats have given fat a bad name, but the truth is that the unsaturated fats found in foods like nuts, salmon, and olive oil are key components of a healthy diet.

Nutrition News Flash #2: BREAD WILL NOT MAKE YOU FAT!

→ The low-carb craze of the early 2000s had people terrified of breaking bread, but eating the right kinds of breads and other grains can actually help you lose weight. An *American Journal of Clinical Nutrition* study found that people who obtained most of their grain servings from whole grains had less belly fat than those who skipped the whole grains. The reason: The fiber found in whole-grain foods helps slow digestion, keeping you fuller longer. You should still avoid refined grains like "enriched" flour, but a moderate amount of whole-grain bread can be a great addition to a balanced diet. Tip: True whole-grain bread products will have "whole wheat" or "whole grain" flour as their first ingredient. If you see anything else, your "wheat" bread is an imposter.

Nutrition News Flash #3: SNACKING WILL NOT MAKE YOU FAT EITHER!

→ Mom may have told you that eating frequently is a surefire way to pack on the pounds, but she probably also told you that your face will freeze that way. In fact, snacking throughout the day is actually one of the best ways to avoid an expanding waistline. In a recent study from Alabama, researchers discovered that people who snacked four or more times a day took in fewer calories and had lower BMIs—a measure of obesity—than those who didn't snack at all. Why? Because consistent snacking helps maintain your blood sugar level, curbs cravings, and prevents your body from storing excess fat. The most effective snacks are high in protein and low in sugar. Two great options: nuts and (low-fat) dairy products, like yogurt (but beware of yogurts with added fruit, which are often high in sugar).

Nutrition News Flash #4: IT'S SAFE TO GO BACK TO STARBUCKS!

→ A 2006 study in the journal *Diabetes Care* showed that coffee drinkers were significantly less likely to develop type 2 diabetes, and other research has linked coffee consumption with reduced risks of Parkinson's disease, dementia, stroke, and depression. And get this: According to researchers from the University of Scranton in Pennsylvania, coffee is the number one source of antioxidants in the American diet. Yes, overdoing it in the morning can lead to the jitters and a bit of withdrawal by lunchtime, but pace your joe consumption throughout the day and you'll be fine.

Nutrition News Flash #5: FOCUSING ON FOOD WILL MAKE YOU SLIM!

→ One of the dumbest dieting tricks ever is the idea of distracting yourself to keep from eating. "Think about other things," you've been told: Your friends. Your 401(k). The game. Grandma's dentures. Anything that will get your mind off food, right? Well, no: According to Dutch researchers, thinking about snacks and meals can actually help you stay lean. The study found that when asked questions like "What will you do if you get hungry 2 hours before your next meal?" thinner participants were better able to give healthy responses, like "eat a handful of nuts." While fantasizing about how many onion rings you could feasibly fit on a double bacon cheeseburger is probably not going to keep the pounds at bay, taking a proactive approach to your diet by thinking ahead will. Try planning nutritious meals for the week or keeping healthy snacks like fruits and nuts on hand to ward off hunger.

Nutrition News Flash #6: DESSERT CAN WHITTLE YOUR WAISTLINE!

→ It doesn't just make life worth living; dessert just might help you stay lean, as well.

Studies have shown that completely eliminating foods you love can send you sailing straight into binge mode. Is chocolate mud pie good for you? No, and if you feel like you want to cut down on indulgences, go right ahead. But try allowing yourself a small dessert every day to satisfy your cravings without doing too much damage. Need help? Try a Breyers Smooth & Dreamy Chocolate Chip Cookie Dough Ice Cream Sandwich. It has a very reasonable 160 calories and 15 grams of sugars. Or try any of the dozens of terrific choices you'll find inside, starting on page 230.

Nutrition News Flash #7: A STEAK IS GOOD FOR YOUR HEART!

→ Harvard researchers recently discovered that while eating processed meats like hot dogs and bacon can contribute to heart disease, there is no such risk for people who consume only unprocessed meats. Meat is also a complete protein, providing all nine essential amino acids, and many studies have linked protein consumption with weight loss. Moreover, meat and other animal products are the only dietary sources of vitamin B12, which helps your body make blood cells and maintain a healthy nervous system. Now, this doesn't mean every meal should feature a T-bone that hangs over the edge of the plate: Leaner cuts are healthier.

Nutrition News Flash #8: CHOLESTEROL ISN'T SO BAD FOR YOU!

→ Perhaps the biggest nutrition myth is that dietary cholesterol is bad for your heart, a fact that's led many of us to cry fowl around eggs. But here's the truth: The dietary cholesterol found in eggs actually has little effect on the amount of cholesterol in your blood. When it comes to increasing LDL ("bad cholesterol"), trans and saturated fats are the real culprits. The incredible, edible egg is actually an excellent, affordable source of protein and B vitamins, and it may help you lose weight. A 2008 study in the *International Journal of Obesity* found that dieters who consumed two eggs for breakfast each day lost significantly more weight than those who consumed bagels.

So, bottom line: It's time to revitalize your relationship with food. It's time to pick out your true friends and cast aside the frenemies. And that's what this book will help you do. By learning a few simple swaps, you'll surround yourself with delicious and nutritious food friends, and you'll start seeing the pounds melt away—effortlessly. Ready to begin? Then just turn the page!

"I can finally wear the kind of clothes I've always wanted!"

Erin Fitzpatrick played basketball and lacrosse during high school and college, but no amount of training could offset the damage of a diet built around soda and fast food. It wasn't that she didn't notice her weight; it just never clicked in her mind how quickly the junk-food calories stacked up.

Erin spent a semester abroad in Ireland, and her willpower wore thin under the novelty of new foods in a new environment. "I told myself it was worth it for this once-in-a-lifetime experience." She returned to school larger than she'd ever been, and for the first time in her life, she felt defeated. It was as if she'd left her confidence behind in Ireland. With money tight, she couldn't justify the expense of Weight Watchers or Jenny Craig, so she graduated unsure of her future and dissatisfied with her body.

BEFORE: 181 pounds

VITALS:
Erin Fitzpatrick, 25
Location: Charleston, SC

HEIGHT: 5'6"

TOTAL WEIGHT LOST: 41 lbs

TIME IT TOOK TO LOSE THE WEIGHT: 11 months

NOW: 140 pounds

A NEW PAGE

A year and a half after graduation, Erin's brother in South Carolina was looking for a nanny. She decided to make the move; she needed a fresh start.

Shortly after her arrival, she discovered that her brother and sister-in-law were using weight-loss advice from *Eat This, Not That!* and making home-cooked meals from *Cook This, Not That!* Erin purchased her own copies and took them home. Every Sunday she sat down with the books and created a week's worth of recipes. "It made it easy—what I had in the house was what I was going to eat for the week," she explains. She was still eating out occasionally, but she relied on *Eat This, Not That!* to guide her to lower-calorie options. As the weight came off, Erin started feeling better about herself. And because she had more energy, she started running and taking group cardio classes.

HAPPINESS RESTORED

Within a year, Erin had reached her target weight, and people took notice. "When I saw friends I hadn't seen since the previous fall, they were floored," she says. One friend did a double take, picked her up, and spun her in the air. "He told me that he'd never seen me so happy."

Although Erin's no longer trying to lose weight, she hasn't given up her favorite *Cook This, Not That!* recipes. "Now I even have my friends cooking from *Cook This, Not That!*" By making smart decisions about what to eat, Erin lost the weight that was dragging her down. "I spent so many years wishing and waiting for when I would feel good about how I looked," she says. "Now I do."

Are You as Tired of Being Lied to as I Am?

AS I WRITE THESE WORDS, the 2012 election season is in full swing. Which means that we've already had our fill of malicious mendacity, dastardly duplicity, and conniving complicity.

Well, I have some good news and some bad news: Election season doesn't go on forever. But lying season is open year-round. Because even after every last bit of confetti has been swept from the floor of some distant convention center, you can bet there will still be a bull market for bull down at your local grocery store or chain restaurant.

You see, many of the barking nutritional claims on the supermarket shelves and the dazzling descriptions on your favorite restaurant menus are nothing but a pile of baloney, sandwiched between two slices of toasted flimflammery. But unless you have a Ph.D. in nutrition, you might not realize that the food world is as full of shysterism as the campaign trail. Every time you walk into a grocery store or a restaurant, food marketers are trying to feed you a line of bull.

That's why we launched the *Eat This, Not That!* book series 5 years ago. By playing David to Big Food's Goliath, we keep the food industry honest. Consider:

- After an April 2008 *Eat This, Not That!* blog post names Baskin-Robbins's 2,310-calorie Health Bar milk shake "the Worst Drink on the Planet," the company pulls the product, and eventually scraps its entire line of "premium" milk shakes.
- A month later, Jamba Juice eliminates its Power (read "enormous") size Chocolate Moo'd Power Smoothie and, in a letter to

Eat This, Not That!, company spokesman Tom Suiter declares the company's goal of becoming "the healthiest restaurant chain in America."

- In June 2009, *Eat This, Not That!* exposes Jack in the Box's Bacon Cheddar Potato Wedges as the Trans Fattiest Food in America. The company responds by replacing its fryer oil with trans-fat-free oil.
- In 2010, after several years of *Eat This, Not That!* demanding restaurants disclose their nutrition content, President Obama signs just such a mandate into law.
- In 2011, Carl's Jr. and Hardee's—whose CEO declared "healthy eating" to be a manufactured media concept back in 2009—go national with their *Eat This, Not That!* menu of burgers, all under 500 calories.
- After a March 2012 *Eat This, Not That!* story calls out the restaurant chains that fudge their serving sizes to make their calorie counts appear lower, both P.F. Chang's and Uno Chicago Grill straighten up and adjust their nutrition information to accurately reflect their generous serving sizes.

More than 6 million books later, the mind set of hungry Americans is clearly changing. For example, recent polls show up to 96 percent of us would like genetically modified foods to be clearly labeled, and 70 percent of U.S. diners want more transparency about the sourcing and nutrition value of menu items.

But until those improvements come to pass, you'll have to take your nutrition fate into your own hands. The shelves of your local supermarket and the pages of your favorite chain's menu are rife with health food impostors, and it's up to you—and me—to call them out. Some of these shady products are so egregious, in fact, that I believe they deserve a swift smack from the heavy hand of the law. Below I throw the book at seven foods that just aren't what they seem.

FOOD LABEL LIE #7
SUNNYD

The Crime: The Day-Glo liquid presents itself as a delicious, nutritious alternative to orange juice, but in truth, it's little more than sweetened water.

The Evidence: Look at the label. The vast majority of this bottle consists of water and corn syrup, with less than 2 percent coming from concentrated juice swirled with artificial colors, sweeteners, canola oil, and sodium hexametaphosphate (don't ask). The beverage company bases its vague nutrition claims ("reverse-engineered from the sun"?) on the fact that SunnyD contains 80 percent of your daily recommended vitamin C. But you know what else has 100 percent of your day's vitamin C? A cup of chopped broccoli, a few thick slices of red bell pepper, a medium orange, or a multivitamin. Also condemnable is SunnyD's current marketing campaign, which encourages children to collect SunnyD labels to exchange for schoolbooks. Care for some diabetes with that diploma?

The Takeaway: "Fruit flavored" is no substitute for real fruit. If you want the full nutritional package, buy fresh, unadulterated produce—or at the very least 100 percent juice.

FOOD LABEL LIE #6

SIMPLY NATURAL CHEETOS WHITE CHEDDAR PUFFS

The Crime: Abuse of the term "natural." Last I checked, Cheetos don't grow in the wild.

The Evidence: When was the last time you saw a flowering field of torula yeast? Or how about a fresh crop of maltodextrin? Didn't think so. These cheese puffs consist largely of corn, but they've been processed to the point that no 20th-century farmer would ever recognize them as food. What's more, compared with regular Cheetos Puffs, they only have about 10 fewer calories per serving. Oh, and see those "natural flavors" on the ingredient statement? By FDA standards, those don't even have to relate to the food in question. For all we know, those are tinctures made from bovine bone marrow.

The Takeaway: Except in the instance of some meat products, the FDA doesn't regulate use of the word "natural," leaving the food industry free to define it on its own terms. In 2008, natural products reached $22 billion in sales. Defend yourself by reading the ingredient statement. If you can't pronounce it, it probably ain't natural.

FOOD LABEL LIE #5

MOTT'S MEDLEYS FRUIT AND VEGETABLE JUICE

The Crime: Although wholesome by juice standards, this one is promoted to parents as a substitute for real fruits and vegetables. But fruits and vegetables have fiber; Mott's has none.

The Evidence: The Mott's label says that 8 ounces contains 2 servings of fruits and vegetables, and sadly, the USDA agrees. The government's MyPlate considers juice to be a suitable substitute for produce. But here's why it's not: One of the biggest health boons of fruits and vegetables is their fiber, which fills the stomach, slows digestion, and fights disease. According to a recent study published in the *Archives of Internal Medicine*, people who consume the most fiber have a 22 percent lower chance of premature death from any cause. Yet at the current rate of consumption, Americans are getting only about half the fiber they need.

A single apple has more than 4 grams of fiber. That's about 4 grams more than a 46-ounce bottle of Mott's Medleys Apple and Carrot Juice Blend.

The Takeaway: Modest amounts of juice can fit into a healthy diet, but it's no substitute for whole produce.

FOOD LABEL LIE #4

MISSION GARDEN SPINACH HERB WRAPS

The Crime: Mission's "Garden Spinach Herb" wraps are guilty of identity theft—there's no spinach to be found in these crooked tortillas!

The Evidence: Along with a ton of unnatural, unhealthy ingredients like enriched flour, these spinach imposters contain 2 percent or less of "spinach powder" seasoning. Yum! And the wraps' green color? Courtesy of food dyes Yellow #5 and Blue #1.

The Takeaway: Don't judge a book by its cover—or a product by its package. The front label is little more than an advertisement for the company, so for legitimately useful information, look to the Nutrition Facts panel and the ingredient statement. And remember: Just because a food is "flavored" like a whole food doesn't mean it contains a whole food.

FOOD LABEL LIE #3

DORITOS

The Crime: On its nutrition label, Frito-Lay reassures us that Doritos contain zero gram of trans fats. Problem is, it's a blatant lie!

The Evidence: Partially hydrogenated oil is the primary source of trans fats, and these cheesy chips contain two types: partially hydrogenated soybean oil and partially hydrogenated cottonseed oil. So how does the company get away with the "zero gram" claim, you ask? The FDA allows manufacturers to market products as trans fat free if they contain less than 0.5 gram of the artery-clogging acids per serving. But get this: The American Heart Association recommends we max out our trans fat intake at about 2 grams per day, so if you're regularly eating foods with 0.49 gram per serving, then you can easily surpass that limit without knowing. That could lead to a host of cardiovascular problems, and one recent Spanish study even linked increased trans fat consumption with a lower quality of life and overall happiness.

The Takeaway: At the risk of belaboring the point: Read the ingredient statement. If you see anything that's been "partially hydrogenated," you have a trans fatty food in your hand. Set it down and nobody will get hurt—least of all you.

FOOD LABEL LIE #2

APPLEBEE'S WEIGHT WATCHERS GRILLED JALAPENO-LIME SHRIMP

The Crime: This Weight Watchers entrée carries a heavy burden of guilt—for containing a shameful amount of salt.

The Evidence: Applebee's loads this dish with 2,950 milligrams of blood-pressure-spiking sodium, far exceeding the USDA's recommended daily limit of 2,300 milligrams (for some people, like those at risk for hypertension, it's only 1,500 milligrams!). And the Applebee's marketing team has the nerve to put this on the restaurant's Weight Watchers menu? Guffaw! Sadly, Applebee's isn't the only guilty restaurant when it comes to the sins of salt. Chains like Chili's and Cheesecake Factory, for example, also pack egregious amounts of sodium into specialty items geared toward health-conscious eaters.

The Takeaway: In terms of calories, diet or "light" options are usually superior to other items on a chain's menu, but almost all major chain restaurants still take a heavy-handed approach with the salt shaker. If you're going to eat out, make an effort to keep your sodium intake as low as possible for the rest of the day.

FOOD LABEL LIE #1

WENDY'S NATURAL-CUT FRIES

The Crime: Wendy's promotes these spuds as a healthy alternative to typical fries—the chain's Web site boasts that they're "naturally cut from whole Russet potatoes" and seasoned with "a sprinkle of sea salt." But there's more to it than that.

The Evidence: A quick skim through Wendy's ingredient statement is all it takes to expose these fraudulent spuds. They contain preservatives, added sugars, and hydrogenated oil. Last I checked, there was nothing remotely natural about infusing vegetable oil with hydrogen. Technically, Wendy's isn't lying when it says that these fries are "natural-cut." But it makes one wonder: What would be the unnatural way to cut a potato?

The Takeaway: Restaurants toss out buzzwords like "natural," "fresh," and "wholesome" as a clever way of making not-so-nutritious items seem closer to what you'd make at home. Truth is, food manufacturers haven't found a way to align your health with their profits, and until they do, the onus of healthy eating is on you and you alone.

6 Gross Things You Didn't Know You Were Eating

Q: What do these things have in common?

- → Mold
- → Maggots
- → Rocket fuel
- → Staph infection bacteria

A: They can all be in your food. Legally.

DISTURBING, RIGHT? Yet researchers for our parent company's Web site, Rodale.com, have discovered that the food you buy in grocery stores isn't nearly as safe or as healthy as you'd like it to be. Perhaps that's why 48,000 Americans develop food poisoning every year.

So what can you do about it? Protect yourself by asking questions. It's your food; you have a right to know what's inside. I'll even give you a head start: Here are the six most gag-inducing foods in your supermarket.

1 PINK SLIME IN BEEF

The Gross Factor: The meat industry likes to call it "lean finely textured beef," but after ABC News ran a story on it, the public just called it what it looks like—pink slime. It's a mixture of waste meat and fatty parts from higher-quality cuts of beef that have had the fat mechanically removed. Afterward, it's treated with ammonia gas to kill salmonella and E. coli bacteria. Then it gets added to ground beef as a filler. Food microbiologists and meat producers insist that it's safe, but based on the public's reaction to the ABC News report, there's an ick factor we just can't overcome. The primary producer of pink slime closed three of the plants where pink slime was produced in May, and Kroger, Safeway, Food Lion, McDonald's, and all but three states participating in the National School Lunch Program (among other outlets) have pulled it from their product offerings.

Eat This Instead: Organic ground beef is prohibited from containing pink slime by the National Organic Program standards, so it's your safest bet. If you can't find organic, ask the butcher at your grocery store whether their products contain the gunk.

2 MERCURY IN FRUIT DRINKS

The Gross Factor: Sugary and calorie laden, those drinks are often sweetened with high-fructose corn syrup (HFCS), which, according to tests from the Institute for Agriculture and Trade Policy, may be contaminated with mercury. The group tested 55 brand-name foods in which HFCS was the leading or second highest ingredient listed and found mercury in a third of them.

Eat This Instead: Buy only 100 percent juice. And opt for HFCS-free versions of other foods as well. The processed sweetener lurks in seemingly all processed foods.

3 MRSA IN MEAT

The Gross Factor: Hard-to-treat, antibiotic-resistant infections are no joke. Superbug strains like MRSA (a form of the bacteria that cause staph infections) infect 90,000 people—and kill 15,000—people annually in the United States. In January 2012, University of Iowa researchers found the dangerous organisms to be prevalent in supermarket meat. One theory is that the overuse of antibiotics on factory farms has caused the MRSA bug to grow resistant and more difficult to kill. In the study, researchers looked specifically at supermarket pork and discovered MRSA in 7 percent of samples tested. The bacteria die during proper cooking, but improper handling could leave you infected.

Eat This Instead: The University of Iowa researchers found conventional meat and store-bought "antibiotic free" meat with MRSA was likely contaminated at the processing plant. Search LocalHarvest.org to source meat from small-scale producers who don't use antibiotics or huge processing plants.

4 ROCKET FUEL IN LETTUCE

The Gross Factor: Lettuce is a great source of antioxidants, and thanks to the great state of California, we can now eat it all year long. However, much of the lettuce grown in California is irrigated with water from the Colorado River. According to the Environmental Protection Agency, Colorado River water is contaminated with low levels of perchlorate, a component of rocket fuel known to harm thyroid function, and perchlorate can be taken up inside lettuce plants. A separate study from the Environmental Working Group found perchlorate in 18 percent of store-bought fall and winter lettuce samples.

Eat This Instead: Perchlorate is hard to avoid, but some of the highest levels in the country have been found in California's agricultural regions. If you eat locally and in season, you can ask your local farmers whether it's a problem in their irrigation water supply.

5 MOLDY BERRIES

The Gross Factor: The FDA legally allows up to a 60 percent mold count in canned or frozen blackberries and raspberries. Canned fruit and vegetable juices are allowed to contain up to 20 percent mold.

Eat This Instead: Go for fresh! When berries are in season, stock up and freeze them yourself to eat throughout the winter. To freeze them, just spread fruits out on a cookie sheet, set the sheet in your freezer for a few hours, then transfer the berries to a glass jar or other airtight, freezer-safe container.

6 BUG PIECES IN... EVERYTHING!

The Gross Factor: I realize that in some parts of the world, bugs are considered a reliable source of protein. But here in America, we like to think our food is relatively bug free. Often, it isn't. Here are some of the gnarliest offenders:

- **THRIPS.** At anywhere from 1/25 to 1/8 of an inch long, these tiny winged parasites are legally allowed in apple butter, canned or frozen asparagus, frozen broccoli, sauerkraut, canned or frozen spinach, and frozen brussels sprouts.
- **APHIDS.** Those same little green or black bugs that can destroy a bouquet of flowers can infiltrate your frozen veggies, particularly spinach, broccoli, and brussels sprouts. And if you home-brew beer, you might consider growing your own hops: The FDA legally allows 2,500 aphids for every 10 grams of hops.
- **MITES.** These tiny white bugs are common in wheat and other grains that have been stored for a while, but expect to eat a few with your frozen vegetables, too. And if you have indoor allergies, that could be a problem. Storage and grain mites can cause the same type of allergic reaction as the dust mites common in homes.
- **MAGGOTS.** If you've ever eaten canned food, you've probably also eaten a maggot. These disgusting little critters abound in things like canned mushrooms, canned tomatoes, tomato paste, and pizza sauces. Mushrooms are by far the worst: 20 maggots are allowed for every 100 grams of drained mushrooms, compared with between 1 and 5 for every 500 grams of tomato products.
- **FRUIT FLIES.** Buy a piece of fruit covered in fruit flies, and you can wash them off. Buy a can of citrus juice, and you'll be swilling 5 fruit-fly eggs with every 8-ounce cup of juice. Grab an 8-ounce handful of golden raisins and you could be eating as many as 35 fruit-fly eggs.
- **COWPEA CURCULIO.** Love black-eyed peas? Buy them dried and cook them yourself, rather than buying them canned. A can of black-eyed peas, cowpeas, or field peas may contain up to an average of five or more cowpea curculio larvae, which would have grown into bronze-black, humpback beetles that infest all manner of peas and beans.
- **CATERPILLARS.** Fuzzy, ugly caterpillars are supposed to turn into beautiful butterflies for people to marvel at—not eat in a mouthful of frozen spinach. But along with the 50 or so aphids, mites, and/or thrips allowed in 100 grams of canned or frozen spinach, you may also find yourself munching on caterpillar larvae and larval fragments. Mmm . . . probably not what was giving Popeye all that strength.

Everything Is BIGGER!

WANT MORE EVIDENCE that our obesity crisis is getting entirely out of hand? Everything around us seems to be getting bigger, except our bank accounts. And there's a direct relationship: Nearly 10 percent of all American medical dollars are now spent on obesity. In fact, people who are obese spend almost $1,500 more each year on health care—about 41 percent more than average-weight people. Everything from our insurance costs to the price of airline tickets is increasing, in part because of obesity. So you can either laugh or get ticked off when you realize...

Buses Are Getting Bigger!

The Federal Transit Administration wants to raise the assumed average weight of bus passengers from 150 to 175 pounds, claiming that previous assumptions were built on people looking as they did during the *Mad Men* era. In addition, the FTA also suggests increasing the space allotment for standing bus passengers to 1.75 square feet of floor space, up from the current 1.5 square feet, "to acknowledge the expanding girth of the average passenger," according to the *New York Times*.

Boats Are Getting Bigger!

The Coast Guard now says that fewer of us can fit on standard-size boats, so it's increased the assumed average weight per person (the aptly abbreviated "AAWPP"!) to 185 pounds. Next Halloween, try the Coast Guard's new game: bobbing for apple-shaped people.

Bosoms Are Getting Bigger!

The bra size needed by the average American woman has gone up 2 cup sizes since the mid-1980s. Fifty years ago, DD was the largest size you could find, but today lingerie shops stock bras with K, L, and even O cups, according to the Intimate Apparel Council. Last year, according to the founder of the Intimacy retail chain, it sold 70,000 bras that were sizes G and up.

Babies Are Getting Bigger!

One-third of infants in the United States are obese or at risk for obesity, according to a Wayne State University study. But don't let your baby get hung up on his or her weight. We've got the perfect solution.

Cats and Dogs Are Getting Bigger!

More than half of all domestic pets are now overweight or obese. "Roll over. Stay. Good dog."

Military Recruits Are Getting Bigger!

Which at first sounds like a good thing—who wouldn't want to send a battalion of supersized soldiers off to face the commies, or the terrorists, or whomever we're fighting next? But our soldiers aren't supersized in quite the right way. "Overall only 1 in 4 of our young adults between the ages of 17 and 24 is eligible for military service," says retired Rear Admiral James Barnett. Obesity is one of the main reasons, he says.

Movie Theaters Are Getting Bigger!

Theaters now spend nearly a third more on their building space than they did just 20 years ago, the result of having to accommodate larger moviegoers. The average seat has increased from 20 inches to as wide as 26 inches. Perhaps smaller tubs of popcorn would help?

Ambulances Are Getting Bigger!

Boston's emergency services retrofitted an ambulance to make it capable of ferrying people of up to 850 pounds. Geez, that's seven 1950s–era humans! But of course, getting an 850-pound patient safely to the hospital is just half the battle . . .

Gurneys Are Getting Bigger!

New "bariatric cots" made to carry patients weighing up to 1,600 pounds are being introduced around the country, although they can cost four times as much as simple cots. Talk about your tax dollars being eaten up!

Coffins Are Getting Bigger!

Just in case your community hasn't invested in one of those bariatric cots, there's a backup plan: Goliath Casket makes models of up to 52 inches wide, capable of holding the massive body those cots would have been transporting. "We sell about 300 caskets per year, and my records show the average age of the deceased is 45 or younger," says Keith Davis, the company's president. Of course, we're going to need some bigger graves . . .

Ultimate Food-Fighting Championships

Tostitos All Natural "Chunky" Salsa takes on Dean's "French" Onion Dip in a classic showdown of fierce competitors. Which one will help you fit into the championship belt?

Hello, folks, and thanks for joining us. I'm Joe Buckwheat....

And I'm Choy Bokman...

And welcome to the Ultimate Food-Fighting Championships, 2013 edition. Choy, it's been a long, hot summer for these two competitors. They've been seen circling one another at pool parties and barbecues. But they don't exactly get along, do they?

Not at all, Joe. In fact, you could say Salsa and Onion Dip both have chips on their shoulders—broken chips.

It's tough to be an afterthought, Choy. When people put together a spread, they want it to be healthy, so they're focusing on the sandwiches, the beverages, the desserts. But nobody realizes that the match is won or lost in the trenches—the trenches you dig with your chips.

This bout could be a make-or-break battle for the belt. Let's go over some UFFC modified ground rules. First, no chokeholds in this food fight.

Choking would be bad, Choy.

Second, the UFFC has suspended cage matches, due to protests by the chicken-fighting contingent.

They've replaced them with a cage-free standard, the Octagon Bowl Match. We fully support the UFFC's decision to insist that competitors beat each other into a bloody pulp in a politically correct way.

And there's the opening bell. Onion Dip comes out strong. You've got to admire Onion Dip's strong, healthy roots. There's nothing better for you than an onion. And Onion Dip strikes first: He tries a flying fiber kick, but no impact!

Salsa seems taken aback, Choy. Given what we know about onions, I think he was expecting Onion Dip to come on stronger. Onion Dip seems to have no nutritional punch at all.

But Onion Dip weighs in at SIX TIMES Salsa's calorie count!

Now Onion Dip is trying the vitamin-and-mineral route, but there's nothing there—zero vitamin A, zero C, zero iron. Salsa senses the weakness: He's countering with a solid dose of lycopene, 10 percent of your vitamin C intake, and now he's pummeling Onion with vitamin A as well.

Onion's trying to grab hold of Salsa, but he can't seem to maintain his grip.

It's the palm oil, Choy! Onion Dip's top four ingredients are skim milk, whey, water and...palm oil.

Salsa's coming on strong with a battery of vegetables—tomatoes, peppers...even onions! Onion Dip is already folding—turns out, it's less than 2 percent onion!

And French Onion Dip taps out! A lot of hype, Choy, but not much French resistance here.

DING!
DING!
DING!

Salsa is the new Ultimate Food-Fighting Champion. And Onion Dip—well, that's a sad case, Joe.

Brings a tear to your eye, Choy.

Onion always does.

How to lose weight with this book

While a lot of factors come into play, the most effective way to lose weight is to take in fewer calories than you burn.

The basic formula is this: Calories in – calories out = total weight loss or gain. This is the equation that determines whether your body will shape up to look more like a slender 1 or a paunchy 0, a flat-bellied yardstick or a pot-bellied protractor. That's why it's absolutely critical that you have some understanding of what sort of numbers you're plugging into this formula.

On the "calories out" side, we have your daily activities: cleaning house, standing in line at the post office, hauling in groceries, and so on. Often when people discover extra flab hanging around their midsections, they assume there's something wrong with this side of the equation. Maybe so, but more likely it's the front end of the equation—the "calories in" side—that's tipping the scale. That side keeps track of all the cookies, fried chicken, and piles of pasta that you eat every day.

In order to maintain a healthy body weight, a moderately active female between the ages of 20 and 50 needs only 2,000 to 2,200 calories per day. A male fitting the same profile needs 2,400 to 2,600. Those numbers can fluctuate depending on whether you're taller or shorter than average or whether you spend more or less time exercising, but they represent reasonable estimations for most people. (For a more accurate assessment, use the calorie calculator at mayoclinic.com.)

Let's take a closer look at the numbers: It takes 3,500 calories to create a pound of body fat. So if you eat an extra 500 per day—the amount in one Dunkin' Donuts' Blueberry Crumb Donut—then you'll earn 1 new pound of body fat each week. Make that a habit—like so many of us do unwittingly—and you'll gain 52 pounds of flab per year!

That's where this book comes in. Within these pages are literally hundreds of simple food swaps that will save you from 10 to 1,000 calories or more apiece. The more often you choose "Eat This" foods over "Not That!" options, the quicker you'll notice layers of fat melting away from your body. Check this out:

- A single cup of APPLE CINNAMON CHEERIOS cereal has 160 calories. Switch to KELLOGG'S APPLE JACKS five times per week and you'll drop 4½ pounds this year.

- A GRANDE JAVA CHIP FRAPPUCCINO from Starbucks has 440 calories. Switch to an ESPRESSO FRAPPUCCINO three times per week and you'll shed 5 pounds in 6 months.

- HAAGEN-DAZS MINT CHIP ICE CREAM has 300 calories. Switch to the Breyers version of the same flavor four times a week and you'll drop more than 2 pounds every 4 months.

- An ORIENTAL CHICKEN SALAD from Applebee's packs an astounding 1,380 calories. Instead, order the ASIAGO PEPPERCORN STEAK three times per week—or make a comparable swap at some other restaurant—and you'll blast away nearly 7 pounds of body fat in just 2 months.

And here's the best news of all: These swaps aren't isolated calorie savers. If you commit yourself to just the four on this list, the cumulative calorie-saving effect will stamp out 1 pound of body fat every week this year. Take that, multigrain bagel! Check out more of our favorite calorie-squashing, fat-melting Top Swaps on the following pages.

TOP SWAPS

BURGER

Eat This!
Steak 'n Shake Double Steakburger with Cheese
440 calories
25 g fat
(11 g saturated, 1 g trans)
590 mg sodium

Save!
233 calories and 18 grams of fat!

Not That!
Five Guys Little Cheeseburger with Lettuce, Tomato, Onions, and Mayo
673 calories
43 g fat
(17 g saturated)
772 mg sodium

In the battle between two of America's fastest-growing burger chains, the East Coast titan gets trounced by the scrappy Midwestern patty shack. Five Guys' smallest, relatively restrained cheeseburger packs more calories than a Big Mac and 233 calories more than a bilevel cheeseburger from Steak 'n Shake. From a sheer flavor standpoint, it's hard to argue that both places aren't putting out burgers superior to the hamburger heavyweights (after all, they're cooking fresh ground beef on flattops to order), but Five Guys proves fresh and healthy often have very little to do with each other.

PASTA

Eat This!
Olive Garden Capellini di Mare
650 calories
18 g fat (5 g saturated)
1,830 mg sodium
Not That!
Romano's Macaroni Grill Pasta di Mare
1,310 calories
57 g fat (16 g saturated)
1,900 mg sodium
Save!
660 calories and 39 grams of fat!

In Italian, *di mare* means "of the sea," and when done correctly, it brings in a load of protein-rich shellfish to offset the starch-heavy noodles. At Romano's, that's not the case. The 1,310-calorie bowl contains 11 times more carbohydrates than protein. Olive Garden's version, on the other hand, packs an impressive 41 grams of protein for a solid one-to-two ratio of protein to carbs. It's shocking just how different these dishes are: Both feature spaghetti, olive oil, wine, garlic, and tomatoes, yet somehow Romano's comes out with twice the calories and an inexplicable glut of saturated fat.

BREAKFAST BURRITO

Eat This!
Burger King Sausage Breakfast Burrito
290 calories
17 g fat (7 g saturated)
830 mg sodium

Not That!
Chick-fil-A Sausage Breakfast Burrito
500 calories
28 g fat (11 g saturated)
880 mg sodium

Save!
210 calories and 11 grams of fat!

When it comes to dependably low-calorie fast-food chicken sandwiches, Chick-fil-A has the market cornered, but if you're on the hunt for sausage and egg wrapped in a warm tortilla, keep on driving. The chicken purveyor's breakfast burrito has as much fat as seven Chargrilled Chicken Sandwiches, not to mention unwholesome injections of partially hydrogenated oils and other unpronounceable chemicals. Burger King's burrito, on the other hand, is surprisingly balanced, relying on just enough sausage to add flavor without excess fat.

CHICKEN ENTRÉE

The difference between these two meals can be only partly explained by the fact that Ruby Tuesday grills its chicken instead of frying it. California Pizza Kitchen's dish looks like an inverted salad, after all. Where could all that fat come from? The chain doesn't provide the data we'd need to explain it, but judging by the numbers, you could expect this dish to have 75 grams of fat—roughly four times what you'll find in Ruby Tuesday's dish. Make this swap twice a week and you'll save 20 pounds within a year.

SALAD

According to Chevys' menu, its Chicken Fajita Salad is "about to go viral it's so good." Which makes us wonder: Do you really want to eat a viral salad? No, you do not. Not if it looks like this, anyway. The dressing alone supplies as many calories as a chicken enchilada with a side of Mexican rice and has more sugar than one and a half bowls of Lucky Charms. And it's a diabolical act of salad engineering that even allows these greens to support such a heavy load of cheese and tortilla chips. Chili's version, on the other hand, relies on low-calorie, high-impact ingredients like chili peppers, pico de gallo, and cilantro to amp up the flavor, and it applies tortilla strips and avocado judiciously to satisfy your taste buds without damaging your waistline.

RIBS

Before there were refrigerators, man preserved meat by packing it in salt. Apparently nobody told Chili's that we don't have to do that anymore. This rack is not only weighed down by more than a full day's worth of sodium, but also packs the maximum amount of saturated fat you should consume in a 24-hour span. There's no escaping the fact that pork ribs are a fatty cut of meat, but there's no excuse for this kind of negligence. Choose Ruby Tuesday's instead and you cut more than 300 calories, roughly 75 percent of which comes from the elimination of excessive fat.

PIZZA

Eat This!
Domino's Artisan Italian Sausage & Pepper Trio (2 slices)
320 calories
14 g fat (5 g saturated)
660 mg sodium
Not That!
Pizza Hut Italian Sausage & Red Onion Pan Pizza (medium, 2 slices)
540 calories
26 g fat (9 g saturated)
1,120 mg sodium
Save!
220 calories and 12 grams of fat!

Pizza Hut's pie represents pizza's two great pitfalls: oversized crust and fatty meat. That pushes carbs and fat to the forefront and relegates protein to a supporting role, a bad strategy if you like to eat pizza regularly (who doesn't?). Domino's exceptional new Artisan line relies on relatively thin crusts and lean toppings, and with this particular pizza, the trio of flavor-dense peppers prevents the heavier sausage from overrunning the pie. The end result is one of the best pizzas in America, decadent enough to crave a serious pizza craving, lean enough to eat on a regular basis.

SUB

Not That!
Quiznos Turkey Bacon Guacamole Sub (regular)
850 calories
42 g fat (11 g saturated, 0.5 g trans)
2,070 mg sodium

Save!
450 calories and 28 grams of fat!

Eat This!
Subway Turkey & Bacon Avocado Sub (6")
400 calories
14 g fat (3.5 g saturated)
1,000 mg sodium

On the nutritional battlefield, Subway's subs win nearly every time, and this is no exception. Quizno's liberal condiment policy allows for two calorie-dense spreads on this sandwich—guacamole and ranch—which combine to sabotage any shot at a light lunch. Subway's version balances indulgence (bacon, avocado) with refreshing simplicity (no excess condiments, all of the fresh vegetables you want). Plus your heart will thank you. Subway slashed sodium from every sandwich last year, minimizing the salty strain on your cardiovascular system.

SMOOTHIE

Eat This!
Jamba Juice Light Strawberry Nirvana
(Power size, 30 fl oz)
300 calories
0.5 g fat
58 g sugars

Not That!
Smoothie King Lemon Twist Strawberry
(32 fl oz)
657 calories
0 g fat
156 g sugars

Save!
357 calories and 98 grams of sugars!

Portion distortion! These two cups differ by only 2 fluid ounces, yet Jamba's is a large and Smoothie King's is a medium. Order a "large" at Smoothie King and you'll receive a 40-ounce bathtub of a smoothie. That would have qualified as slapstick comedy 50 years ago, but today it's become standard fare. What is shocking is the part you can't see; roughly a quarter of the sugar in the Lemon Twist Strawberry comes from added sweeteners. That's 150 unnecessary calories. In contrast, Jamba's smoothie earns the majority of its 58 grams of sugar from real fruit or fruit juice. And the 30-ounce cup you see here? It's the biggest you can order. That's good, because if you need more than 30 ounces of smoothie, you should probably consider sitting down to a real meal.

KID'S MEAL

Consider this: America's obesity rate is nearly three times that of Italy's. If that doesn't convince you to aim for authentic Italian pizzas (or to move to Tuscany), nothing will. Although Uno's Kid's pizza is a vast improvement over the chain's adult individual deep dish, it still packs more than 90 calories per ounce, making it more calorie dense than a Dairy Queen Blizzard. Mac Grill approaches its pie as an Italian would, stretching the crust thin, allowing it to puff up, and then applying just the right amount of pepperoni and cheese.

DESSERT

Eat This!
Jack in the Box Chocolate Overload Cake
302 calories
7 g fat (2 g saturated)
57 g carbohydrates
Not That!
Applebee's Triple Chocolate Meltdown
830 calories
48 g fat (30 g saturated)
97 g carbohydrates
Save!
528 calories and 41 grams of fat!

It's not often we suggest that people turn to Jack in the Box for nutritional refuge, but in a minor miracle the West Coast behemoth has managed to produce one of the lowest-calorie chocolate treats we've ever come across. Skip the medium fries and order this instead and you'll take in fewer carbs and a third fewer calories. The scariest thing about Applebee's Chocolate Meltdown is that despite sharing the same general makeup as the Chocolate Overload cake (look at it!), it somehow packs 15 times the saturated fat. This is what a good swap is all about: Eating the healthiest possible versions of the foods you really want to eat (burgers! pizza! chocolate cake!).

What If Food Ads Told The TRUTH?

SoBe
STRAWBERRY
BANANA
SoBe
100%
FRUIT FREE

BIG MOUTH
BURGER
Recession Special!
EVERY BURGER PACKS ENOUGH CALORIES
TO FEED A FAMILY OF FOUR!
chilis

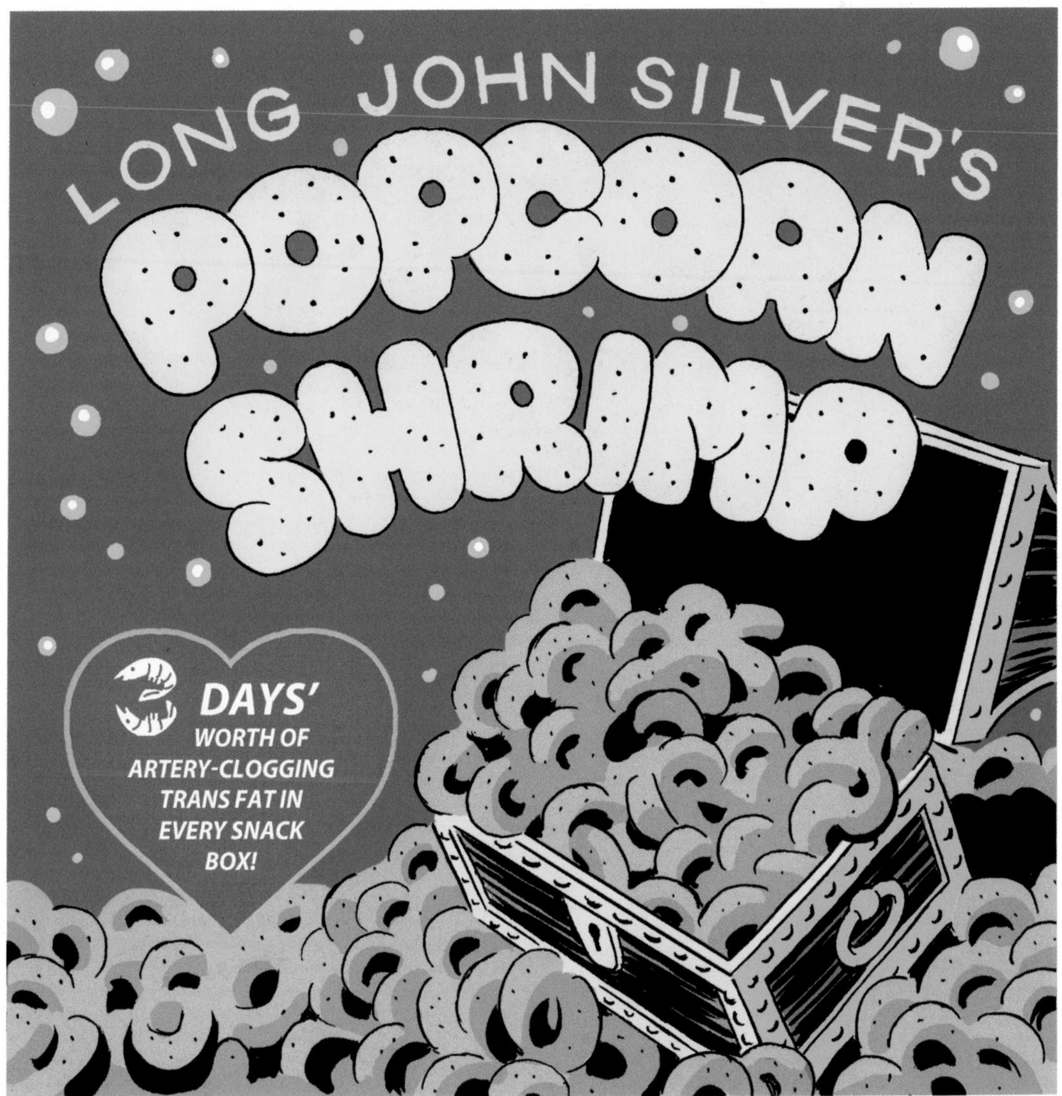
LONG JOHN SILVER'S
POPCORN SHRIMP
3 DAYS'
WORTH OF
ARTERY-CLOGGING
TRANS FAT IN
EVERY SNACK
BOX!

DOMINO'S

Bread Bowl

PASTA

Your insulin levels will never be the same!

SMUCKER'S
UnCrustables
•LESS FIBER!
•LESS PROTEIN!
•MORE HIGH-FRUCTOSE CORN SYRUP than those impossible-to-make peanut butter and jelly sandwiches!

1

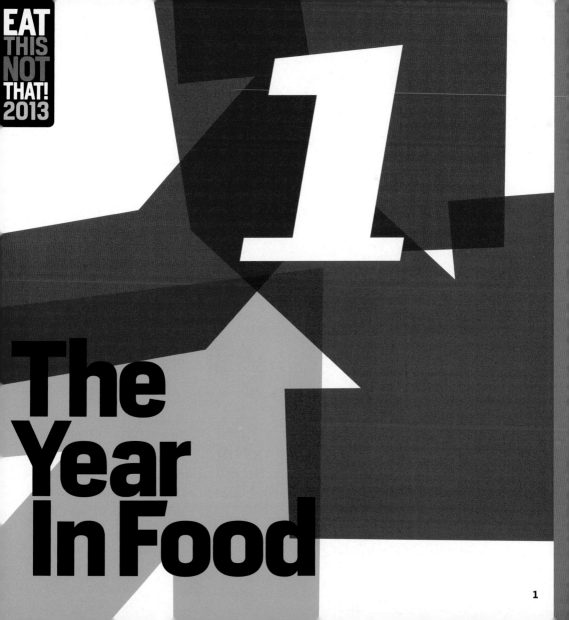

The Year In Food

The YEAR In Food

In the world of food, 12 months is an eternity. Menus are overhauled, supermarket aisles are reshuffled, and government regulations alter how products are made and distributed. Some changes are for the betterment of American eating habits, while others threaten our waistlines and well-being. Here now are the best and worst changes in the food industry over the past year.

CONSUMERS LAY THE SNACKDOWN ON "ALL NATURAL" FOOD FRAUDS

IN 2011 FRITO-LAY slapped an "all natural" label on half its products, and in January 2012 a New York man responded with a class action lawsuit. His chief complaint was that Tostitos and SunChips are made with corn and oils derived from genetically modified plants and therefore aren't deserving of the "all natural" claim.

The man has a point: If nature didn't make it that way, how can Frito-Lay call it "natural"? The answer: The FDA doesn't regulate the use of the word "natural" on packaged foods, so the food industry is free to define it at will. The is the latest in an ongoing battle against "natural" abuse. Over the past few years, disgruntled consumers have blown the whistle on AriZona Beverage Company, Kashi Company, and Coca-Cola for similarly inflated claims.

We're happy to see consumers taking action against dishonest claims, but the real issue here lies with the FDA's inaction. The USDA regulates "natural" labels on meat products, but the FDA refuses to do the same for packaged foods. The food industry has been pumping out highly processed junk disguised as healthy fare for years, and until the FDA steps in, consumers will continue to be misled into buying these frauds. Without a legal definition of the term "natural," it's tough to say how the Frito-Lay plaintiffs will fare, but we hope the recent string of consumer suits will be the push the FDA needs to finally get its act together.

☑ ETNT APPROVED

SCIENTISTS DECLARE CALORIE-GATE!

YOUR GOOD-FAITH EFFORT to make smart menu selections could be in vain. In a recent study published in *JAMA: The Journal of the American Medical Association*, a team of Tufts University researchers looked at 269 menu items at 42 popular chains and found that nearly 20 percent of the dishes contained at least 100 calories more than posted, with one side item containing more than 1,000 additional calories!

What's worse, the study showed that low-calorie dishes like soups and salads—foods people generally choose when trying to lose weight—had the biggest calorie discrepancies. The researchers also found that sit-down restaurants were more likely than fast-food joints to display inaccurate calorie counts. This likely stems, they say, from the leeway line cooks at those restaurants have in the food-preparation process, which allows them to act carelessly with big-calorie ingredients like oil, butter, and salad dressing.

Study coauthor Susan Roberts, PhD, told CNN, "I think restaurants have a lot to answer for here," and we agree. When the number of calories is continuously understated, restaurants need to either reel in the calories being tossed around their kitchens or adjust the numbers on their nutritional reports. A couple extra calories here and there aren't devastating, but 100 calories per meal most certainly can be. If you add that just once a day, you'll pack on 10 extra pounds this year. It's bad enough that healthy chain offerings are few and far between, but punishing patrons for choosing the garden salad over the cheeseburger? It's a nutritional travesty!

CONSUMERS VS. THE PINK SLIME!

EVER HEARD OF lean finely textured beef (LFTB)? It's a paste-like meat filler comprised of ground-up beef scraps that have been warmed and spun in a centrifuge (to remove fat) and treated with ammonium hydroxide gas (to eliminate bacteria). Gross, right? And you've probably been eating the stuff for years; until recently, it was extremely common in fast-food burgers and pre-ground supermarket beef.

This year LFTB made headlines after the USDA announced that it planned to buy 7 million pounds of the stuff to serve to children in schools, prompting one blogging mother to start a Change.org petition asking the agency to rethink the purchase and ban LFTB from schools. The term "pink slime" was culled from an internal USDA e-mail, and after a series of ABC exposés made it popular, consumers nationwide turned to Twitter to voice their opposition. Nobody, it seemed, was happy to learn they'd been eating pink slime.

Left with no choice, the food industry reacted. Wendy's took out newspaper ads announcing that it had never used the stuff, while McDonald's, Burger King, and Taco Bell all said they were planning to stop. Major meat processors applied to the USDA for labeling that would force competitors to alert consumers to pink slime's presence, and the USDA announced that schools would be able to opt out of purchasing beef that contained it.

Still, meat producers insist that pink slime is safe, and while some scientists agree, others claim the goop is at best nutritionally inferior to raw meat and at worst harmful to our health. Either way, the recent controversy serves as yet another illustration of how little we truly know about what goes into the food we eat, and we couldn't be happier to see this slimy beef exposed.

☑ ETNT APPROVED

IS RONALD McDONALD A SAD CLOWN?

IN A GROUNDBREAKING STUDY published in *Public Health Nutrition* this year, scientists found the first direct link between fast-food consumption and clinical depression. In the study, Spanish researchers followed 9,000 people over 6 months and along the way, they asked them how frequently they ate junk foods like burgers, fries, and commercial baked goods. At the beginning of the study, none of the participants were depressed, but by the end, nearly 500 suffered from clinical depression. And here's the interesting part: Compared to those who ate the least fast food, those who ate the most were about 50 percent more likely to develop depression.

Scary? Definitely. Surprising? Not really. If you eat too much junk, you're going to feel like junk. It's the old you-are-what-you-eat principle. And sure, you can eat healthy at the drive-thru, but most consumers opt for oversized burgers, greasy french fries, and the biggest soda cups they can get with their value meals. Eat like that regularly and you're bound to feel the brunt of a high-calorie diet with a scarcity of nutrients.

The way we see it, this new research on the fast-food blues offers further evidence of what *Eat This, Not That!* has been saying all along: Staying healthy (and happy) is about making smart choices. Whether at the drive-thru, in the supermarket aisle, or in the restaurant booth, eating to fuel your body and slim your waistline is the best way to stay healthy and happy.

☑ ETNT APPROVED

"I got back the confidence to be who I am."

Stephen Gardner was an outgoing kid with a sharp sense of humor. He was heavy for his age, but he supported his big frame with an even bigger personality. He had a close group of friends, a girlfriend he adored, and an adult-size appetite. "I didn't want the kids' meal from McDonald's," he says. "I wanted a regular meal."

By the time he reached college, he was eating without restraint, supplementing a dubious dorm-food diet with fast food, chips, and Cheez-Its. In a short time his weight had climbed to nearly 300 pounds, but even that didn't slow his eating. Before that could happen, Stephen needed a slap from reality, and that slap came when his girlfriend of 4 years broke up with him. Stephen was crushed, but decided to use his grief to fuel a positive transition. "I wanted to look my best and be as healthy as possible for the next woman I met," Stephen recalls. He was ready to start losing weight.

BEFORE: 290 pounds

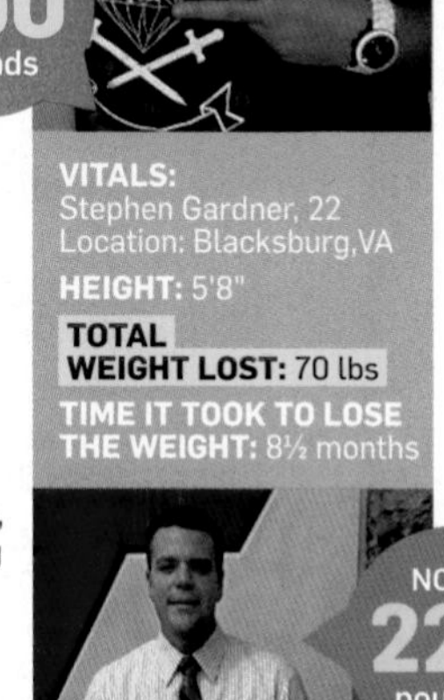

VITALS:
Stephen Gardner, 22
Location: Blacksburg, VA

HEIGHT: 5'8"

TOTAL WEIGHT LOST: 70 lbs

TIME IT TOOK TO LOSE THE WEIGHT: 8½ months

NOW: 220 pounds

HITTING THE BOOKS

Stephen had occasionally flipped through the stack of *Eat This, Not That!* books that his mom kept in the house, but he hadn't taken them to heart. Now, resolved to lose weight, he returned to the stack. He suddenly become aware of how many superfluous calories he consumed every day. "The things you think are healthy—things like smoothies and salads—you have no idea how bad they can be," he says.

With hard numbers at his fingertips, Stephen was able to start whittling down his portions. He wrote out shopping lists, running through the breakfast swaps, lunch meat upgrades, and—newly 21 years old—the best low-calories beers. Following one of the book's recommendations, Stephen began regular dinnertime visits to his campus Chick-fil-A. He was cutting calories out of his life without changing his daily routine. "What I like most about *Eat This, Not That!* is that it's not a diet; it just shows you better ways to eat," he says.

LITTLE BIG MAN ON CAMPUS

Over the span of a school year, Stephen shed 70 pounds, and he intends to keep losing until he's at 200 flat. "It was hard for me to see the day-to-day changes, but every time I go home for a break, my family and friends just say, 'Wow!'" As for his romantic prospects? "A girl in my class messaged me on Facebook, telling me I was cute." They're now a couple. "This never would have happened before my transformation," he says.

AN END TO MYSTERY MEAT

IN MARCH 2012, the USDA implemented a provision requiring grocers to display nutritional information for raw meat. Under the new policy, nutrition labels will now be featured on 40 of the most common cuts, as well as on all ground meat products.

So what does the new law mean for us lowly supermarket shoppers? For one, it makes it easier for consumers to mine the meat aisle for healthy choices. The difference between 8 ounces of sirloin and 8 ounces of ribeye, for instance, is nearly 300 calories and 20 grams of saturated fat. Plus the sirloin has more protein. Who knew, right? Not the average shopper.

And another reason we're digging the policy: It takes the guesswork out of portion control. Research shows that, without guidance, people are inherently bad at estimating calorie counts. In fact, one *American Journal of Public Health* study found that people regularly underestimate calories in foods by nearly 50 percent. That's why we need nutrition labels—so we know what we're eating.

Adding nutrition labels to meat will make it easier for you to avoid dangerous caloric mishaps, and as any *Eat This, Not That!* reader knows, any rule that makes it easier for consumers to make healthy choices is okay in our, um, book.

☑ ETNT APPROVED

THE KING OVERHAULS HIS KINGDOM (BUT FAILS TO MAKE IT HEALTHIER)

IN APRIL, Burger King launched a massive brand reinvention that included new "premium" food offerings, a trendy new look, and a series of national TV spots featuring A-list celebs like Jay Leno and David Beckham. Consider this the King's attempt to rescue an ailing empire: According to *USA Today*, BK has experienced steadily declining sales, and in 2011 Wendy's bumped the Whopper creator out of the No. 2 spot among fast-food chains (McDonald's still sits comfortably at No. 1). As Burger King's North America president Steve Wiborg told *USA Today*, the new brand strategy was devised with a single goal in mind: "Getting to be No. 1."

Truth be told, we couldn't care less about celebrity-driven advertisements and fancy new menu boards. What we care about is the food, and the real question here is whether BK's new menu truly provides, as the restaurant claims, "a variety of better-for-you options." The short answer: not really. A few of the salads aren't terrible—if not a little high in sugar and sodium—but the "snack" wraps hover around a meal-worthy 400 calories, the smoothies are loaded with added sugar, and the coffee drinks can pack as much as 600 calories in a 20-ounce cup. Whether BK's fancy new image will help it rise from the flame-broiled ashes remains to be seen, but if we had it our way, progress in the fast-food world would mean better nutrition, not better PR.

CONGRESS DECLARES PIZZA A VEGETABLE

IN JANUARY 2012, after much debate from Congress, Michelle Obama unveiled a major overhaul of the National School Lunch Program. In many ways, the new plan is a victory in the battle against childhood obesity. It calls for more vegetables and whole grains, and it sets limits on fats and sodium. It's the biggest upgrade the lunch program has seen in more than 15 years. But as with any good food fight, there's still a mess to clean up.

Despite all that the new plan does well, it left in two senseless exceptions for french fries and pizza, the two favorite foods of kids and the school cafeterias that serve them. First, Congress blocked a provision that would have limited starchy vegetables—namely fries—to 1 cup per week. Then, lawmakers denied the USDA's request to amend a long-standing rule that counts pizza sauce as a serving of vegetables. If the USDA had its way, tomato paste would count as a vegetable only if it amounted to ½ cup or more. Congress struck that notion, allowing instead ⅛ cup of sauce—an amount that can be reasonably smeared over a small slice of pizza dough and covered with cheese—to count as a serving of vegetables.

Nutrition advocates blasted Congress for siding with frozen-pizza producers and potato farmers over our nation's kids, and we agree wholeheartedly. First, Americans eat more fried potatoes than any fruit or vegetable, and allowing fries in school only perpetuates the problem. And second, ⅛ of a cup is the equivalent of 2 tablespoons. To say that 2 tablespoons of tomato sauce is equal to a whole tomato is not only inane but also deceptive, and it fails to teach our children the value of proper nutrition and healthy eating. So let's call this what it is: another instance of politics trumping advocacy on Capitol Hill. If the health of American children—20 percent of whom are obese—were really Washington's top priority, french fries and pizza would certainly make fewer appearances on the lunch line.

"I'm reaching goals I never thought I would."

Her family encouraged her to lose weight, but **Lindsey Morrison** ignored them. She felt confident enough as she was. Even in high school it didn't particularly bother her that her weight fluctuated between 250 and 275 pounds. She played field hockey and lacrosse and had a great group of friends, so why worry?

But when Lindsey left for college, her eating habits started to cause problems. She was living in the dorms, so her meal planning was little more than a short walk to the cafeteria. Her Freshman 15 was more like a Freshman 50. Within the first year and a half of college, her weight spiked to 310 pounds. She'd never seen herself so big. She started feeling lethargic and suffering from daily headaches. "Suddenly it hit me," she says. "I didn't like how I felt."

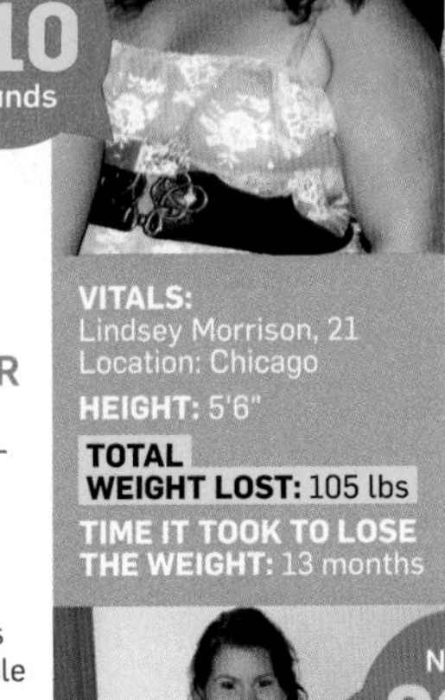

BEFORE:
310
pounds
VITALS:
Lindsey Morrison, 21
Location: Chicago
HEIGHT: 5'6"
TOTAL
WEIGHT LOST: 105 lbs
TIME IT TOOK TO LOSE
THE WEIGHT: 13 months
NOW:
205
pounds

A HEALTHIER OUTLOOK

While still in the dorms, Lindsey started reading the *Eat This, Not That!* that her cousin had given her as a gift. In her room, she relied on a healthy-food delivery service, and when she ate out, she used the book to guide her. After 3 months, she was steadily losing weight, but she was bored with the drab delivery food. She decided to ditch the service and rely entirely on Eat This, Not That! "I didn't really like only eating what was prescribed," she says. "With the books, you're learning."

Lindsey discovered that some of her favorite health foods—salads, yogurts, and smoothies—weren't always healthy. She also learned that she had been making some devastating serving-size blunders. To keep her diet exciting, she started preparing recipes from *Cook This, Not That!* As a college student, she appreciated that each recipe had a full breakdown of price. To her delight, the weight continued to fall off. Lindsey started feeling healthier, and last summer she completed three 5-K races, her time for each better than the last.

SOCIAL MEDIA STAR

When Lindsey started posting pictures of her slimmer body on Facebook, she found her page flooded with congratulatory messages from people she hadn't seen in years. "I was shocked by how many people reached out because they were inspired by me losing so much," she says. "It's a great feeling." But there's nothing better than feeling healthy. Lindsey is now more than 100 pounds lighter and plans to lose 30 more. "I have a lot more energy, I look better, and my mood is better," she says.

THE FDA GIVES BPA THE A-OK

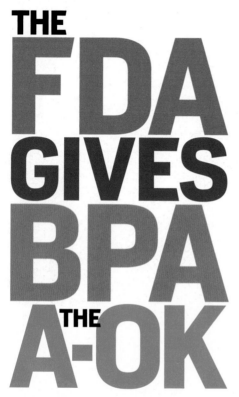

IN MARCH, the FDA rejected a petition by the Natural Resources Defense Council to prohibit the use of bisphenol A (BPA), a potentially dangerous compound used commonly in plastic containers and tin cans. The agency's claim was this: There's not enough scientific evidence against BPA to warrant a ban, but, that said, the decision is "not a final safety determination on BPA."

Wait—what? What the FDA is essentially saying here is this: We can't tell if it's safe or not, so we're going to let it stay in the food supply until we figure it out. So here's the gist of the science on BPA safety: There's a growing body of research showing that BPA exposure may cause reproductive and nervous system damage, particularly in infants and children. But some scientists (including those at the FDA) contest these findings on the basis that most BPA testing has been done on animals, not people, and that the trace amounts of BPA that enter our bodies via food containers are quickly broken down and eliminated. The FDA's official stance on BPA research: "While evidence from some studies have raised questions as to whether BPA may be associated with a variety of health effects, there remain serious questions about these studies, particularly as they relate to humans."

Our take: The innocent-until-proven-guilty philosophy shouldn't apply to food. The fact that there's even a possibility that BPA could cause major health damage is enough to turn us off to the substance. We don't know about you, but we think the food industry should have to prove that a chemical is safe before it starts dumping it in our food.

THE FDA ASKS THE MEAT INDUSTRY TO "JUST SAY NO"

THIS YEAR, in yet another victory for the country's carnivores, the FDA took a major step toward improving the meat supply. In April the government agency called on food manufacturers and pharmaceutical companies to voluntarily curb the use of antibiotics in farm animals—a practice that's already been banned in Europe.

Food processors have for years been lacing animal feed with antibiotics in order to promote weight gain and prevent disease in livestock, but the problem has spiraled out of control. The FDA estimates that as much as 80 percent of the antibiotics produced in the United States end up on feedlots. The problem is, pumping animals full of antibiotics—often the same drugs doctors prescribe for humans—promotes the growth of antibiotic-resistant bacterial strains that can infect humans, sometimes with deadly results. The superbug MRSA, for example, claims roughly 15,000 American lives each year, and it's quite likely that our inability to eradicate it owes to our dependence on antibiotics.

Critics of the new rule say the FDA's call to action was too soft because the guidelines simply ask—but don't require—food and drug companies to stop using and selling antibiotics for the purpose of animal production. We hear their cries, and we want more, too, but we still consider the move a consumer victory. The FDA's giving companies 3 years to implement the changes, and plans to explore further regulatory action for companies that don't comply. This type of government pressure, coupled with public support, just might be enough to make the food industry think twice about popping pills in the trough.

☑ ETNT APPROVED

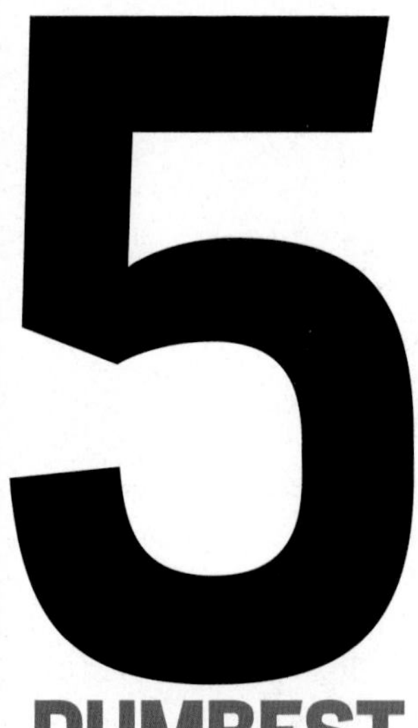

5 DUMBEST THINGS SAID ABOUT FOOD (RECENTLY)

WHAT THEY SAID:

"Fat makes you fat."
—University of Iowa Hospitals and Clinics

"If we're supposed to go out and eat nothing, if we're supposed to eat roots and berries and tree bark and so forth, show us how."
—Radio talk show host Rush Limbaugh

FOOT-IN-MOUTH ALERT!

Fat contains more calories by weight than carbohydrates, true. But fat is also filling, and certain fats—like those found in nuts, olives, and fish—are really good for you. When will so-called experts learn: Eating fat won't make you fat any more than eating money will make you rich.

In our ridiculously partisan world, Michelle Obama could save Washington by catching a nuclear bomb in her teeth and Limbaugh would somehow find fault with her dental work. But in criticizing Obama's crusade against childhood obesity, the rotund radio ranter just looks silly. Nobody's recommending a menu of tree bark, least of all the burger-loving Obamas.

WHAT THEY SHOULD HAVE SAID:

"Eating too much—of any kind of food—makes you fat."

"As someone who's struggled with my own weight-related health issues—from a heart scare to painkiller addiction caused by back pain—I know firsthand that overweight children carry a heavy health burden into adulthood. Trying to change all that sounds like a good idea."

"High-fructose corn syrup...provides many consumer benefits."
—SweetSurprise.com, a publicity front for—you guessed it—the Corn Refiners Association

"No consumer could reasonably be misled into thinking Vitaminwater was a healthy beverage."
—Attorney representing the beverage's maker, Coca-Cola

"I am eating a healthy diet."
—Ninety percent of the 1,234 American adults surveyed by *Consumer Reports*

Besides changing the group's name from "Sweet Surprise" to "Nasty Surprise," this corn syrup flack attack would be much more honest if it admitted that HFCS has allowed the food industry to cheaply oversweeten legions of our snacks and staples, accelerating our junk-food-fueled descent into obesity.

"High-fructose corn syrup is not that different from sugar. And neither one is good for you."

Really? "Vitaminwater" doesn't sound like "a healthy beverage"? What's their next marketing strategy, renaming Fanta "Nice Shiny Teeth Drink"? In reality, Vitaminwater is nothing more than the latest slick sugar-delivery vehicle. The minor benefits of the vitamins mixed in are vastly outweighed by the damage these sweetened drinks can cause. We were relieved when a federal judge ruled the packaging misleading.

"Vitaminwater? Oh, we meant to call it 'Sugarwater.' Our bad!"

Two out of three women and three out of four men in America are overweight or obese. We have become so fat that even contestants on *The Biggest Loser* look somewhat normal. In reality, only about 33 percent of Americans eat enough fruits and 27 percent eat enough vegetables every day, according to the Centers for Disease Control and Prevention.

"Eating a healthy diet is very difficult in America today. But having* Eat This, Not That! *sure helps!"

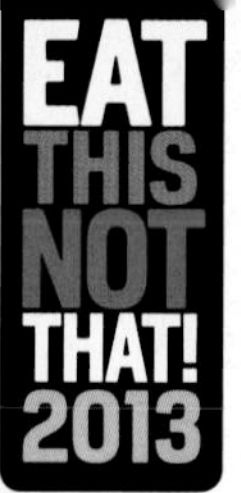

2

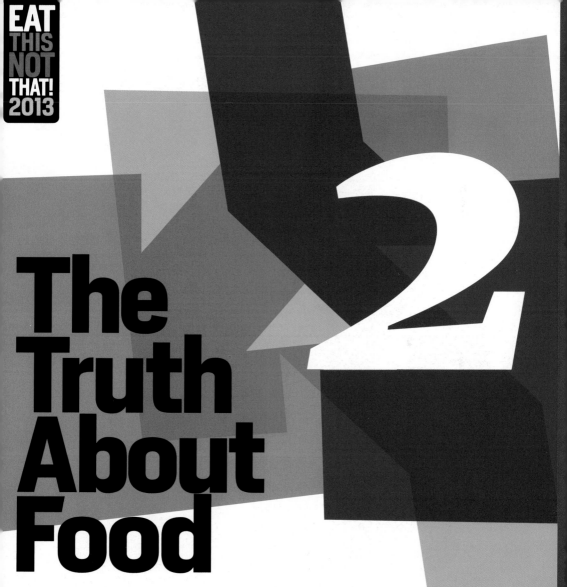

The Truth About Food

What's Really in Your Food?

LIFE USED TO BE SO SIMPLE.

Home ownership was the best way to invest a paycheck; *Leave It to Beaver* represented the classic American family; and "eating out" meant gathering the family into the old Buick, cruising down to the local diner, and sipping a small soda while a clean-cut fella in a paper hat hand-pressed raw chuck into hamburger patties.

Somewhere between then and now, life took a sharp left turn toward chaos. Home ownership became more volatile than Texas hold'em, the Cleavers were replaced by the Kardashians, and that local burger was ousted by a frozen hockey puck shaped halfway across the country.

More than credit default swaps and Kim and Khloe chicanery, it's the changes in our food that have had the most impact on our happiness and well-being. Compared with their normal-weight peers, overweight people are 30 percent more likely to have asthma, 44 percent more likely to have high blood pressure, and 64 percent more likely to be hospitalized for diabetes. The fact is, we're heavier than we've been at any other time in history.

Sure, Americans have changed, but not nearly as much as American food has. Consider this: A 1950s ice cream sundae contained about 8 or 9 different ingredients. Today you can walk into any Baskin-Robbins in the country and order a sundae with 50 or more additives, most of them junk-food fillers that you would never stock in your pantry at home (unless of course you cook with polysorbate 80 and hydrogenated coconut oil).

The point is, food today is nothing like it was 60 years ago. The portions are bigger, the nutrients are fewer, and it requires a PhD in food chemistry to understand the intricacies of half the ingredients. More and more of our favorite foods are being tweaked and manipulated in laboratories rather than roasted and sautéed in kitchens. And that has serious implications for all of us.

So before you mindlessly chew your way through another value meal, turn the page to unravel the mysteries behind these freakish foods. Sometimes the truth is tough to swallow.

What's Really in... Kentucky Fried Chicken's Chunky Chicken Pot Pie?

CHICKEN POT PIE FLAVOR Food processors know that if the flavor isn't correct, sales will suffer, and that presents a formidable challenge. See, after making room for emulsifiers, stabilizers, thickeners, and preservatives, the natural flavors in this pie are muted. To battle the blandness, KFC turned to chemists who specialize in what food should taste like. That means that when you take a bite, you're tasting the result of meetings and e-mails exchanged between KFC execs and guys in lab coats. Your taste buds register something like chicken and vegetables, but the driving force is an onslaught of chemicals derived from cheap commodity crops—corn, soy, and wheat—that have been laced with a proprietary "flavor," steeped in stock, and thickened with carbohydrates. It underscores the vicious cycle of our industrial food system: When artificial additives create problems, the solution is to invent more artificial additives.

Their ingredient list...

Chicken Stock

Potatoes (with sodium acid pyrophosphate to protect color)

Carrots

Peas

Heavy Cream

Modified Food Starch

Contains 2% Or Less Of Wheat Flour, Salt, Chicken Fat, Dried Dairy Blend (whey, calcium caseinate)

Butter (cream, salt)

Natural Chicken Flavor With Other Natural Flavors (salt, natural flavoring, malto-dextrin, whey powder, nonfat dry milk, chicken fat, ascorbic acid [to help protect flavor], sesame oil, chicken broth powder)

Monosodium Glutamate

Liquid Margarine (vegetable oil blend [liquid soybean, hydrogenated cottonseed, hydrogenated soybean], water, vegetable mono and diglycerides, beta carotene [color])

Roasted Garlic Juice Flavor (garlic juice, salt, natural flavors)

Gelatin

Roasted Onion Juice Flavor (onion juice, salt, natural flavors)

Chicken Pot Pie Flavor (hydrolyzed corn, soy and wheat gluten protein, salt, vegetable stock [carrot, onion, celery], maltodextrin, flavors, dextrose, chicken broth)

Sugar

Mono and Diglycerides

Spice

Seasoning (soybean oil, oleoresin turmeric, spice extractives)

Parsley

Citric Acid

Caramel Color

Yellow 5

Enriched Flour Bleached (wheat flour, niacin, ferrous sulfate, thiamin mononitrate, riboflavin, folic acid)

Hydrogenated Palm Kernel Oil

Water

Nonfat Milk

Maltodextrin

Salt

Dextrose

Sugar

Whey

Natural Flavor

Butter

Citric Acid

Dough Conditioner

L-Cysteine Hydrochloride

Potassium Sorbate and Sodium Benzoate (preservatives)

Colored With Yellow 5 & Red 40

Fresh Chicken Marinated With:
Salt
Sodium Phosphate and Monosodium Glutamate
Breaded With:
Wheat Flour
Salt
Spices
Monosodium Glutamate
Leavening (sodium bicarbonate)
Garlic Powder
Natural Flavorings
Citric Acid

L-CYSTEINE HYDRO-CHLORIDE Used as a dough conditioner in industrial food production, this nonessential amino acid is most commonly derived from one of three equally surprising sources: human hair, duck feathers, or a fermented mutation of E. coli. Yum.

Maltodextrin
Sugar
Corn Syrup Solids
With Not More Than 2% Calcium Silicate Added as an Anti Caking Agent
OR
Fresh Chicken Marinated With:
Salt,
Sodium Phosphate and Monosodium Glutamate
Breaded With:
Wheat Flour
Salt, Spices
Monosodium Glutamate
Corn Starch

GELATIN Hard to believe, but the stuff that gives Jell-O its jiggle comes from the collagen found inside animals' skin and bones. Here, it's used as a gelling agent to give the sauce a more viscous consistency.

RED 40 (NATURAL RED #40)

Red 40 is a crimson pigment extracted from the dried eggs and bodies of the female Dactylopius cocus, a beetlelike insect that preys on cactus plants. It's FDA-approved and widely used as a dye in various red foods, especially yogurts and juices. Still, it's hard to get excited about a beetle pot pie.

Our ingredient list...

chicken
celery
carrot
onion
potato
chicken broth
butter
flour
milk
salt
black pepper

Leavening (sodium bicarbonate)
Garlic Powder
Modified Corn Starch
Spice Extractives,
Citric Acid
2% Calcium Silicate added as Anticaking Agent

OR

Fresh Chicken Marinated With:
Salt
Sodium Phosphate and Monosodium Glutamate
Breaded With:
Wheat Flour
Sodium Chloride and Anti-caking Agent (tricalcium phosphate)
Nonfat Milk
Egg Whites
Colonel's Secret Original Recipe Seasoning

OR

Potato Starch
Sodium Phosphate
Salt
Breaded With:
Wheat Flour
Sodium Chloride and Anticaking agent (tricalcium phosphate)
Nonfat Milk
Egg Whites
Colonel's Secret Original Recipe Seasoning

OR

Potato Starch
Sodium Phosphate
Salt
Breaded With:
Wheat Flour
Salt
Spices
Monosodium Glutamate
Leavening (sodium bicarbonate)
Garlic Powder
Natural Flavorings
Citric Acid
Maltodextrin
Sugar
Corn Syrup Solids With Not More Than 2% Calcium Silicate Added as an Anti-caking Agent

OR

Potato Starch
Sodium Phosphate
Salt
Breaded With:
Wheat Flour
Salt
Spices
Monosodium Glutamate
Corn Starch
Leavening (sodium bicarbonate)
Garlic Powder
Modified Corn Starch
Spice Extractives
Citric Acid
and 2% Calcium Silicate Added As Anticaking Agent

OR

Seasoning (salt, monosodium glutamate, garlic powder, spice extractives, onion powder)
Soy Protein Concentrate
Rice Starch and Sodium Phosphates
Battered With:
Water
Wheat Flour
Leavening (sodium acid pyrophosphate, sodium bicarbonate, monocalcium phosphate)
Salt
Dextrose
Monosodium Glutamate
Spice and Onion Powder
Predusted With:
Wheat Flour
Wheat Gluten
Salt
Dried Egg Whites
Leavening (sodium acid pyrophosphate, sodium bicarbonate)
Monosodium Glutamate
Spice and Onion Powder.
Breaded With:
Wheat Flour
Salt
Soy Flour
Leavening (sodium acid pyrophosphate, sodium bicarbonate)
Monosodium Glutamate
Spice
Nonfat Dry Milk
Onion Powder
Dextrose
Extractives of Turmeric and Extractives of Annatto.
Breading Set in Vegetable oil.

What's Really in... Dunkin' Donuts' Boston Kreme Donut

Their ingredient list...

Donut:

enriched unbleached wheat flour(wheat flour, malted barley flour, niacin, iron as ferrous sulfate, thiamin mononitrate, enzyme, riboflavin, folic acid)

palm oil

water

dextrose

soybean oil

whey (a milk derivative)

skim milk

yeast

contains less than 2% of the following: salt

leavening (sodium acid pyrophosphate, baking soda)

defatted soy flour

wheat starch

mono and diglycerides

sodium stearoyl lactylate cellulose gum

soy lecithin

guar gum

xanthan gum

artificial flavor

sodium caseinate (a milk derivative)

enzyme

colored with (turmeric and annatto extracts, beta carotene)

eggs

Boston Kreme Filling:

water

sugar syrup

modified food starch

corn syrup

palm oil

contains 2% or less of the following: natural and artificial flavors

glucono delta lactone

salt

potassium sorbate and sodium benzoate (preservatives)

yellow 5

yellow 6 titanium dioxide (color)

agar

Chocolate Icing:

sugar

water

cocoa

high-fructose corn syrup

soybean oil

corn syrup

contains 2% or less of: maltodextrin

dextrose

corn starch

partially hydrogenated soybean and/or cottonseed oil

salt

potassium sorbate and sodium propionate (preservatives)

soy lecithin (emulsifier)

artificial flavor

agar

XANTHAN GUM It's not dangerous, but it is funky. Xanthan gum is a thickener and emulsifier derived from sugar through a reaction with *Xanthomonas campestris*, a slimy bacterial strain that often appears as black rot on broccoli and cabbage. Worldwide production of xanthan gum is about 20,000 tons a year, so there's a decent chance you'll find some in whatever you eat next today.

ARTIFICIAL FLAVOR Denotes any of hundreds of allowable chemicals such as butyl alcohol, isobutyric acid, and phenylacetaldehyde dimethyl acetal. The exact chemicals in flavorings are the propriety information of food processors, and they use them to imitate specific fruits, spices, fats, and so on. Ostensibly every ingredient hiding under the blanket of "artificial flavor" must be approved by the FDA, but because you have no way of knowing what those ingredients are, you can't simply avoid something you'd rather not eat.

Our ingredient list...

flour
milk
sugar
yeast
eggs
butter
cream
whipped cream

BOSTON KREME FILLING Note the "K" in "Kreme." That's a not-so-subtle acknowledgement that there's no actual dairy in this filling. Bavarian cream, the real stuff, is made with milk, eggs, and cream. But those are high-dollar ingredients that require special storage accommodations, so Dunkin' Donuts stocks its doughnut case with a loose interpretation. Gone are the simple ingredients that make Bavarian cream a deeply satisfying and memorable indulgence, and in their place is a crude sludge made mostly from palm oil, modified food starch, and two types of syrup. There's also the dynamic duo of yellow 5 and yellow 6 to make sure the cream-like substance looks like cream. If it weren't for the "natural and artificial flavorings" injected alongside it, your tongue wouldn't pick up much besides fat and sugar.

What's Really in... McDonald's Big Mac?

Their ingredient list...

Beef patty:

100% pure USDA inspected beef

seasoning (salt, black pepper)

Bun:

enriched flour (bleached wheat flour, malted barley flour, niacin, reduced iron, thiamin mononitrate, riboflavin, folic acid, enzymes)

water

high-fructose corn syrup

sugar

soybean oil and/or partially hydrogenated soybean oil

contains 2% or less of the following: salt

calcium sulfate

calcium carbonate

wheat gluten

ammonium sulfate

ammonium chloride

dough conditioners (sodium stearoyl lactylate, datem, ascorbic acid, azodicarbonamide, mono- and diglycerides, ethoxylated monoglycerides, monocalcium phosphate, enzymes, guar gum, calcium peroxide, soy flour)

calcium propionate and sodium propionate (preservatives)

soy lecithin

sesame seed

Pasteurized Process American Cheese:

milk

water

milkfat

cheese culture

sodium citrate

salt

citric acid

sorbic acid (preservative)

sodium phosphate

artificial color

lactic acid

acetic acid

enzymes

soy lecithin (added for slice separation)

Big Mac Sauce:

soybean oil

pickle relish [diced pickles, high fructose corn syrup, sugar, vinegar, corn syrup, salt, calcium chloride, xanthan gum, potassium sorbate (preservative), spice extractives, polysorbate 80]

distilled vinegar

water

egg yolks

high-fructose corn syrup

onion powder

100% PURE USDA INSPECTED BEEF The fact that McDonald's beef is "USDA inspected" isn't surprising; it would be illegal to sell it otherwise. By dropping this trivial detail into the official ingredient statement, McDonald's seems to be trying to distance itself from the criticisms facing industrially processed beef. For starters, the cows killed for industrial beef are routinely treated with antibiotics, a practice that cuts costs for farmers but leads to resistant strains of bacteria that doctors can't effectively treat. But what's equally odious—and less acknowledged—is what happens to this antibiotic-fueled beef after slaughter. Before making its way onto the value menu, fast-food beef passes through the hands of a company called Beef Products, which specializes in cleaning slaughterhouse trimmings traditionally reserved for pet food and cooking oil. The fatty deposits in these trimmings are more likely to harbor *E. coli* and salmonella, so Beef Products cleans the meat with the same stuff the cleaning crew at Yankee Stadium might use to scrub the toilets—ammonia. Every week, Beef Products pumps some 7 million pounds of ground beef through pipes that expose it to ammonia gas that could potentially blind a human being. The tradeoff is that we don't have to worry about pathogens, right? Wrong. According to documents uncovered by the *New York Times*, since 2005 Beef Products' beef has tested positive for E. coli at least three times and salmonella at least 48 times.

BIG MAC SAUCE Mickey D's so-called "secret sauce" turns out to be more prosaic than years' worth of myth and mystery suggest. Soybean oil combines with egg yolk to make mayonnaise, which is in turn spiked with mustard, high-fructose corn syrup, and pickle relish. Surprisingly enough, the pink hue appears to come from two relatively nutritious spices, paprika and turmeric, not ketchup as most people assume. While a few of the industrial additives (like propylene glycol alginate, a thickener derived from kelp) creep us out, it's a relatively innocuous concoction that contains fewer calories than straight mayonnaise.

mustard seed
salt
spices
propylene glycol alginate
sodium benzoate (preservative)
mustard bran
sugar
garlic powder
vegetable protein (hydrolyzed corn, soy and wheat)
caramel color
extractives of paprika
soy lecithin
turmeric (color)
calcium disodium EDTA (protect flavor)

Lettuce

Pickle Slices:

cucumbers
water
distilled vinegar
salt
calcium chloride
alum
potassium sorbate (preservative)
natural flavors (plant source)
polysorbate 80
extractives of turmeric (color)

Chopped Onions

Our ingredient list...

ground beef
salt
pepper
Thousand Island dressing
shredded lettuce
American cheese
pickles
onion
hamburger buns (one top and two bottoms)

CALCIUM DISODIUM EDTA

This compound is complex, but here's all you need to know: It's really good at gathering metal ions in liquid. This gives it many functions, but in food, the trait allows it to prevent microscopic pieces of metals from discoloring or spoiling the liquid.

What's Really in... Chick-fil-A's Chicken Sandwich

Their ingredient list...

Chicken:

100% natural whole breast filet

seasoning (salt, monosodium glutamate, sugar, spices, paprika)

seasoned coater (enriched bleached flour {bleached wheat flour, malted barley flour, niacin, iron, thiamine mononitrate, riboflavin, folic acid}, sugar, salt, monosodium glutamate, nonfat milk, leavening {baking soda, sodium aluminum phosphate, monocalcium phosphate}, spice, soybean oil, color {paprika})

milk wash (water, whole powdered egg and nonfat milk solids)

peanut oil (fully refined peanut oil with TBHQ and citric acid added to preserve freshness and methylpolysiloxane an anti-foaming agent added)

SODIUM/ SALT More than three-quarters of the sodium in the American diet comes from processed, packaged, and prepared foods, and here's a perfect example of why. Salt is undoubtedly the predominant source of dietary sodium, but it doesn't act alone. The chicken by itself, before you add bun and pickles, delivers three other sources of sodium: baking soda, monosodium glutamate (aka "MSG"), and sodium stearoyl lactylate. Fast-food chains regularly brine their patties, and in many instances they rely on mechanically operated syringes to drive sodium deep into the muscle tissue. All told, this sandwich has 10 sources of sodium and 1,410 milligrams total—just 90 milligrams shy of a full day's take.

TBHQ (TERT-BUTYLHYDROQUINONE) An organic preservative that also can be found in dog food, perfumes, varnishes, and resins. Due to potential links with cancer and DNA damage, the FDA limits the use to 0.02 percent of the oil or fat in any single food item. Studies on its long-term safety have been contradictory, but as with all dubious additives, it's best to limit your exposure whenever possible.

DIMETHYLPOLYSILOXANE Go ahead, try to pronounce it. We'll wait... Ready? Okay, dimethylpolysiloxane is a silicone-based antifoaming agent added to fried foods to keep the oil from turning frothy. You'll also find it in a range of products from shampoos to Silly Putty. While no adverse health effects have been identified, there's something unsettling about the thought of Silly Putty in our chicken.

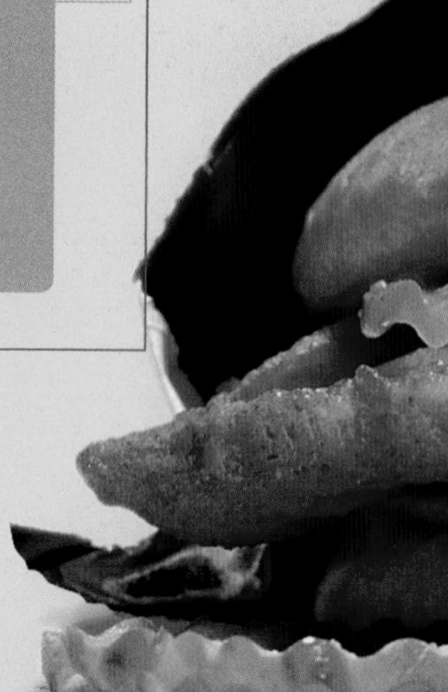

Bun:

enriched flour (wheat flour, malted barley flour, niacin, reduced iron, thiamin mononitrate {Vitamin B1}, riboflavin {Vitamin B2}, folic acid)

water

high fructose corn syrup

yeast

contains 2% or less of each of the following: liquid yeast

soybean oil

nonfat milk

salt

wheat gluten

soy flour

dough conditioners (may contain one or more of the following: mono- and diglycerides, calcium and sodium stearoyl lacty-lates, calcium peroxide)

soy flour

amylase

yeast nutrients (monocalcium phosphate, calcium sulfate, ammonium sulfate)

calcium propionate added to retard spoilage

soy lecithin

cornstarch

butter oil (soybean oil, palm kernel oil, soy lecithin, natural and artificial flavor, TBHQ and citric acid added as preservatives, and artificial color)

Pickle:

cucumbers

water

vinegar

salt

lactic acid

calcium chloride

alum

sodium benzoate and potassium sorbate (preservatives)

natural flavors

polysorbate 80

yellow 5

blue 1

Our ingredient list...

chicken patty
egg whites
bread crumbs
cooking oil
pickles
bun

BLUE #1 (BRILLIANT BLUE)

In an effort to make listless food look more appealing, processors regularly add artificial coloring to everything from breads and crackers to fruits and vegetables. The reason is simple: They know that we taste first with our eyes. If food looks boring, it's liable to taste boring, too. The problem is that many artificial colors have been linked to health problems. The Center for Science in the Public Interest recom-mends caution in consuming brilliant blue and avoidance of its cousin indigotin (blue #2) because they've been loosely linked to cancer in animal studies. And two British studies implicated the dye along with yellow #5 (also in Chick-fil-A's pickles) as possible causes of hyperactiv-ity in children. But as long as it's legal and it makes food look pretty (though it's still unclear exactly why Chick-fil-A would choose blue to gussy up its iconic sandwich), don't expect fast-food companies to stop coloring anytime soon.

What's Really in... Baskin-Robbins' Oreo Layered Sundae

Their ingredient list...

Oreo Cookies 'n Cream Ice Cream:

cream

nonfat milk

oreo chocolate cookies pieces (sugar, enriched flour [wheat flour, niacin, reduced iron, thiamine mononitrate, riboflavin, folic acid] vegetable shortening [partially hydrogenated soybean oil], cocoa [processed with alkali], high fructose corn syrup, corn flour, whey [from milk], corn starch, baking soda, salt, soy lecithin [emulsifier], vanillin—an artificial flavor, chocolate)

sugar

corn syrup

whey

n&a vanilla flavor

cellulose gum

mono and diglycerides

guar gum

carrageenan

polysorbate 80

annatto color

Oreo Cookies:

sugar

enriched flour (wheat flour, niacin, reduced iron, thiamine mononitrate (vitamin b1)riboflavin (vitamin b2), folic acid)

palm and/or high oleic canola and/or soybean oil, cocoa processed with alkali

high-fructose corn syrup

baking soda

cornstarch

salt

soy lecithin (emulsifier)

vanillin—an artificial flavor

chocolate

Hot Fudge Sauce:

sugar

corn syrup

water

partially hydrogenated coconut oil

partially hydrogenated soybean oil

cocoa (treated with alkali)

nonfat milk solids

modified food starch

salt

VEGETABLE SHORTENING Shortening is simply a code name for partially hydrogenated oil, which shows up three times on this ingredients list. The reason that's bad: Partially hydrogenated oils are the predominant source of trans fats in our diet, and research has shown a strong link between trans fat consumption and heart disease. A few years back the Institute of Medicine issued a report that stated that the only sensible trans fat recommendation the organization could make was zero grams. This sundae may only have 1 gram, but in our book, that's 1 gram too many.

SUGAR Sugar, in its various forms, appears 12 times in this sundae. That's 146 grams in total, which is more than you'd consume if you sat down to two full pints of Häagen-Dazs Butter Pecan ice cream. The impact of that sugar can't be overstated; if you stripped this cup of every ingredient except sugar, you'd still be left with nearly 675 calories. (As it's served, this sundae packs a staggering 1,330.) So why does Baskin-Robbins go to such destructively sweet lengths? Think about it: The store attracts customers on the promise of sugar, but outside of a few whole foods, almost everything we eat is loaded with the stuff. Bagels, deli meats, canned fruits, condiments, peanut butter—they're all laced with sugar. In order to create novelty, ice cream shops have to push the sugar to increasingly dangerous heights. The more sugar you eliminate from your diet, the less you'll need to satisfy your sweet tooth.

CELLULOSE GUM This additive is made from cotton or wood pulp, and in Baskin's sundae, it helps prevent the formation of ice crystals. Cellulose gum isn't dangerous, but its versatility as an additive makes for some strange applications. Toothpaste, shampoo, detergent, laxatives, and lubricant are but a few of the products in which it's used. When lumped in with that disparate group, this sundae begins to look less like food and more like any other commodity.

sodium bicarbonate

potassium sorbate (as preservative)

natural and artificial flavors

lecithin

propyl paraben—as a preservative)

Marshmallow Sauce:

corn syrup

sugar

egg whites

modified food starch

artificial flavor

sodium sulfite & sodium bisulfite (preservatives)

Whipped Cream:

cream

milk

sugar

dextrose

nonfat dry milk

artificial flavor

mono and diglycerides

carrageenan

mixed tocopherols [vitamin e] to protect flavor

propellant: nitrous oxide

Our ingredient list...

milk
vanilla
sugar
chocolate
Oreos
whipped cream

PROPYL PARABEN

Parabens are a class of compounds used to preserve food, cosmetics, and pharmaceuticals. It's been well documented that parabens act as mild estrogens, and according to the Environmental Working Group, they can disrupt the natural balance of hormones in your body. In a Japanese study, male rats fed propyl paraben daily for 4 weeks suffered lower sperm and testosterone production, and other studies have found that the compounds concentrate in breast cancer tissues.

The Worst Foods in America

WE, THE AMERICAN EATERS,

are the perky blondes in horror movies who are always running up the stairs when we should run down. We never fail to unlock the dietary door when a knock comes in the middle of the night. And we continue to peek at the darkest corners of the appetizer menu even though we are suspicious of what's lurking behind those sordid descriptions. Because we, like the slasher-film scream queens, are notorious for ignoring imminent danger. We need help.

Research says we are woefully ill-equipped to calculate what we're putting in our bodies. A 2006 study in the *American Journal of Public Health* showed that unhealthy restaurant foods contained an average of 642 calories more than people estimated. If you're like the average American who eats out five times a week, that's 47 pounds a year you didn't know you were consuming.

Now look at what our ignorance has wrought: The top three killers of Americans are heart disease, cancer, and stroke—all three of which are strongly rooted in lifestyle. Translation: Our diets stink. It's time for us to put an end to the horror show. The list on the following pages presents the 20 most cunning villains in a world filled with shadowy characters. So be wise. Next time one of these nutrition nightmares comes knocking on your door, double-bolt it and turn off the lights.

No. 20 WORST FRANKENFOOD

This appetizer sounds like a fantasy food dreamed up in the early morning hours at a college frat house: "Dude, imagine if you took hunks of lasagna, dipped them in batter, and tossed them in the deep fryer." Unfortunately, Olive Garden's crazy pasta creation is the real deal, and so is its cost to your health. A meal starter with half a day's calories and a day's saturated fat? That's one fantasy we'd rather not fulfill.

Olive Garden Lasagna Fritta
1,030 calories
63 g fat
(21 g saturated)
1,590 mg sodium

Olive Garden Stuffed Mushrooms
280 calories, 19 g fat (5 g saturated), 720 mg sodium

WORST PASTRY

The cinnamon bun is an inherently unscrupulous pastry—there's just no way to slather big blobs of dough with butter and frosting and end up with a sensible treat—but this caramel catastrophe from Cinnabon is just plain inexcusable. Here, Cinnabon, that peddler of so much dietary mischief, takes its classic bun—which already packs an astounding 880 calories—and defiles it with a dousing of caramel syrup and a pile of pecans. This type of shameless excess results in a day's saturated fat, half a day's calories, and nearly 20 teaspoons of sugar. Save your own buns and indulge elsewhere.

Cinnabon Caramel Pecanbon
1,080 calories
50 g fat (20 g saturated)
76 g sugars

Cinnabon Classic Bites (4)
420 calories, 17 g fat (7 g saturated), 25 g sugars

No. 18 WORST FRIES

Here's the most distressing dietary fact we know: French fries are the most consumed "vegetable" in America. They also happen to be one of the most dubious caloric investments in the nutrition world. Bad enough on their own, but when doused with trans-fatty processed cheese and loaded with greasy ground beef, you get a side dish so twisted it'll make a burger blush. In fact, you could scarf three Steakburgers with cheese and still take in fewer calories than you would with these spuds. Our advice: If you're really hungry, skip fries altogether and order another burger.

Steak 'n Shake Chili Cheese Fries (large)
1,170 calories
67 g fat
(22 g saturated, 3.5 g trans)
2,150 mg sodium

Bacon Cheese Fries (small)
360 calories, 20 g fat (6 g saturated, 1.5 g trans), 710 mg sodium

No. 17 WORST SUB

Quiznos Chicken Carbonara (large)
1,280 calories
61 g fat (27 g saturated, 1 g trans)
2,920 mg sodium

Carbonara is code for cream, cream, and more cream. Grilled chicken is usually a safe sandwich stuffer, but a smothering of Parmesan Alfredo sauce—along with the fatty one-two punch of bacon and cheese—makes for a chicken sub with more than a day's allotment of saturated fat. A 160-pound person would have to go on a 3-hour hike just to burn off this sandwich's calorie load. There are much smarter ways to spend your lunch money.

Eat This Instead! Chicken Milano (small)
450 calories, 18 g fat (9 g saturated), 1,060 mg sodium

No. 16 WORST FAST-FOOD BURGER

"Monster" is right. This burger beast comes at your diet full force, saddling your gut with four strips of bacon, three slices of processed cheese, and two ⅓ -pound slabs of greasy ground beef. Coincidentally, ⅓ of a pound is exactly how much flab you'll add to your middle if you inhale one of these bad boys. At Hardee's, consider "little" a relative term. The Little Thick Cheeseburger is one of the only ways to leave the chain's drive-thru window with your waistline intact.

Hardee's Monster Thickburger
1,290 calories
92 g fat (35 g saturated)
2,840 mg sodium

Little Thick Cheeseburger
430 calories, 23 g fat (9 g saturated), 1,090 mg sodium

No. 15 WORST DESSERT

The word "Thunder" is a pretty clear indicator that you're about to do some serious damage to your diet, but this sundae's nutrition stats are impressively heinous. The calorie culprits: a brick of a brownie, a hefty scoop of vanilla ice cream, a crown of whipped cream, and a deluge of chocolate sauce. Even if you split this dessert with three friends, you'll still take in a meal's worth of calories and a day's saturated fat. When you consider that the Classic Cheesecake is one of the great caloric bargains in America, there's no excuse to throw away 1,200 calories.

Outback Steakhouse Chocolate Thunder from Down Under
1,554 calories
106 g fat (53 g saturated)
133 g carbohydrates

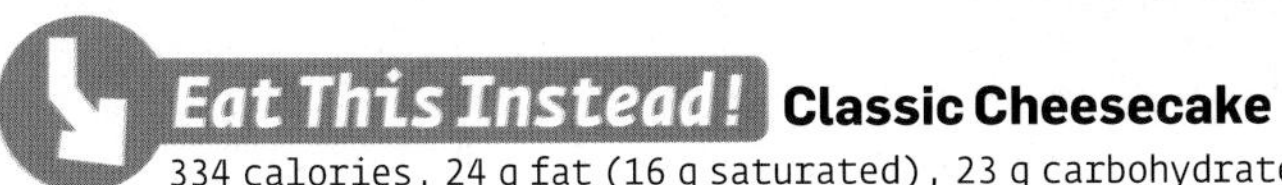

Eat This Instead! Classic Cheesecake
334 calories, 24 g fat (16 g saturated), 23 g carbohydrates

No. 14

WORST SALAD

The poor spinach never saw it coming. The simple menu description screams wholesome and healthy, but nothing could be further from the truth. With this bowl of mischief, IHOP debases one of the most nutritious greens on the planet by suffocating it with deep-fried chicken, bacon, and one too many handfuls of Cheddar cheese. You could order the chain's worst burger—the Monster Bacon'N Beef Cheeseburger made with Bacon Patties—and a side of fries—and still not reach the calorie load of this health-food fraud. Unfortunately, other than the basic Simple & Fit House Salad and the Side Caesar Salad, none of the pancake purveyor's salads come with fewer than 700 calories.

IHOP Chicken & Spinach Salad
1,600 calories
118 g fat
(32 g saturated, 0.5 g trans)
2,340 mg sodium

Eat This Instead! **Simple & Fit Simply Chicken Sandwich** with Fresh Fruit
500 calories, 10 g fat (3.5 g saturated), 840 mg sodium

No. 13 WORST MILK SHAKE

Baskin-Robbins Chocolate Chip Cookie Dough Shake (large)

1,600 calories
72 g fat (46 g saturated, 2 g trans)
181 g sugars

We're thankful that Baskin ditched the 2,310-calorie Heath Bar Shake that used to haunt our every waking moment, but there are still more than a few nutritional nightmares to be found on its menu. Even an average small shake at the chain houses 16 teaspoons of sugar! Order a large cookie dough and you'll gulp down more than 2 days' worth of saturated fat, 56 Chips Ahoy! cookies' worth of sugar, and enough calories to add half a pound to your gut. A word of caution: When you can drink your dessert, you're asking for trouble.

Eat This Instead! **Chocolate Chip Cookie Dough Ice Cream** (1 large scoop, 4 oz)
300 calories, 15 g fat (10 g saturated), 30 g sugars

No. 12 WORST CHIPS & DIP

Chili's Skillet Queso with Chips

1,710 calories
101 g fat
(37 g saturated)
3,490 mg sodium

Cheese dips are bad news to begin with—their fluid consistency can fool you into downing more calories than you realize—and the addition of fatty ground beef makes Chili's version the most hazardous chip sauce in America. Order this little cheese pot and you risk scooping up almost 2 days' worth of saturated fat and nearly a day's calories. Those would be some seriously sad stats for an entrée, but for an appetizer, they're downright deplorable. Other than its rib and burger plates, this is the most offensive item Chili's has to offer.

Eat This Instead! **Fried Cheese with Marinara Sauce**

660 calories, 35 g fat (15 g saturated), 2,040 mg sodium

No. 11 WORST HEALTH-FOOD FRAUD

The folks at the Cheesecake Factory aren't exactly forthcoming about what goes on behind their culinary curtain, so we're honestly not sure how they managed to take grilled chicken and avocado—two of the healthiest foods on the planet—and turn them into a sandwich with more calories than their worst burger. The bacon, cheese, and mayo certainly don't help matters, but the Factory must be hiding a secret ingredient that magically turns any reasonable food into a nutritionist's nightmare. We may never know the truth, but all you need to know is this: Stay away from this sandwich.

Cheesecake Factory Grilled Chicken and Avocado Club

1,750 calories
N/A g fat
(28 g saturated)
2,306 mg sodium

Eat This Instead! Factory Burger

730 calories, N/A g fat (15 g saturated), 1,016 mg sodium

No. 10 WORST BREAKFAST

Unless you're stocking up to hibernate for the winter, there's no reason to ever order a menu item that contains the word "platter." Your cholestrol could shoot up just reading the menu description: fried chicken, biscuits, fried eggs, cheese, gravy, bacon, and hash browns. The collective impact translates into 4 days' worth of sodium, 2 days' worth of saturated fat, and a calorie count fit for a family of four. We can't think of a worse way to start your day.

Perkins Southern Fried Chicken Biscuit Platter

1,860 calories

86 g fat (43 g saturated, 0.5 g trans)

6,680 mg sodium

Eat This Instead! **Classic Eggs** and Smoked Bacon with Breakfast Potatoes and Fresh Fruit

620 calories, 37 g fat (11.5 g saturated), 1,280 mg sodium

No. 9 WORST BURRITO

The trouble with burritos? It takes a whole lot of food to fill out those big tortillas. And when chains opt for particularly fattening fillers—which, let's be honest, is often the case—it's a recipe for a full-scale caloric assault. Case in point: This Baja burrito bomb is stuffed with creamy salsa, cheese sauce, and shredded Jack and Cheddar cheeses. As if that weren't bad enough, the chain offers patrons the option to order their burrito "Enchilado" style, which translates to a smearing of cheese and salsa, a pile of deep-fried chips, and a glob of sour cream. Ay caramba!

Baja Fresh Enchilado Style Nacho Burrito
1,670 calories
82 g fat (36 g saturated)
4,650 mg sodium

Eat This Instead! Chicken Americano Soft Tacos (2)
460 calories, 20 g fat (9 g saturated), 1,180 mg sodium

No. 8 WORST CHICKEN

It takes guts to name your restaurant Friendly's and then dish out this type of vicious waistline attack. Any food that's been smothered in batter and dunked in the deep fryer is a nutritional loser by default, but the added blow of oily, sugary sauces makes this poultry plate a particularly fattening failure. Order this combo and you'll wolf down nearly a day's calories and more sugar than you'd find in 150 Honey Teddy Grahams. Doesn't get much more unfriendly than that.

Friendly's Create Your Own Combo Chicken Strips Entrée Honey BBQ and Kickin' Buffalo Flavors (6)

1,780 calories

115 g fat (18 g saturated)

2,630 mg sodium

Half Turkey Club SuperMelt Sandwich with Chili

620 calories, 33 g fat (12 g saturated), 2,050 mg sodium

No. 7 WORST BURGER

A typical burger at Chili's will cost you a cool 1,400 calories—without fries!—and with this ground-beef bomb, the chain pulls out all the gut-busting stops: cheese, bacon, fried onions, barbecue sauce, and mayo. This blatant display of excess translates into a sandwich with more calories than seven McDonald's cheeseburgers and more than four times your recommended daily allotments of salt and saturated fat. There's only one way to safely get your meat fix at Chili's: Order a steak and pair it with respectable sides.

Chili's Southern Smokehouse Bacon Burger
2,290 calories
139 g fat
(46 g saturated)
6,500 mg sodium

Eat This Instead! Custom Combinations Classic Sirloin
500 calories, 22 g fat (7 g saturated), 1,720 mg sodium

No. 6 WORST FISH

Attack of the beige! Whenever your dinner is monochromatic (in this case, the off-brown hue of deep-fried junk), you know you're in trouble. Don't blame the fish—seafood is packed with lean, muscle-building protein and heart-healthy fats. No, the trouble here lies with a massively unbalanced fish-to-fat ratio. A coating of crispy batter and a heaping pile of deep-fried potatoes is no way to treat the golden child of nutrition. Plus, trans fats? Really? That's so 2005! When it comes to seafood, always abandon ship on fried fish and opt for grilled instead.

Applebee's New England Fish & Chips

1,930 calories

138 g fat (24 g saturated, 1.5 g trans)

3,180 mg sodium

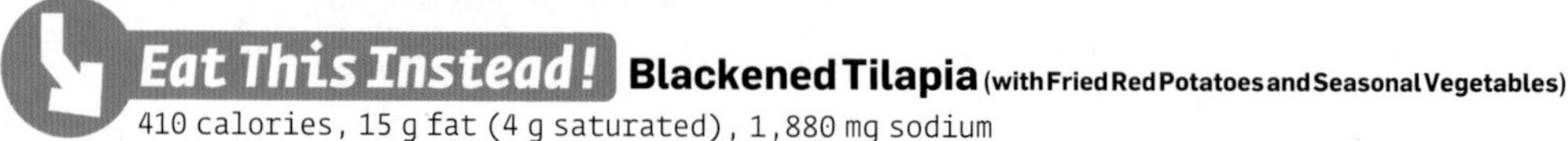

Blackened Tilapia (with Fried Red Potatoes and Seasonal Vegetables)

410 calories, 15 g fat (4 g saturated), 1,880 mg sodium

No. 5 WORST APPETIZER

According to Outback's Web site, its signature starter is "hand-carved by a dedicated bloomologist." We have no idea what that means, but consider bloomology the science of diet destruction. This bouquet of batter-dipped produce is the caloric equivalent of eating an entire medium Pizza Hut pepperoni pizza—before your dinner! What's more, it also delivers 2 days' worth of cholesterol-boosting trans fats and enough sodium to keep your cardiologist up at night.

Outback Steakhouse Bloomin' Onion

1,949 calories

161 g fat (48 g saturated, 4 g trans)

4,100 mg sodium

Eat This Instead! Shrimp on the Barbie

295 calories, 16 g fat (3.5 g saturated), 867 mg sodium

No. 4 WORST PIZZA

This atrocious pie has been dishonored with our distinction of the single worst pizza in America for 5 years running, since the inception of *Eat This, Not That!*. Truth be told, we're running out of ways to express its nutritional transgressions, so we'll break it down like this: If you ate just one of these "individual" pies each week, you'd take in enough calories to gain 34 pounds in a year. 'Nuff said.

Uno Chicago Grill Chicago Classic Individual Pizza

2,300 calories
164 g fat
(53 g saturated, 1 g trans)
4,910 mg sodium

Eat This Instead! **Sausage Thin Crust Pizza (½ pie)**

540 calories, 26 g fat (11.5 g saturated), 1,360 mg sodium

No. 3 WORST PASTA DISH

Aside from the Atkins craze, Alfredo sauce is the worst thing to ever happen to pasta. You'd be better off bathing the noodles in a bowl of butter (seriously—this dish has more fat than a full stick of butter!). Thankfully, the Cheesecake Factory recently took a break from destroying the hearts and guts of the American public to unveil its lower-calorie SkinnyLicious menu. We're not crazy about the name (though it's an improvement on the denigratory name of its old low-cal menu, the Weight Management Menu), but we love its nutrition stats: The pasta plate below will save you 1,760 (!) calories.

The Cheesecake Factory Fettuccini Alfredo with Chicken

2,300 calories
N/A g fat
(103 g saturated)
1,297 mg sodium

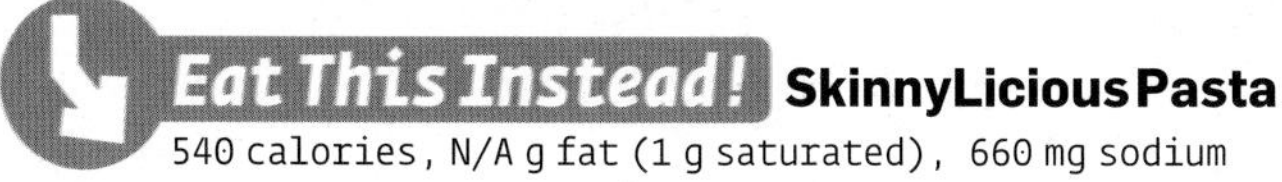

Eat This Instead! SkinnyLicious Pasta

540 calories, N/A g fat (1 g saturated), 660 mg sodium

No. 2 WORST GRILLED ENTRÉE

Tasty as they are, ribs are one of the fattiest cuts on the pig, so when they get the big-chain treatment (monster portions, excess sauce, and lackluster sides), they're pure nutritional mayhem. The heart-rattling stats here: more than a day's calories and more than 2 days' saturated fat. And, as if that's not enough, if you order this ridiculous rib plate, you'll also take in four times the recommended daily dose of sodium. Consider this dish cardiac kryptonite. If you want ribs, try our baby backs in *Grill This, Not That!* (they'll save you nearly 2,000 calories). Otherwise, stick with grilled chicken or steak at Chili's.

Chili's Shiner Bock BBQ Ribs (full rack) with Cinnamon Apples and Homestyle Fries

2,310 calories
123 g fat (44 g saturated)
6,340 mg sodium

Eat This Instead! Chili's Margarita Grilled Chicken

550 calories, 14 g fat (3.5 g saturated), 1,870 mg sodium

No. 1 WORST FOOD IN AMERICA

For the 3rd year in a row, the bastion of gluttony known as the Cheesecake Factory has received the top prize in our contest of diet debauchery. We give the chain props for rolling out some lighter options as of late, but its menu is still home to the most caloric fare in the country. What's worse, the Factory insists on keeping its nutrition info under lock and key. And we can't say we blame them. True to its namesake, this breakfast plate attempts to make up for its nutritional shortcomings by enticing diners with indulgent ingredients like cream-drenched bread, piles of pecans, and a snowstorm of powdered sugar. The result: a breakfast with as many calories as 3 dozen eggs.

The Cheesecake Factory French Toast Napoleon
2,530 calories
N/A g fat
(65 g saturated)
1,930 mg sodium
253 g carbohydrates

Energy Breakfast
690 calories, 4 g saturated, 1,288 mg sodium

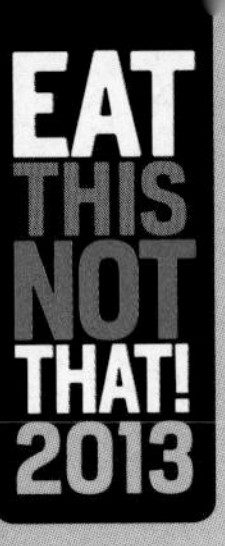

3

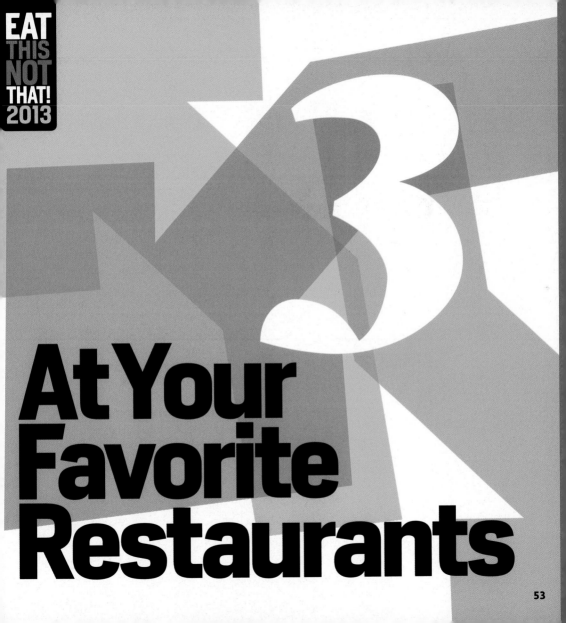

At Your Favorite Restaurants

YOU SURVIVED A TOUGH DAY AT WORK/ a challenging commute/another family drama/a 6-hour marathon of *Keeping Up with the Kardashians*!

You deserve to celebrate/cut loose/drown your sorrows/indulge while you dissect Khloè's relationship!

You should order the appetizer/all-you-can-eat platter/dessert special/enormous pitcher of fizzy stuff!

It's a special occasion!

Okay, really, it's not. It's just dinner. Or lunch. Or even breakfast. But if you've gone out to a restaurant for this meal, chances are you're going to feel like celebrating—even if there isn't anything to really celebrate. Experts call it the "special occasion mentality," and it sets in almost every time we set foot in a restaurant.

Of course, all restaurant meals feel special—the clinking of the glasses, the wafting scent of a sizzling supper, the overtired waitstaff marching down the aisle singing that happy-birthday song, over and over. Restaurants want us to feel special, sure. But they also want us to order more food. And creating a party atmosphere inspires us to throw caution to the wind. In fact, a 2008 study in the *International Food Research Journal* found that people are less likely to make healthy restaurant choices when they feel they're dining out for a special occasion.

In theory, it's great: Go out to celebrate, indulge for the night, and then go back to normal life. But sitting in a restaurant is normal life for most people: In fact, 1 in 10 Americans eats out almost every single day. That means that your "special occasion" is about as special as taking a shower.

In this chapter, you'll discover exactly how not-so-special some of your restaurant favorites really are, and some easy ways to make sure the terrific spread at the buffet doesn't turn into a terrific spread at your waistline. See, most of your favorite eating establishments have great options on the menu; you just need to know how to spot them.

But it's not just about knowing the right foods to eat: Restaurants have their own special challenges, too. So while you're perusing the menu, keep these points in mind:

Don't assume that slow food is healthier food.

The idea that fast food is bad for us has been beaten into our heads for a generation. But just because you're sitting down and being waited on by an aspiring musician doesn't mean you're eating healthier. In fact, our analysis of 24 national chains revealed that the average sit-down restaurant entrée boasted a whopping 867 calories, compared with 522 in the typical fast-food-franchise dinner.

AT YOUR FAVORITE RESTAURANTS

Don't get up-sold.

The kids at the drive-thru are like dastardly little mortgage brokers, looking to squeeze you into a great deal that you actually can't afford. Studies show that people are more likely to order the sides or supersize their orders when prompted by the helpful young lass in the paper hat. But it's a bad investment: Indeed, supersizing your meal costs you an average of 67 more cents, but loads you up with 397 more calories. Talk about a balloon payment!

Don't order dessert.

No dessert? Oh, come on! You suck, *Eat This, Not That!* guys! Hey, let us rephrase: An indulgent scoop of chocolate ice cream is one of the true pleasures in life. Of course you should have dessert. But here's an awesome weight-loss trick: Pay for your dinner, leave the restaurant, and then go somewhere else for dessert. The reason? First, a change of scenery may short-circuit your cravings. Second, it takes about 20 minutes for your body to signal that you've had enough to eat. By the time you're on the road to Heidi's House of Hot Fudge, you may discover that you weren't as hungry as you thought. That's calories off your belly—and money in your pocket! (And if you're still hungry when you get there? Then go ahead!)

A&W

C- A&W's Canadian outlets have ditched the trans-fatty frying oil, so why do the American stores continue to soak its rings, fries, and chicken strips in this hazardous liquid? Beyond the trans fat issues, A&W offers little refuge for the health-conscious eater. The menu is long on old-time classics (burgers, fries, shakes) with new-age nutritionals (760-calorie burgers, 900-calorie milk shakes). The grilled chicken sandwich may be your only salvation.

Eat This

Original Bacon Cheeseburger

530 calories
30 g fat
(10 g saturated, 0.5 g trans)
1,160 mg sodium

This isn't the healthiest burger on A&W's menu—that title belongs to the basic Hamburger—but 500 calories is a reasonable price to pay for a substantial patty crowned with cheese and bacon.

SURVIVAL STRATEGY

The best item on the entire menu is the Grilled Chicken Sandwich. Start with that or a small burger, skip the sides and the regular root beer, and finish (if you must have something sweet) with a small sundae or a vanilla cone.

OTHER PICKS

Grilled Chicken Sandwich
400 calories
15 g fat
(3 g saturated)
820 mg sodium

Corn Dog Nuggets
(regular)
280 calories
13 g fat
(3 g saturated, 0.5 g trans)
830 mg sodium

Hot Fudge Sundae
350 calories
11 g fat
(6 g saturated)
15 g sugars

690 calories
39 g fat
(14 g saturated,
1 g trans)
1,350 mg sodium

Not That!

Papa Burger

A prime example of why singles trump doubles at the drive-thru. Double doses of meat and cheese up your burger's calorie load without adding much flavor, while a single patty leaves room for more exciting toppers. Who needs extra beef when you can have bacon?

WEAPON OF MASS DESTRUCTION

Cheese Curds

(large)

1,140 calories
80 g fat
(42 g saturated,
2.5 g trans)
2,440 mg sodium

We can't say we're surprised that deep-fried cheese blobs aren't the health food of the year, but half a day's calories, 2 days' worth of saturated fat, and 2.5 grams of dangerous trans fats in a single side dish is downright preposterous, even by junk-food standards.

Ice Cream STACKUP

Signature Soft Serve Cone
200 calories
22 g sugars

Root Beer Float
(medium)
350 calories
64 g sugars

Vanilla Shake
(medium)
900 calories,
71 g sugars

OTHER PASSES

Reese's Polar Swirl

740 calories
31 g fat
(14 g saturated,
0.5 g trans)
85 g sugars

Chili Cheese Fries

410 calories
17 g fat
(5 g saturated,
3.5 g trans)
990 mg sodium

Chicken Strips

with Ranch Dipping Sauce

660 calories
46 g fat
(7.5 g saturated,
2 g trans)
1,290 mg sodium

APPLEBEE'S

D+ It's easy to see why it took Applebee's so many years to release their nutritional information. The 1,180-calorie Riblets Basket, the 1,380-calorie Oriental Chicken Salad, and the 2,530-calorie Appetizer Sampler are just a few of the little nightmares lurking on the menu. The bright spots on their menu include the steaks and the ever-expanding Under 550 Calories menu (despite some serious sodium issues).

SURVIVAL STRATEGY

Skip the meal-wrecking appetizers, pastas, and fajitas, and be very careful with salads, too; half of them pack more than 1,000 calories. Concentrate on the excellent line of lean steak entrées, or anything from the fantastic 550-calorie-or-less menu.

Eat This

Creamy Parmesan Chicken

470 calories
13 g fat
(6 g saturated)
1,510 mg sodium

Cream-based sauces usually come with a hefty calorie load—as do the majority of plates at Applebee's—but this dish is a welcome exception. Only about 25 percent of its calories come from fat, compared to nearly 50 percent for the pasta on the right.

OTHER PICKS

Asiago Peppercorn Steak
380 calories
14 g fat
(6 g saturated)
1,520 mg sodium

Classic Wings with Southern BBQ Sauce
660 calories
35 g fat
(9 g saturated)
1,060 mg sodium

Garlic Mashed Potatoes
250 calories
15 g fat
(4.5 g saturated, 1 g trans)
870 mg sodium

1,460 calories
74 g fat
(36 g saturated,
2 g trans)
2,140 mg sodium

Not That!
Three Cheese Chicken Penne

The average Applebee's pasta entrée packs a staggering 1,400 calories. The reason? They're all drowning in cream and butter. This penne packs nearly 2 days' worth of saturated fat, and a 160-pound person would have to swim laps for 3.5 hours straight just to burn off its calorie load.

Loaded Mashed Potatoes
460 calories
33 g fat
(15 g saturated,
1.5 g trans)
1,230 mg sodium

Boneless Wings
with Honey BBQ Sauce
1,250 calories
55 g fat
(11 g saturated,
0.5 g trans)
3,060 mg sodium

Steak Sizzling Skillet Fajitas
1,400 calories
54 g fat
(25 g saturated,
1.5 g trans)
5,460 mg sodium

Santa Fe Chicken Salad
1,280 calories
92 g fat
(24 g saturated,
1.5 g trans)
3,360 mg sodium

How can grilled chicken on a bed of greens possibly do this much damage? Blame the high-fat trifecta of guac, cheese, and sour cream. Add on fried tortilla strips, and you have the worst grilled chicken salad on the menu (and one of the worst in the country!).

Guilty Pleasure

Garlic Mashed Potatoes
250 calories
15 g fat
(4.5 g saturated,
1 g trans)
870 mg sodium

Mashed potatoes at sit-down chains are usually loaded with cream and butter, but Applebee's managed to make their version with fewer calories and fat grams than a baked potato or small Caesar salad.

ARBY'S

C+ Arby's offers a long list of sandwiches with fewer than 500 calories, including a trio of new roast chicken sandwiches. Problem is, there's an even longer list of sandwiches with considerably more than 500 calories. Credit Arby's for nixing the trans fat from their frying oil years ago, but it seems they might be a little too proud of that fact; the restaurant doesn't offer a single side that hasn't had a long soak in a bath of hot oil.

SURVIVAL STRATEGY

You're not doing yourself any favors by ordering off the Market Fresh sandwich menu. You're better off with a regular roast beef or Melt Sandwich, which will save you an average of nearly 300 calories over a Market Fresh sandwich or wrap.

Eat This

Roast Chicken Club Sandwich

460 calories
19 g fat
(6 g saturated)
1,440 mg sodium

Healthy compromise at its finest. Bacon and cheese are usually considered indulgences, but the roasted chicken balances this sandwich out with a solid serving of lean protein. Which reminds us: Always go "roast" over "crispy" (aka deep-fried) at the Arby's drive-thru.

OTHER PICKS

Beef 'n Cheddar Classic
440 calories
18 g fat
(5 g saturated, 0.5 g trans)
1,290 mg sodium

Roast Chopped Farmhouse Salad
with Balsamic Vinaigrette Dressing
390 calories
26 g fat
(9 g saturated)
1,140 mg sodium

Potato Cakes
(small)
230 calories
14 g fat
(2 g saturated)
460 mg sodium

800 calories
36 g fat
(9 g saturated, 0.5 g trans)
2,200 mg sodium

Not That!

Market Fresh Roast Turkey, Ranch & Bacon Sandwich

With an average of 648 calories, Arby's healthy-sounding Market Fresh sandwiches are the worst items on the menu. This turkey option has roughly the same fillings as the club, but it packs nearly double the calories and fat. The honey wheat bread alone contains a staggering 380 calories and the same amount of sugar as a Hostess Ho Ho.

Ham & Swiss Melt

300 calories
8 g fat
(3.5 g saturated)
1,070 mg sodium

The best bang for your nutritional buck at Arby's. It not only is low in calories and fat, but also delivers 18 grams of protein to help keep hunger pangs at bay.

Beef Sandwich STACKUP

Jr Roast Beef
210 calories
6 g fat

Roast Beef Classic
350 calories
12 g fat

French Dip and Swiss
430 calories
14 g fat

Bacon Beef 'n Cheddar
510 calories
23 g fat

Beef 'n Cheddar Max
650 calories
29 g fat

OTHER PASSES

Steakhouse Onion Rings
410 calories
20 g fat
(3 g saturated)
1,690 mg sodium

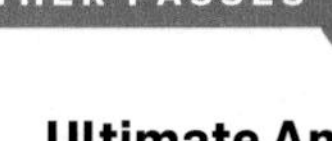

Crispy Chopped Farmhouse Salad
with Honey Mustard Dressing
610 calories
40 g fat
(11.5 g saturated, 0.5 g trans)
1,230 mg sodium

Ultimate Angus Three Cheese & Bacon Sandwich
640 calories
33 g fat
(12 g saturated, 0.5 g trans)
1,820 mg sodium

AU BON PAIN

B+ There are plenty of ways you could go wrong here, but Au Bon Pain couples an extensive inventory of healthy items with an unrivaled standard of nutritional transparency. Use the on-site nutritional kiosks to seek out one of dozens of paths to a sensible meal. Or simply opt for one of the excellent soups or salads, or pair two smaller items from the All Portions menu.

SURVIVAL STRATEGY

Banish bagels and baked goods from your breakfast routine and opt for eggs instead. As for lunch, the café sandwiches come in around 530 calories, so make a lean meal instead by combining soup with one of the many low-calorie options on the All Portions menu.

Eat This

Black Angus Roast Beef & Cheddar Sandwich

480 calories
17 g fat
(8 g saturated)
1,670 mg sodium

Our kind of sandwich: substantial, flavorful, packed with 32 grams of protein and just 480 calories.

OTHER PICKS

Classic Chicken Salad Sandwich

450 calories
11 g fat
(2 g saturated)
960 mg sodium

Chicken Gumbo Soup (medium)

190 calories
9 g fat
(1 g saturated)
930 mg sodium

Chocolate Chip Cookie

280 calories
13 g fat
(7 g saturated)
24 g sugars

740 calories
30 g fat
(16 g saturated,
0.5 g trans)
1,490 mg sodium

Not That!
Turkey and Swiss Sandwich

You think white meat is healthier than red meat? Think again. When it comes to deli slices, turkey, ham, and roast beef all pack about the same amount of calories, fats, and protein per serving, which means when you're looking for the healthiest option, it all comes down to bread and condiments.

OTHER PASSES

Double Chocolate Chunk Muffin
620 calories
25 g fat
(8 g saturated)
47 g sugars

BBQ Chicken and Beef Stew
(medium)
300 calories
10 g fat
(4 g saturated)
1,150 mg sodium

Grilled Chicken Avocado Sandwich
690 calories
25 g fat
(6 g saturated)
1,960 mg sodium

WEAPON OF MASS DESTRUCTION
Pecan Roll

810 calories
41 g fat
(14 g saturated,
0.5 g trans)
47 g sugars

You could eat two Double Chocolate Cupcakes and still not reach the calorie load of this pecan-encrusted disaster. Unless you want to cultivate rolls of your own, avoid this pastry at all costs.

Side STACKUP

Chicken Noodle Soup
110 calories
2 g fat

Beef Chili
300 calories
13 g fat

Turkey Chili
380 calories
14 g fat

Lobster Bisque
410 calories
30 g fat

Macaroni & Cheese
560 calories
35 g fat

BAJA FRESH

D Baja Fresh is like communism or friends with benefits: In theory, it sounds great, but in practice, it fails miserably. It's nice that Baja makes all of its menu items fresh on-site, but why can't it make a simple chicken burrito for under 600 calories? And what's up with all of the "naturally occurring" trans fats in their quesadillas and nachos? To minimize damage, turn to the tacos—then turn for the door.

SURVIVAL STRATEGY

Unless you're comfortable stuffing 108 grams of fat into your arteries, avoid the nachos at all costs. In fact, avoid almost everything on this menu. The only safe options are the tacos, the torta, or a salad topped with salsa verde and served without the elephantine tortilla bowl.

Eat This

Savory Pork Carnitas Baja Ensalada
with Salsa Verde

385 calories
18 g fat
(6 g saturated)
1,780 mg sodium

The Baja Ensalada menu offers the chain's only salad options with fewer than 600 calories. And though salsa is known for its excellence as a chip dip, it also makes a super light salad dressing that, in this case, adds a mere 15 calories to your meal.

OTHER PICKS

Steak Original Baja Taco (2)
460 calories
16 g fat
(4 g saturated)
520 mg sodium

Shrimp Americano Soft Taco (2)
460 calories
20 g fat
(9 g saturated)
1,280 mg sodium

Side Salad
130 calories
6 g fat
(1.5 g saturated)
430 mg sodium

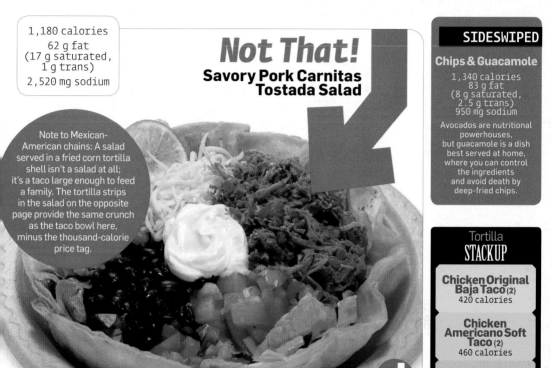

1,180 calories
62 g fat
(17 g saturated, 1 g trans)
2,520 mg sodium

Not That!

Savory Pork Carnitas Tostada Salad

Note to Mexican-American chains: A salad served in a fried corn tortilla shell isn't a salad at all; it's a taco large enough to feed a family. The tortilla strips in the salad on the opposite page provide the same crunch as the taco bowl here, minus the thousand-calorie price tag.

OTHER PASSES

Chips and Salsa Baja
810 calories
37 g fat
(4 g saturated, 1.5 g trans)
1,140 mg sodium

Shrimp Fajitas with Flour Tortillas
1,120 calories
32 g fat
(10 g saturated)
3,410 mg sodium

Charbroiled Steak Quesadilla
1,430 calories
87 g fat
(41 g saturated, 3 g trans)
2,600 mg sodium

SIDESWIPED

Chips & Guacamole
1,340 calories
83 g fat
(8 g saturated, 2.5 g trans)
950 mg sodium

Avocados are nutritional powerhouses, but guacamole is a dish best served at home, where you can control the ingredients and avoid death by deep-fried chips.

Tortilla STACKUP

Chicken Original Baja Taco (2)
420 calories

Chicken Americano Soft Taco (2)
460 calories

Chicken Baja Burrito
790 calories

Charbroiled Chicken Quesadilla
1,330 calories

Charbroiled Chicken Nachos
2,020 calories

BASKIN-ROBBINS

C- Baskin-Robbins has a long tradition of carrying some of the worst frozen fare in the country. Sure, they shed their atrocious line of Premium Shakes, but it's going to take a lot more downsizing to earn a higher grade from us. The Premium Sundae line averages 1,015 calories, and even the average small Fruit Blast Smoothie contains 71 grams of sugars. If not for the frozen yogurt and sherbet, this grade would be even worse.

SURVIVAL STRATEGY

With choices like frozen yogurt, sherbet, and no-sugar-added ice cream, Baskin's lighter menu is the one bright spot in this otherwise dark world. Beyond that, look to the freezer for a Grab-N-Go treat. Stacked next to a shake, sundae, or even a smoothie, these are great bets.

Eat This

Oreo Cookies 'n Cream Ice Cream in a Cake Cone
(two 2.5-oz scoops)

365 calories
18 g fat
(10 g saturated)
34 g sugars

Keep it simple at the scoop shop. Most BR flavors weigh in at under 200 calories per scoop, so when you pile two of 'em on a 25-calorie cake cone, you get a classic American treat with a reasonable calorie load.

OTHER PICKS

Cappuccino Blast Made with Soft Serve
(small)
280 calories
8 g fat
(6 g saturated)
41 g sugars

Chocolate Chip Cookie Dough Ice Cream
in a Cake Cone
(two 2.5-oz scoops)
405 calories
18 g fat
(12 g saturated)
38 g sugars

Soft Serve Cookie Sandwich
190 calories
5 g fat
(3 g saturated)
21 g sugars

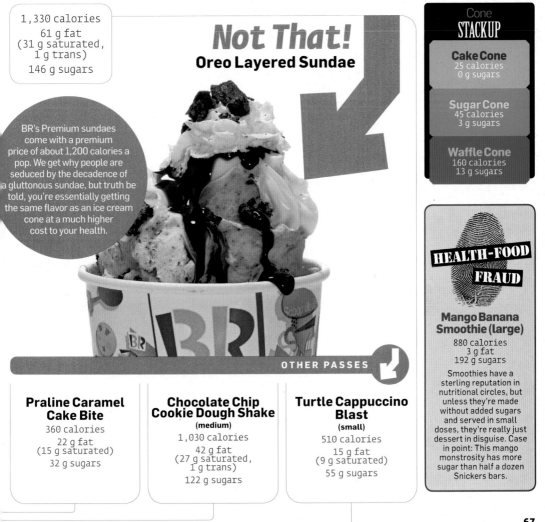

1,330 calories
61 g fat
(31 g saturated,
1 g trans)
146 g sugars

Not That!

Oreo Layered Sundae

BR's Premium sundaes come with a premium price of about 1,200 calories a pop. We get why people are seduced by the decadence of a gluttonous sundae, but truth be told, you're essentially getting the same flavor as an ice cream cone at a much higher cost to your health.

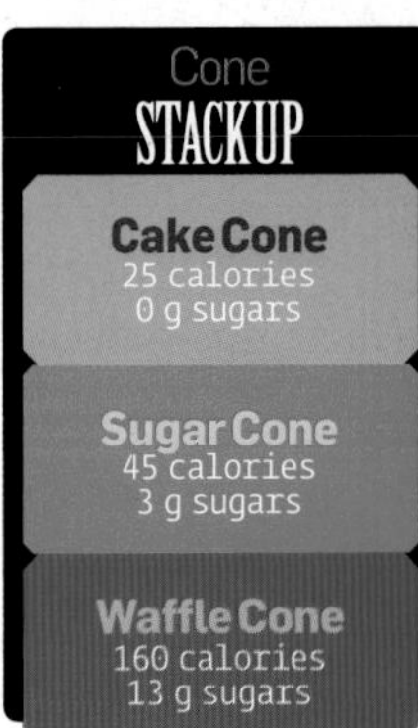

Cone
STACKUP
Cake Cone
25 calories
0 g sugars
Sugar Cone
45 calories
3 g sugars
Waffle Cone
160 calories
13 g sugars

Mango Banana Smoothie (large)

880 calories
3 g fat
192 g sugars

Smoothies have a sterling reputation in nutritional circles, but unless they're made without added sugars and served in small doses, they're really just dessert in disguise. Case in point: This mango monstrosity has more sugar than half a dozen Snickers bars.

OTHER PASSES

Praline Caramel Cake Bite

360 calories
22 g fat
(15 g saturated)
32 g sugars

Chocolate Chip Cookie Dough Shake
(medium)

1,030 calories
42 g fat
(27 g saturated,
1 g trans)
122 g sugars

Turtle Cappuccino Blast
(small)

510 calories
15 g fat
(9 g saturated)
55 g sugars

BEN & JERRY'S

C What sets Ben & Jerry's apart from the competition amounts to more than just an affinity for jam bands and hacky sacks. The company remains committed to the quality of its ingredients. All dairy is hormone free and the chocolate, vanilla, and coffee ingredients are all Fair Trade Certified. From a strictly nutritional standpoint, though, it's still just an ice cream shop, and Ben & Jerry's average scoop is packed with more fat and sugar than most of its competitors.

SURVIVAL STRATEGY

With half of the calories of the ice cream, sorbet makes the healthiest choice on the menu. If you demand dairy, the frozen yogurt can still save you up to 100 calories per scoop.

Eat This

Banana Peanut Butter Greek Frozen Yogurt
(½ cup)

210 calories
9 g fat
(2.5 g saturated)
22 g sugars

We were glad to see Ben & Jerry's introduce its new line of Greek frozen yogurt flavors this year. Greek fro yo offers the same creamy goodness of regular ice cream, minus most of the saturated fat.

OTHER PICKS

Rocky Road-ish Ice Cream
(½ cup)
250 calories
12 g fat
(7 g saturated)
24 g sugars

Super Pomegranate Smoothie
(large)
190 calories
0 g fat
36 g sugars

Dave Matthews Band's Magic Brownies Ice Cream
(½ cup)
230 calories
12 g fat
(7 g saturated)
22 g sugars

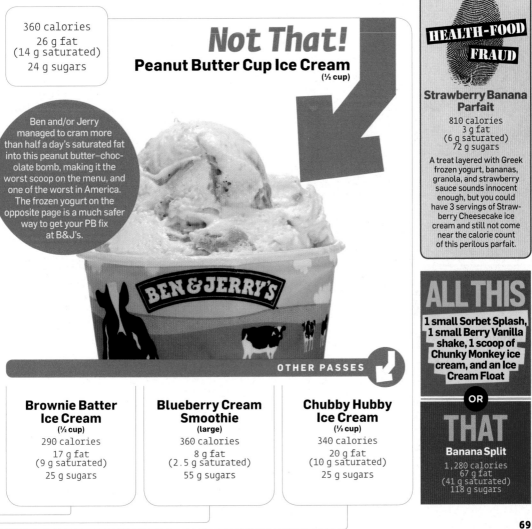

360 calories
26 g fat
(14 g saturated)
24 g sugars

Not That!

Peanut Butter Cup Ice Cream
(½ cup)

Ben and/or Jerry managed to cram more than half a day's saturated fat into this peanut butter–chocolate bomb, making it the worst scoop on the menu, and one of the worst in America. The frozen yogurt on the opposite page is a much safer way to get your PB fix at B&J's.

OTHER PASSES

Brownie Batter Ice Cream
(½ cup)
290 calories
17 g fat
(9 g saturated)
25 g sugars

Blueberry Cream Smoothie
(large)
360 calories
8 g fat
(2.5 g saturated)
55 g sugars

Chubby Hubby Ice Cream
(½ cup)
340 calories
20 g fat
(10 g saturated)
25 g sugars

Strawberry Banana Parfait
810 calories
3 g fat
(6 g saturated)
72 g sugars

A treat layered with Greek frozen yogurt, bananas, granola, and strawberry sauce sounds innocent enough, but you could have 3 servings of Strawberry Cheesecake ice cream and still not come near the calorie count of this perilous parfait.

ALL THIS
1 small Sorbet Splash, 1 small Berry Vanilla shake, 1 scoop of Chunky Monkey ice cream, and an Ice Cream Float

OR

THAT
Banana Split
1,280 calories
67 g fat
(41 g saturated)
118 g sugars

BLIMPIE

B- In the past, we admonished Blimpie for its love of trans fat. Since then, the chain has quietly removed all the dangerous oils of its menu and earned itself a place of honor in our book. But that doesn't mean the menu is free of danger. Blimpie likes to splash oil on just about everything containing deli meat, and there are a handful of sinful subs that top the 1,000-calorie mark.

SURVIVAL STRATEGY

A Bluffin makes a solid breakfast, and the Grilled Chicken Teriyaki Sandwich is one of the best in the business. But skip the wraps and most of the hot sandwiches. And no matter which sandwich you choose, swap out mayo and oil for mustard or light dressing.

Eat This

French Dip Ciabatta Panini Sandwich (6")

410 calories
11 g fat
(5 g saturated)
1,650 mg sodium

Shavings of fatty prime rib and blankets of cheese usually make French dips menu items to avoid, but a Blimpie dip turns out to be a respectable sandwich. Much of the sodium comes from the side of au jus, so go easy on the dunking.

OTHER PICKS

Hot Pastrami Sandwich (6")

430 calories
16 g fat
(7 g saturated)
1,350 mg sodium

Ham Egg & Cheese Bluffin

280 calories
10 g fat
(5 g saturated)
1,050 mg sodium

Chocolate Chunk Cookie

180 calories
10 g fat
(5 g saturated)
14 g sugars

590 calories
35 g fat
(11 g saturated)
1,410 mg sodium

Not That!

Philly Steak & Onion Sandwich (6")

This is what we like to call a Top Swap, a painless substitution between two nearly identical menu items that will save you major calories. Both subs here are substantial steak sandwiches, but opting for the cheese-covered French Dip over the Philly will save you 180 calories and cut your fat by a third.

SALT LICK

SUPER STACKED TURKEY & BACON SANDWICH (12")

5,250 mg sodium
1,250 calories
57 g fat
(21 g saturated)

Blimpie loves the salt shaker, so anything Super Stacked will come at a cost to your blood pressure. This particular sub has more sodium than 138 Saltine Crackers.

Guilty Pleasure

Roast Beef & Provolone Sub (6")

430 calories
15 g fat
(5 g saturated)
1,020 mg sodium

Roast beef gets a bad rap at the deli counter, but its calorie count and fat content are usually on par with turkey, ham, and other lean cold cuts. This sub has the same amount of saturated fat as Blimpie's Turkey & Provolone, but it feels a little more indulgent.

OTHER PASSES

Sugar Cookie
320 calories
15 g fat
(6 g saturated)
23 g sugars

Sausage Grilled Breakfast Sandwich
710 calories
45 g fat
(18 g saturated)
1,920 mg sodium

Meatball Sandwich (6")
560 calories
29 g fat
(13 g saturated)
1,820 mg sodium

BOB EVANS

C- No menu in America is more perplexing than Bob's. On one hand, the Ohio-based chain offers up an array of great entrées and side options, making it easy to cobble together a well-balanced meal. On the other, the menu is littered with land mines like 1,200-calorie multigrain pancakes and 1,000-calorie chicken salads. Until Mr. Evans shows us some consistency, we'll be showing him a lousy report card.

SURVIVAL STRATEGY

Breakfast should consist of staples like oatmeal, eggs, fruit, and yogurt (with maybe a slice or two of bacon); for lunch and dinner, stick with grilled chicken or fish paired with one of the non-fried vegetable sides. Or opt for one of Bob's perfectly portioned Savory Size entrées.

Eat This

Sunshine Skillet

(without Biscuits)

436 calories
24 g fat
(10 g saturated)
1,410 mg sodium

An omelet with fewer than 500 calories is a rarity at American breakfast chains, but this open-faced version at Bob Evans requires fewer eggs, so the sausage, potato, and cheese fillings don't take it over the caloric edge.

OTHER PICKS

Pot Roast Stroganoff
(Savor Size)
431 calories
26 g fat
(10 g saturated)
1,121 mg sodium

The Farm Favorite Fried Chicken Sandwich
658 calories
26 g fat
(8 g saturated)
1,578 mg sodium

Fruit & Yogurt Crepe and Quaker Oatmeal
612 calories
17 g fat
(4 g saturated)
343 mg sodium

884 calories
56 g fat
(14 g saturated)
2,124 mg sodium

Not That!

2 Scrambled Eggs

with 3 Sausage Links and Hash Browns

Ordering à la carte is usually your best strategy at big breakfast chains, but a couple of misguided choices can take your custom creation into dangerous territory. Switch the sausage to bacon and the hash browns to home fries, and you'll bring this meal down to a much more reasonable 418 calories.

MENU MAGIC

Opting for mashed potatoes over french fries at Bob Evans will save you more than 300 calories and 12 g of fat. But be warned: This strategy won't work its magic everywhere. Many chains jack their mashed taters with copious amounts of cream and butter.

OTHER PASSES

Cranberry Multigrain Hotcakes

(3) with Butter and Syrup

1,247 calories
16 g fat
(6 g saturated)
1,537 mg sodium

The Smokehouse Grilled Chicken Sandwich

890 calories
47 g fat
(17 g saturated)
2,642 mg sodium

Slow Roasted Chicken Pot Pie

862 calories
56 g fat
(22 g saturated)
2,623 mg sodium

HIDDEN DANGER

Buttermilk Biscuit

Many of the breakfast items come with a side of two biscuits, which may feel like a bonus to hungry eaters, but the damage is often worse than the breakfast itself. Remember, it's these items—the bread basket, the chips and salsa, the "free" biscuits—that do the most damage to your waistline.

476 calories
24 g fat
(14 g saturated)
1,570 mg sodium

BOSTON MARKET

B With the addition of two new sides containing 7 and 9 grams of saturated fat, Boston Market's menu continues to head in the wrong direction. Healthy combination platters can still be had, but more dietary land mines is not what this menu needs. What it does need? Less butter, less cheese, and makeovers of the Meatloaf, Pastry Top Chicken Pot Pie, and the entire line of Boston Carver sandwiches.

SURVIVAL STRATEGY

Pair roasted turkey, ham, white-meat chicken, or even beef brisket with a vegetable side or two, and you've got a solid dinner. But avoid calorie-laden dark-meat chicken, meat loaf, potpie, and almost anything served between two pieces of bread. And choose your sides carefully.

Eat This

Roasted Turkey Breast

(large) with Garlic Dill New Potatoes and Mediterranean Green Beans

520 calories
17 g fat
(5.5 g saturated)
1,210 mg sodium

The piecemeal approach is still the best way to go at Boston Market, and there's no better place to start than with turkey breast. A 7-ounce piece contains 54 grams of protein, meaning that an astounding 83 percent of the turkey's 260 calories come from the metabolism-spiking macronutrient.

OTHER PICKS

Beef Brisket

(regular) with Fresh Vegetable Stuffing

420 calories
21 g fat
(4.5 g saturated)
1,150 mg sodium

Turkey Breast

(regular)

180 calories
3 g fat
(1 g saturated)
620 mg sodium

Cinnamon Apples

210 calories
3 g fat
15 mg sodium

1,110 calories
50 g fat
(17 g saturated)
2,500 mg sodium

Not That!

Half Rotisserie Chicken

with Mashed Potatoes and Cornbread

Peel aside the skin on this rotisserie bird and you'll save 200 calories and 21 grams of fat. But if you just can't resist, order a quarter bird instead. More importantly, find some better partners for the bird. The cornbread and mashed potatoes combine for 470 calories and 1,120 milligrams of sodium—and that's before you add gravy.

OTHER PASSES

Sweet Potato Casserole
460 calories
16 g fat
(4.5 g saturated)
270 mg sodium

Quarter White Rotisserie Chicken
320 calories
13 g fat
(4 g saturated)
710 mg sodium

Meatloaf
(regular)
with Mashed Potatoes
750 calories
41 g fat
(18 g saturated, 2 g trans)
1,910 mg sodium

FrankenFood

Meatloaf
(large)

720 calories
45 g fat
(20 g saturated, 3 g trans)
1,635 mg sodium

Meatloaf might be comfort food, but the recipe for Boston Market's loaf boasts a 45-ingredient lineup of additives you won't find in your kitchen. That is, unless your mom's recipe calls for modified starch, maltodextrin, and xantham gum.

Side STACKUP

Fresh Steamed Vegetables
60 calories

Sweet Corn
170 calories

Mashed Potatoes
270 calories

Creamed Spinach
280 calories

Half Caesar Salad
360 calories

BURGER KING

C- BK may have switched its motto, but it's still serving a menu long on nutritional losers. If anything, matters have only deteriorated, with the emergence of 400-calorie wraps, sugar-loaded smoothies, and coffee drinks with nearly as many calories as a Whopper. Add to that the normal oversized burgers and chicken sandwiches and BK is lucky to escape with a C-. Thankfully, standbys like the Whopper Jr., Chicken Tenders, and Apple Fries give you a way out.

SURVIVAL STRATEGY

Start your day with a Muffin Sandwich. For lunch, match the regular hamburger, the Whopper Jr., or the Tendergrill Sandwich with Apple Fries and water, and you'll escape for under 600 calories.

Eat This

Western BBQ Cheeseburger BK Toppers Burger

with Lettuce, Tomato, and Onions

400 calories
23 g fat
(9 g saturated, 1 g trans)
720 mg sodium

It's tough to find even a basic fast-food burger with fewer than 450 calories and 10 grams of saturated fat, but a burger that meets those criteria and comes souped up with barbecue sauce, onion rings, and cheese? We're impressed. If only we could say the same for the rest of BK's new menu lineup.

OTHER PICKS

TenderGrill Chicken Sandwich

470 calories
18 g fat
(3.5 g saturated)
1,330 mg sodium

Chicken Tenders

with Sweet and Sour Sauce (6 pieces)

335 calories
17 g fat
(3 g saturated)
515 mg sodium

Sausage, Egg & Cheese Muffin Sandwich

390 calories
23 g fat
(9 g saturated)
960 mg sodium

770 calories
50 g fat
(21 g saturated, 0.5 g trans)
1,820 mg sodium

Not That!
BK Chef's Choice Burger

BK recently joined its Golden Arches rival in offering specialty burgers designed to imitate the more substantial burgers offered by sit-down chains. The problem? These pseudo-gourmet burgers translate into nothing more than bigger portions (aka bigger calorie loads). BK is not the place to go gourmet.

Whopper Jr. (without Mayo)

260 calories
10 g fat
(4 g saturated)
460 mg sodium

Sans mayo, the Whopper Jr. is a star beyond just the realm of Burger King. Order it solo for a solid snack or pair it with Chicken Tenders or a side garden salad for a satisfying meal.

OTHER PASSES

Southwestern Breakfast Burrito

620 calories
37 g fat
(14 g saturated, 0.5 g trans)
1,740 calories

TenderCrisp Chicken Sandwich

750 calories
45 g fat
(8 g saturated, 0.5 g trans)
1,560 mg sodium

Chicken Apple & Cranberry Garden Fresh Salad
with TenderCrisp Chicken and Dressing

700 calories
41 g fat (9 g saturated)
1,090 mg sodium

ALL THIS

1 Hamburger, Chicken Tenders (4 pieces), Onion Rings (small), Mozzarella Sticks, and a Strawberry Sundae

OR

THAT

Triple Whopper with Cheese

1,230 calories

CALIFORNIA PIZZA KIT

D+ CPK's newest menu items include 1,000-calorie tacos, a 950-calorie peach salad, and a 1,439-calorie plate of mac and cheese. The rest of the menu looks just as bad: The pastas, salads, and entrées are still horrible, and the spaghettini still ruins every meal it touches. The bright spots on CPK's rather dismal menu are the Small Cravings Menu, and, surprisingly enough, the pizza itself, as long as you order the right pie.

SURVIVAL STRATEGY

Either turn a healthier appetizer (like the Dynamite Shrimp, Lettuce Wraps, or dumplings) or something from the new Small Cravings Menu into an entrée, or pair a few slices of Thin Crust Pizza with the Wedge Salad or a cup of Artichoke and Broccoli Soup.

Eat This

Original BBQ Chicken Pizza

(3 slices)

528 calories
N/A g fat
(8 g saturated)
1,281 mg sodium

With no shortage of pastas and salads that break the 1,000-calorie mark, eating a few slices of pizza is your safest move at CPK. Chicken makes a great low-calorie, high-protein topper, and this is among the lightest pies on the menu.

OTHER PICKS

Pepperoni Pizza
(3 slices)
555 calories
N/A g fat
(9.5 g saturated)
1,335 mg sodium

Baja Chicken Tortilla Spring Rolls
(2)
602 calories
N/A g fat
(12 g saturated)
1,364 mg sodium

Mediterranean Plate
368 calories
N/A g fat
(4 g saturated)
690 mg sodium

1,280 calories
N/A g fat
(19 g saturated)
1,732 mg sodium

Not That!

Full Original BBQ Chicken Chopped Salad with Avocado

That's right, you could eat an entire BBQ Chicken Pizza and still not come close to the calorie count of this salad. Time and again CPK manages to take some of the world's healthiest ingredients—like avocados and black beans—and serve them up in dishes that sport eye-popping calorie counts.

WEAPON OF MASS DESTRUCTION
Traditional Mac 'N' Cheese

1,439 calories
N/A g fat
(54 g saturated)
1,674 mg sodium

No sane person considers macaroni and cheese a healthy dish, but with half a day's calories and more than 2 days' worth of saturated fat, CPK's version takes the classic comfort food from fattening to downright frightening.

OTHER PASSES

Tuscan Hummus
with Traditional Pita
862 calories
N/A g fat
(4 g saturated)
1,515 mg sodium

Avocado Club Egg Rolls
1,224 calories
N/A g fat
(22 g saturated)
2,079 mg sodium

The Meat Cravers Pizza
(3 slices)
745 calories
N/A g fat
(15.5 g saturated)
2,082 mg sodium

Crust SELECTOR

Thin
440 calories
N/A g fat (0 g saturated)
958 mg sodium

Honey-Wheat with Whole Grain
594 calories
N/A g fat (1 g saturated)
948 mg sodium

Traditional
614 calories
N/A g fat (2 g saturated)
1,115 mg sodium

CARL'S JR.

C+ For a place that used to be an unabashed peddler of problematic foods, Carl's Jr. has shown a surprisingly strong desire to right its nutritional wrongs. Now, to balance out a menu still littered with some of the worst burgers and breakfast options in America, Carl's offers a line of grilled chicken sandwiches, salads, and, most impressively, the fast-food industry's first successful line of turkey burgers.

SURVIVAL STRATEGY

There are three clear-cut paths to salvation at Carl's: the Original Grilled Chicken Salad with low-fat balsamic dressing, the Charbroiled BBQ Chicken Sandwich, or any of the four turkey burgers. Stray from these paths at your own calorie-laden, fat-riddled peril.

Eat This

Single Teriyaki Burger

630 calories
29 g fat
(11 g saturated)
1,060 mg sodium

Certainly not the healthiest drive-thru burger around, but other than the ultra-basic Big Hamburger, it's the only beef burger on the menu that falls below 700 calories. Plus, the grilled pineapple topper adds a gourmet twist you won't find at most fast-food joints.

OTHER PICKS

Santa Fe Turkey Burger
490 calories
22 g fat
(6 g saturated)
1,010 mg sodium

Sourdough Breakfast Sandwich
450 calories
21 g fat
(8 g saturated)
1,470 mg sodium

Hand-Breaded Chicken Tenders (3)
260 calories
13 g fat
(2.5 g saturated)
770 mg sodium

940 calories
59 g fat
(24 g saturated,
1.5 g trans)
1,560 mg sodium

Not That!
Super Star with Cheese

From jumbo patties to superfluous toppings, excess is the standard at Carl's Jr. Case in point: The double whammy of Special Sauce and mayo makes this basic double cheese-burger one of the worst you'll find.

Breakfast Burger

810 calories
42 g fat
(16 g saturated,
1 g trans)
1,480 mg sodium

A plate of eggs, bacon, and hash browns is a simple breakfast meal. A plain cheeseburger is a simple lunch choice. But when you merge them together, you get a freaky creation that's simply one of the worst fast-food breakfast sandwiches in America.

Charbroiled Turkey Burgers

(4 varieties)

470 to 490 calories
14 to 23 g fat
(4.5 to 6 g saturated)
960 to 1,120 mg sodium

In 2011, we worked with Carl's to design a line of turkey burgers, which continues to be a top seller. Lean, juicy turkey with toppings like teriyaki and guacamole—what's not to love?

OTHER PASSES

Sweet Potato Fries

(small)

450 calories
21 g fat
(8 g saturated)
1,470 mg sodium

Big Country Breakfast Burrito

750 calories
44 g fat
(14 g saturated)
1,520 mg sodium

Charbroiled Santa Fe Chicken Sandwich

640 calories
36 g fat
(8 g saturated)
1,370 mg sodium

THE CHEESECAKE FAC

F With more calories than a county fair concession stand and more sodium than a salt flat, the Cheesecake Factory's menu is in desperate need of an overhaul. They made some progress this year by introducing the new SkinnyLicious menu, but most entrées still come with quadruple digit calorie counts. Once again, the Cheesecake Factory retains the title of Worst Restaurant in America.

Eat This

Factory Burger

780 calories
N/A g fat
(15 g saturated)
1,157 mg sodium

You'll seldom find a burger at any sit-down chain with fewer than 800 calories, so to find one at the most calorie-infested restaurant in the country is quite a feat. But be warned: With an average of 1,260 calories, the other burgers on the menu are more in line with the Cheesecake Factory's standard fare.

SURVIVAL STRATEGY

Your best survival strategy is to turn your car around and head home for a meal cooked in your own kitchen. Failing that, skip pasta, specialties, combos, and sandwiches at all costs. Split a pizza or a salad, or look to the new SkinnyLicious menu.

OTHER PICKS

Seared Tuna Tataki Salad
580 calories
N/A g fat
(4 g saturated)
1,761 mg sodium

Crispy Crab Bites
360 calories
N/A g fat
(5 g saturated)
498 mg sodium

Mini Egg Breakfast
240 calories
N/A g fat
(6 g saturated)
473 mg sodium

ORY

1,560 calories
N/A g fat
(26 g saturated)
1,927 mg sodium

Not That!

Grilled Chicken and Avocado Club

Only in the bizarro world of the Cheesecake Factory could a grilled chicken sandwich house more than double the calories of a burger. We're consistently baffled by the chain's ability to cram staggering amounts of calories, fat, and salt into ordinary-sounding dishes. Add fries and you're looking at 2,470 calories on a single plate.

OTHER PASSES

Brioche Breakfast Sandwich
1,190 calories
N/A g fat
(27 g saturated)
2,292 mg sodium

Warm Crab & Artichoke Dip
760 calories
N/A g fat
(22 g saturated)
985 mg sodium

Chicken Caesar Salad
1,400 calories
N/A g fat
(21 g saturated)
1,351 mg sodium

WEAPON OF MASS DESTRUCTION

Fettuccini Alfredo with Chicken

2,300 calories
N/A g fat
(103 g saturated)
1,297 mg sodium

Fettuccine Alfredo's one of the worst dishes you can order at any chain, but leave it to the Cheesecake Factory to take the creamy catastrophe to new heights. An entire day's calories in a single bowl of pasta? No thanks.

Pasta STACKUP

Pasta Marinara
1,100 calories
12 g saturated fat

Shrimp with Angel Hair
1,150 calories
6 g saturated fat

Garlic Noodles
1,540 calories
20 g saturated fat

Pasta Carbonara
2,200 calories
83 g saturated fat

CHICK-FIL-A

A-

Chick-fil-A ranks among the best of the country's major fast-food establishments, thanks to a line of low-calorie chicken sandwiches and an impressive roster of healthy sides like fruit cups and various salads. But a revision to their nutritional information last year revealed a menu inching ever upward in the calorie and sodium departments. Any more movement and this A- becomes a B.

SURVIVAL STRATEGY

Instead of nuggets or strips, look to the Chargrilled Chicken sandwiches or the classic fried chicken sandwich. And sub in a healthy side—fruit or soup—for the standard fried fare. Just don't supplement your meal with a shake—none has fewer than 500 calories.

Eat This

Chick-fil-A Chicken Sandwich

440 calories
16 g fat
(3.5 g saturated)
1,400 mg sodium

You'll rarely find anything deep-fried on this side of the page, but Chick-fil-A's classic sandwich is a surprisingly modest indulgence. The 290-calorie grilled chicken sandwich is still your lightest option, but there are much worse ways you could get your fried-chicken fix.

OTHER PICKS

Chargrilled Chicken Sandwich
290 calories
4 g fat
(1 g saturated)
780 mg sodium

Bacon, Egg, and Cheese Biscuit
440 calories
22 g fat
(11 g saturated)
1,160 mg sodium

Hearty Breast of Chicken Soup
140 calories
4 g fat
(1 g saturated)
1,110 mg sodium

610 calories
39 g fat
(9 g saturated)
1,240 mg sodium

Not That!

Chick-fil-A Chick-n-Strips Salad

with Buttermilk Ranch Dressing

A prime example of how fast-food chains turn salads into junk food. High-fat toppings like ranch dressing, fried chicken, and shredded cheese make this salad the most caloric entrée on the menu.

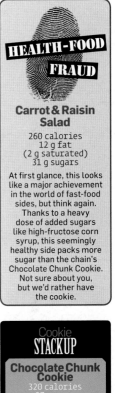

Carrot & Raisin Salad

260 calories
12 g fat
(2 g saturated)
31 g sugars

At first glance, this looks like a major achievement in the world of fast-food sides, but think again. Thanks to a heavy dose of added sugars like high-fructose corn syrup, this seemingly healthy side packs more sugar than the chain's Chocolate Chunk Cookie. Not sure about you, but we'd rather have the cookie.

OTHER PASSES

Chicken Salad Cup

350 calories
22 g fat
(4 g saturated)
1,130 mg sodium

Sausage, Egg, and Cheese Biscuit

670 calories
45 g fat
(19 g saturated)
1,420 mg sodium

Chicken Salad Sandwich

510 calories
19 g fat
(3.5 g saturated)
1,120 mg sodium

Chocolate Chunk Cookie
320 calories
27 sugars

Cookie Sundae
390 calories
52 sugars

Cookies & Cream Milkshake
(small)
520 calories
69 sugars

CHILI'S

D+ From tacos to salads to baby back ribs, Chili's serves up some of the country's saltiest, fattiest, most calorie-laden fare. Worst among the offenders are the burgers, fajitas, and appetizers, including the 2,120-calorie Texas Cheese Fries. The Lighter Choices menu is Chili's attempt to offer healthier meals, but with only a handful of options and a sky-high average sodium count, it's a meager attempt at nutritional salvation.

SURVIVAL STRATEGY

There's not too much to choose from after you eliminate the ribs, burgers, fajitas, and starters. Your best bet is a salad or the Create Your Own Combo section. Pair a spicy shrimp skewer with Margarita Chicken or sirloin and a side of black beans and salsa.

Classic Sirloin

(6 oz) with Sweet Corn on the Cob, Butter, and Steamed Broccoli

500 calories
22 g fat
(7 g saturated)
1,720 mg sodium

At Chili's—where the average burger plate packs 1,786 calories—creating your own steak combo is the safest way to meet your meat craving. Just be sure to stay away from 400-calorie accompaniments like the fries and Loaded Mashed Potatoes.

OTHER PICKS

Fried Cheese
with Marinara Sauce

660 calories
35 g fat
(15 g saturated)
2,040 mg sodium

Margarita Grilled Chicken

550 calories
14 g fat
(3.5 g saturated)
1,870 mg sodium

Caribbean Salad
with Grilled Chicken

610 calories
25 g fat
(4 g saturated)
810 mg sodium

1,570 calories
90 g fat
(29 g saturated)
3,170 mg sodium

Not That!

Avocado Burger on Wheat Bun

with Fries

This option stands out among the bevy of burgers topped with bacon and deep-fried onions. Unfortunately, the wheat bun and fresh avocado slices can't save it from the Chili's treatment: huge portions, fatty sauces, and a heaping pile of greasy fries. They don't call 'em Big Mouth Burgers for nothin'.

SALT LICK

Jalapeño Smokehouse Burger with Fries

6,600 mg sodium
2,210 calories

A typical Chili's burger plate packs a shameful 4,500 milligrams of sodium, and with nearly 3 days' worth of salt, this disaster is the worst of the lot. There's more salt here than you'd find in 2 pounds of roasted peanuts.

OTHER PASSES

Boneless Buffalo Chicken Salad
990 calories
68 g fat
(14 g saturated)
4,320 mg sodium

Monterey Chicken
890 calories
48 g fat
(20 g saturated)
2,920 mg sodium

Classic Nachos (large)
1,410 calories
96 g fat
(50 g saturated)
2,580 mg sodium

Appetizer STACKUP

Classic Nachos (regular)
960 calories
66 g fat

Loaded Potato Skins
1,050 calories
84 g fat

Skillet Queso with Chips
1,710 calories
101 g fat

Texas Cheese Fries with Ranch Sauce (half order)
1,960 calories
136 g fat

CHIPOTLE MEXICAN GR

C We've always commended Chipotle for the integrity of its ingredients and the flexibility of its menu. And the addition this year of soft corn tortillas is a big nutritional step forward. But this burrito bar could still do a lot better. After years of telling people to avoid the meal-wrecking chips (570 calories), flour burrito tortillas (290 calories), and vinaigrette (260 calories), we have a challenge for Chipotle: Offer a smaller version of your belly-busting burrito.

SURVIVAL STRATEGY

Chipotle assures us that they'll make anything a customer wants, as long as they have the ingredients. With fresh salsa, beans, lettuce, and grilled vegetables, you can do plenty of good. Skip the 13-inch tortillas, white rice, and sour cream and you'll do well.

Eat This

Soft Corn Tortilla Tacos

with Steak, Cheese, Lettuce, and Fresh Tomato Salsa

495 calories
16.5 g fat
(7 g saturated)
1,045 mg sodium

Chipotle scores big points in our book for finally offering up soft corn tortillas as an alternative to the flour vessels normally on the menu at Mexican-American restaurants. Ordering these instead of a burrito tortilla will boost fiber and save you 110 calories and 7.5 grams of fat.

OTHER PICKS

Burrito Bowl

with Barbacoa Beef, Black Beans, Cheese, Lettuce, and Fresh Tomato Salsa

415 calories
16.5 g fat
(7.5 g saturated)
1,410 mg sodium

Salad

with Chicken, Black Beans, Cheese, and Fresh Tomato Salsa

440 calories
16 g fat
(7 g saturated)
1,275 mg sodium

Guacamole (side order) and Crispy Corn Taco Shell (3)

330 calories
19 g fat
(3.5 g saturated)
220 mg sodium

ILL

1,070 calories
40.5 g fat
(18 g saturated)
2,060 mg sodium

Not That!

Burrito

with Steak, Black Beans, Cilantro-Lime Rice, Cheese, Sour Cream, and Roasted Chili-Corn Salsa

Chipotle prides itself on serving "Food with Integrity." We appreciate the chain's commitment to high-quality ingredients, but all the integrity in the world won't make sour cream less fattening or giant flour tortillas less caloric.

OTHER PASSES

Chips with Fresh Tomato Salsa

590 calories
27 g fat
(3.5 g saturated)
890 mg sodium

Salad

with Chicken, Black Beans, Cheese, and Vinaigrette

680 calories
40.5 g fat
(11 g saturated)
1,505 mg sodium

Soft Tacos

with Barbacoa Beef, Black Beans, Cheese, Lettuce, and Fresh Tomato Salsa

685 calories
24 g fat
(10.5 g saturated)
2,010 mg sodium

Salsa SELECTOR

Green Tomatillo (2 oz)
15 calories
230 mg sodium

Fresh Tomato (3.5 oz)
20 calories
470 mg sodium

Red Tomatillo (2 oz)
40 calories
510 mg sodium

Roasted Chili-Corn (3.5 oz)
80 calories
410 mg sodium

Tortilla STACKUP

Soft Corn Tortilla (3)
180 calories
1.5 g fat

Crispy Corn Taco Tortilla (3)
180 calories
6 g fat

Flour Taco Tortilla (3)
270 calories
7.5 g fat

Flour Burrito Tortilla
290 calories
9 g fat

COLD STONE CREAMERY

C– What makes Cold Stone novel is also what makes it so dangerous. The regular ice cream is fatty enough, but calorie counts quickly escalate when the mix-ins and toppings come into play. Sundaes are a total mess, small shakes average more than 950 calories, and cakes and plated desserts don't fare much better. Either stick to sorbet, frozen yogurt, and Sinless Sans Fat ice cream, or save this spot for (very) special occasions.

SURVIVAL STRATEGY

Keep your intake under 400 calories by filling a 5-ounce Like It–size cup with one of the lighter scoops, and then sprinkle fresh fruit on top. Or opt for one of the creamery's 16-ounce real-fruit smoothies, which average just 242 calories apiece.

Eat This

Double Chocolate Devotion Cupcake

360 calories
19 g fat
(13 g saturated)
40 g sugars

It's a sure sign that a menu is serious trouble when a big, choco-tastic cupcake emerges on the Eat This side of the page. Beyond the sorbets and Sinless Sans Fat ice creams, you won't find many items with fewer than 360 calories.

OTHER PICKS

Milk Caramel Latte
with Whipped Topping
(Like It size)
360 calories
17 g fat
(13 g saturated)
37 g sugars

Cookies & Creamery Frozen Yogurt
(Like It size)
210 calories
2 g fat
(0.5 g saturated)
33 g sugars

Sweet Cream Cupcake
390 calories
21 g fat
(15 g saturated)
44 g sugars

810 calories
55 g fat
(40 g saturated, 0.5 g trans)
75 g sugars

Not That!
Brownie a La Cold Stone

We've rarely seen a brownie that can earn our approval, much less a brownie smothered in hot fudge, caramel, and whipped cream that can. The net result of this concoction delivers more saturated fat than you'd find in a full cup of mayonnaise. Why do the damage when you can satisfy your chocolate craving for so much less?

1,427
The average number of calories in one of Cold Stone Creamery's Love It size milk shakes

OTHER PASSES

Hot for Cookie Warm Dessert
730 calories
38 g fat
(23 g saturated, 0.5 g trans)
67 g sugars

Oreo Crème Ice Cream
(Like It size)
440 calories
31 g fat
(14 g saturated, 0.5 g trans)
38 g sugars

Lotta Caramel Latte Shake
(Like It size)
1,100 calories
58 g fat
(38 g saturated, 1.5 g trans)
119 g sugars

The Topping STACKUP

Cinnamon
0 calories, 0 g fat
0 g sugar

Blueberries
10 calories, 0 g fat
2 g sugars

Chocolate Sprinkles
25 calories, 0 g fat
6 g sugars

Cherry Pie Filling
50 calories, 0 g fat
0 g sugars

Fudge
90 calories, 2 g fat
16 g sugars

Kit Kat Candy Bar
110 calories
5 g fat, 10 g sugars

Cookie Dough
180 calories
8 g fat, 26 g sugars

Reese's Peanut Butter Cup
190 calories
11 g fat, 17 g sugars

Peanuts
210 calories
18 g fat, 0 g sugars

COSÌ

B It's unfortunate that some of Così's best fare is available only during certain seasons. The year-round items aren't horrible compared with the industry status quo, but the majority could stand to shed a couple hundred calories. This includes a handful of sandwiches and salads; all of the melts, omelette sandwiches, muffins, and scones; and especially the flatbread pizzas, which average 831 calories per pie.

SURVIVAL STRATEGY

Only two items on Così's Lighter Side menu top the 500-calorie mark: the Così Cobb Light Salad and the Chicken T.B.M. Light. The remaining five items are your best bet for a low-calorie lunch or dinner. As for breakfast, oatmeal, parfaits, and wraps are all sound starts to your day.

Eat This

Tuscan Pesto Chicken Sandwich

511 calories
18 g fat
(6 g saturated)
454 mg sodium

With options ranging from the 350-calorie Fire-Roasted Veggie to the 854-calorie Steak & Brie, Così's sandwich menu is hit or miss, but the bold pesto flavor and sub-600 calorie count make this Tuscan chicken offering a hit. Plus, a chicken sandwich with fewer than 500 milligrams of sodium is a minor miracle.

OTHER PICKS

Shrimp Caesar Sandwich
481 calories
22 g fat
(8 g saturated)
902 mg sodium

Santa Fe Breakfast Wrap
470 calories
29 g fat
(12 g saturated)
1,005 mg sodium

Arctic Latte
189 calories
5 g fat
(3 g saturated)
34 g sugars

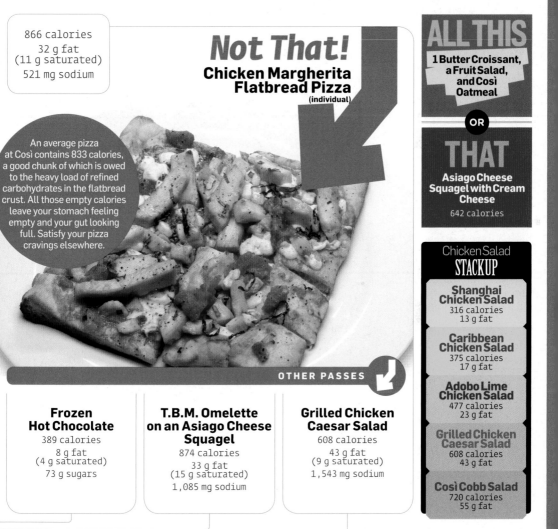

866 calories
32 g fat
(11 g saturated)
521 mg sodium

Not That!

Chicken Margherita Flatbread Pizza
(individual)

An average pizza at Così contains 833 calories, a good chunk of which is owed to the heavy load of refined carbohydrates in the flatbread crust. All those empty calories leave your stomach feeling empty and your gut looking full. Satisfy your pizza cravings elsewhere.

OTHER PASSES

Frozen Hot Chocolate
389 calories
8 g fat
(4 g saturated)
73 g sugars

T.B.M. Omelette on an Asiago Cheese Squagel
874 calories
33 g fat
(15 g saturated)
1,085 mg sodium

Grilled Chicken Caesar Salad
608 calories
43 g fat
(9 g saturated)
1,543 mg sodium

ALL THIS

1 Butter Croissant, a Fruit Salad, and Così Oatmeal

OR

THAT

Asiago Cheese Squagel with Cream Cheese
642 calories

Chicken Salad STACKUP

Shanghai Chicken Salad
316 calories
13 g fat

Caribbean Chicken Salad
375 calories
17 g fat

Adobo Lime Chicken Salad
477 calories
23 g fat

Grilled Chicken Caesar Salad
608 calories
43 g fat

Così Cobb Salad
720 calories
55 g fat

DAIRY QUEEN

C- By offering a few decent sandwiches, a Mini Blizzard, and reasonable-size 300-calorie sundaes, DQ has inched their way into C territory. Still, a wide array of bad burgers, bulging chicken baskets, and blindingly sweet concoctions leave plenty of room for error. Here's a look at one hypothetical meal: a Mushroom Swiss Burger with regular onion rings and a small Snickers Blizzard—a shocking 1,600 calories.

SURVIVAL STRATEGY

Your best offense is a solid defense: Skip elaborate burgers, fried sides, and specialty ice cream concoctions. Order a Grilled Chicken Sandwich or an Original Burger, and if you must have a treat, stick to a soft-serve cone or a small sundae.

Eat This

Hot Fudge Sundae
(small)

300 calories
10 g fat
(8 g saturated)
36 g sugars

A hot fudge sundae was once the epitome of decadence, but thanks to the invention of candy-infused soft-serve disasters like the Blizzard to your right, traditional sundaes are often the most prudent treats at big ice cream chains.

OTHER PICKS

Original Cheeseburger
400 calories
18 g fat
(9 g saturated, 0.5 g trans)
930 mg sodium

Grilled Chicken Sandwich
360 calories
15 g fat
(2.5 g saturated)
1,040 mg sodium

DQ Sandwich
190 calories
5 g fat
(3 g saturated)
18 g sugars

680 calories
35 g fat
(13 g saturated, 0.5 g trans)
63 g sugars

Not That!

Georgia Mud Fudge Blizzard
(small)

Same fudge-y flavor with more than triple the fat and roughly double the sugar and calories. Blizzard, McFlurry, 31° Below—whatever you call it, it's not worth the caloric investment.

OTHER PASSES

Buster Bar
460 calories
28 g fat
(16 g saturated)
36 g sugars

Iron Grilled Turkey Sandwich
550 calories
23 g fat
(7 g saturated)
1,600 mg sodium

¼ Pound GrillBurger
with Cheese
540 calories
30 g fat
(11 g saturated, 1 g trans)
1,020 mg sodium

WEAPON OF MASS DESTRUCTION
Chicken Strip Basket
(6 strips) with Country Gravy

1,260 calories
66 g fat
(11 g saturated, 0.5 g trans)
3,500 mg sodium

This bird basket houses more calories than a Bacon Double Cheeseburger with a large order of fries. Here's some quick math: Fried chicken + a pile of greasy fries + a cup of creamy gravy + 2 slices of butter-drenched toast = one of the worst chicken meals in America.

Guilty Pleasure

Corn Dog with Fries
(regular)

570 calories
28 g fat
(6 g saturated)
1,090 mg sodium

A battered and deep-fried hot dog doesn't exactly scream "healthy," but compared to DQ's 1,200-calorie basket meals, this corn dog-and-fry combo is surprisingly sensible.

DENNY'S

C- It's been a busy few years for Denny's. First came its $4 Fried Cheese Melt with four fried cheese sticks tucked inside a grilled cheese sandwich. Then came Baconalia, Denny's perverse seven-dish celebration of all things bacon. Just as it appeared the diner had hit rock bottom, it bounced back with a newly expanded line of first-rate Fit Fare entrées. It's just enough for Denny's to salvage a C-.

SURVIVAL STRATEGY

Look for the Fit Fare menu, which gathers together all the healthiest options at Denny's. Outside of that, stick to the shrimp skewers, grilled chicken, or soups. For breakfast, order a Veggie Cheese Omelette or create your own meal from à la carte options.

Eat This

Grand Slam

with 2 Eggs, 2 Strips of Bacon, an English Muffin, and Seasonal Fruit

520 calories
27 g fat
(7 g saturated)
722 mg sodium

The smartest approach at big breakfast chains? Bypass in-house creations and build your own balanced meal. You'll get more nutritional bang for your buck, and you'll avoid dessert-worthy pancakes and breakfast-sandwich bombs like the disaster on the opposite page.

OTHER PICKS

Prime Rib Philly Melt
(without sides)
670 calories
36 g fat
(11 g saturated)
1,770 mg sodium

Three-Dip & Chips
560 calories
25 g fat
(11 g saturated)
1,430 mg sodium

Prime Rib Skillet
585 calories
38 g fat
(12.5 g saturated)
1,460 mg sodium

1,520 calories
101 g fat
(44 g saturated, 1 g trans)
3,550 mg sodium

Not That!

The Grand Slamwich

with Hash Browns

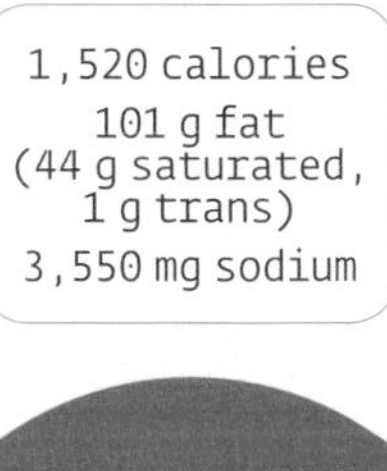

We slammed this Slamwich in 2011 and it's only gotten worse since then, picking up an additional 200 calories and 11 grams of fat. Eggs, bacon, sausage, ham, mayo, and cheese crammed between two butter-soaked slices of toast? It remains the worst breakfast sandwich in the country, and the single worst way to start your day.

OTHER PASSES

Ultimate Skillet
740 calories
56 g fat
(17 g saturated)
1,470 mg sodium

Zesty Nachos
1,340 calories
61 g fat
(29 g saturated)
2,800 mg sodium

Spicy Buffalo Chicken Melt
(without sides)
860 calories
48 g fat
(12 g saturated)
3,760 mg sodium

FrankenFood

Fried Cheese Melt
with Marinara Sauce

830 calories
40 g fat
(17 g saturated, 1 g trans)
2,920 mg sodium

Denny's received a lot of attention in 2010 when it released this cheesy creation. We're not sure what's worse: The fact that it's a grilled cheese sandwich stuffed with deep-fried mozzarella cheese sticks, or that the meal only costs $4.

Starch STACKUP

Grits with Margarine
90 calories
1 g fiber

Oatmeal with Milk
200 calories
4 g fiber

Hash Browns
210 calories
2 g fiber

Toast with Margarine (2 slices)
270 calories
1 g fiber

Buttermilk Pancakes (2)
330 calories
2 g fiber

DOMINO'S

B Domino's has been busy these past few years, first successfully rolling out bolder sauce and better-seasoned dough, then adding the new Artisan line of pizzas, which, along with the Crunchy Thin Crust pizzas, provide some of the lightest slices in America. But there is still plenty of trouble afoot at the pizza juggernaut—namely, a line of high-calorie specialty pies and breadsticks and Domino's appalling line of pasta bread bowls and oven-baked sandwiches.

SURVIVAL STRATEGY

The more loaded a pie is at Domino's, the fewer calories it tends to pack. That's because more vegetables and lean meats mean less space for cheese. It doesn't hold true for greasy meats, so choose wisely.

Eat This

Brooklyn Style Crust Grilled Chicken and Jalapeño Pepper Pizza
(2 slices, large pie)

560 calories
23 g fat
(10 g saturated)
1,720 mg sodium

Designing your own pie is the best approach at Domino's—or any pizza chain, for that matter—and this is one of the healthiest custom creations you can order. The Brooklyn crust is among is the chain's lightest, and grilled chicken is one of the leanest meat toppings on the menu.

OTHER PICKS

Hand Tossed Crust Chorizo and Bacon Pizza
(2 slices, large pie)

620 calories
24 g fat
(10 g saturated)
1,530 mg sodium

Crunchy Thin Crust Sliced Sausage, Onions, and Green Peppers Pizza
(2 slices, large pie)

480 calories
26 g fat (9 g saturated)
890 mg sodium

Fire Chicken Wings
(4)

200 calories
13 g fat
(3.5 g saturated)
1,350 mg sodium

700 calories
34 g fat
(17 g saturated)
1,760 mg sodium

Not That!

Hand Tossed Crust Buffalo Chicken American Legends Pizza
(2 slices, large pie)

This is why specialty pizzas fail our nutrition test. You have essentially the same flavor as the pizza on the left, but superfluous additions like multiple cheeses and a Cheddar-infused crust translate to nearly 150 additional calories and 11 extra grams of fat. The novelty's just not worth it.

OTHER PASSES

Cheesy Bread
(4)
480 calories
24 g fat
(8 g saturated)
560 mg sodium

Italian Sausage Marinara Breadbowl Pasta
1,460 calories
54 g fat
(20 g saturated)
2,760 mg sodium

Hand Tossed Crust MeatZZa Feast Pizza
(2 slices, large pie)
760 calories
38 g fat (16 g saturated)
2,060 mg sodium

FrankenFood

Chicken Carbonara Breadbowl Pasta
1,480 calories
56 g fat
(24 g saturated)
2,220 mg sodium

Domino's already doubled down on carbs with this bready pasta vessel, but by brushing it with an oil blend, they add 44 difficult-to-pronounce ingredients like "oleoresin garlic" and "lipolyzed butter oil" to the mix. Consider this preposterous pasta dish a science experiment gone horribly wrong.

ALL THIS

9 pieces Boneless Chicken, 1 slice medium Crunchy Thin Crust Ham and Pineapple Pizza, 1 Garden Fresh Salad
with Light Italian dressing

OR

THAT

Italian Sausage and Peppers Sandwich
860 calories

DUNKIN' DONUTS

B+ The doughnut king cast out the trans fats in 2007, and they've been pushing the menu toward healthier options ever since—including the DDSmart Menu, which emphasizes the menu's nutritional champions and introduces the low-fat and protein-packed flatbread sandwiches. Now there's no excuse to settle for bagels, muffins, doughnuts, and over-sweetened coffee drinks, which are as bad as ever.

SURVIVAL STRATEGY

Use the DDSmart Menu as a starting point, then stick to the sandwiches served on flatbread or English muffins. Beware: Beverages like Coolattas and souped-up coffee drinks can do even more damage than the food here, so keep your joe as plain as possible.

Eat This

Sugar Raised Donut and Iced Latte

(small, with skim milk)

300 calories
14 g fat
(6 g saturated)
14 g sugars

If poorly choosen (a Crumb donut, say, and a medium Coolatta) this same approach could yield a 1000-calorie breakfast. But this sugar-dusted donut and Iced Latte are both best in their respective classes, making this an acceptable start to your day.

OTHER PICKS

Apple 'n Spice Donut

270 calories
14 g fat
(6 g saturated)
8 g sugars

Caramel Mocha Iced Coffee

with Cream (medium)

260 calories
9 g fat
(6 g saturated)
36 g sugars

Triple Chocolate Chunk Cookie

340 calories
11 g fat
(6 g saturated)
34 g sugars

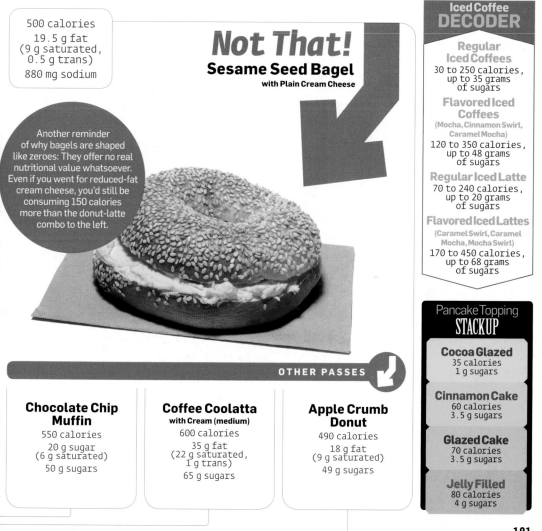

500 calories
19.5 g fat
(9 g saturated, 0.5 g trans)
880 mg sodium

Not That!

Sesame Seed Bagel

with Plain Cream Cheese

Another reminder of why bagels are shaped like zeroes: They offer no real nutritional value whatsoever. Even if you went for reduced-fat cream cheese, you'd still be consuming 150 calories more than the donut-latte combo to the left.

Iced Coffee DECODER

Regular Iced Coffees
30 to 250 calories, up to 35 grams of sugars

Flavored Iced Coffees (Mocha, Cinnamon Swirl, Caramel Mocha)
120 to 350 calories, up to 48 grams of sugars

Regular Iced Latte
70 to 240 calories, up to 20 grams of sugars

Flavored Iced Lattes (Caramel Swirl, Caramel Mocha, Mocha Swirl)
170 to 450 calories, up to 68 grams of sugars

OTHER PASSES

Chocolate Chip Muffin
550 calories
20 g sugar
(6 g saturated)
50 g sugars

Coffee Coolatta
with Cream (medium)
600 calories
35 g fat
(22 g saturated, 1 g trans)
65 g sugars

Apple Crumb Donut
490 calories
18 g fat
(9 g saturated)
49 g sugars

Pancake Topping STACKUP

Cocoa Glazed
35 calories
1 g sugars

Cinnamon Cake
60 calories
3.5 g sugars

Glazed Cake
70 calories
3.5 g sugars

Jelly Filled
80 calories
4 g sugars

FIVE GUYS

Without much more than burgers, hot dogs, and french fries on the menu, it's difficult to find anything nutritionally redeeming about Five Guys. The only option geared toward health-conscious consumers is the Veggie Sandwich. The burgers range from 480 to 920 calories, so how you order can make a big difference to your waistline. Keep your burgers small, choose your topping wisely, and skip the fries.

Eat This

Little Bacon Burger with Lettuce, Ketchup, and Onions

589 calories
33 g fat
(14.5 g saturated)
834 mg sodium

What's in a name? At Five Guys, apparently not much. The chain's regular burgers are doubles and its "Little" burgers are singles. The menu is high in calories and low in choices, so if you want to escape without consuming more than 600 calories, stick with a Little Burger topped with either cheese or bacon (but not both!).

OTHER PICKS

Hot Dog
545 calories
35 g fat
(15.5 g saturated)
1,130 mg sodium

Little Cheeseburger
550 calories
32 g fat
(15 g saturated)
690 mg sodium

Veggie Sandwich
440 calories
15 g fat
(6 g saturated)
1,040 mg sodium

SURVIVAL STRATEGY

The regular hamburger is actually a double, so order a Little Hamburger and load up on the vegetation. Or skip the patty entirely and play around with the huge variety of toppings—it's not hard to create a solid sandwich.

620 calories
30 g fat
(6 g saturated)
90 mg sodium

Not That!
Five Guys Style Fries (regular)

Okay, so there are only 30 more calories in the fries and they have less fat and sodium than the burger, but here's our point: The burger has nearly three times the belly-filling protein. Fries are nothing but blood sugar–spiking carbs soaked in oil. They offer far fewer nutrients than the burger, and you'll be hungry soon after you scarf them. Lay off the fries!

MEET YOUR MATCH
Five Guys Style Fries (large) 1,474 calories
33 Wendy's Chicken Nuggets

ALL THIS
Cheese, Jalapeno Peppers, Onions, Grilled Mushrooms, A.1. Steak Sauce

OR

THAT
Mayonnaise
100 calories

OTHER PASSES

Grilled Cheese
470 calories
26 g fat
(9 g saturated)
715 mg sodium

Cheese Dog
615 calories
41 g fat
(19 g saturated)
1,440 mg sodium

Hamburger
700 calories
43 g fat
(19.5 g saturated)
430 mg sodium

(5) The number of Five Guys locations that open every week

FRIENDLY'S

D For the health-conscious eater, there's nothing particularly friendly about this joint. Breakfast is a sordid affair of fat and refined carbs with few options under 1,000 calories, while lunch and dinner are headlined by a roster of hypercaloric sandwiches, salads, and chicken dishes. Even the Under 555 Calories menu, the only bastion of decent eating, has just 4 items. The best thing we can say about Friendly's is they have good sides.

SURVIVAL STRATEGY

Take advantage of Friendly's massive menu by honing in on the few relatively safe zones. For breakfast, that means eggs à la carte with a side of bacon or ham. For lunch and dinner, turn to the Under 555 Calories menu, or combine a cup of soup with a small salad or a few sides.

Eat This

Chicken Caprese Sandwich

with a Side Salad and Fat-Free Italian Dressing

550 calories
13 g fat
(3 g saturated)
1,970 mg sodium

The key to this sandwich's nutritional success lies in its condiments. Bruschetta and light balsamic vinaigrette offer bold flavor at a fraction of the fat and calories found in more traditional toppings like cheese and creamy dressings. It's also the only sandwich plate at Friendly's that falls under 800 calories.

OTHER PICKS

Broccoli Cheddar Soup
(bowl)

390 calories
25 g fat
(14 g saturated)
1,560 mg sodium

Ginger Chicken Stir-Fry

550 calories
13 g fat
(3 g saturated)
1,970 mg sodium

Happy Ending Hot Fudge Sundae

330 calories
17 g fat
(11 g saturated)
30 g sugars

1,140 calories
55 g fat
(10 g saturated)
1,620 mg sodium

Not That!

Crispy Chicken Wrap

with Fries

Grilled chicken is usually a sensible sandwich filler, but a high-calorie dose of honey mustard dressing and 340 calories of fries bring this chicken wrap to a burger-worthy calorie count. And a word to the wise: Despite their miniscule thickness, wraps often have the same or more calories than standard bread.

WEAPON OF MASS DESTRUCTION Honey BBQ Chicken SuperMelt Sandwich

1,500 calories
78 g fat
(24 g saturated)
2,410 mg sodium
41 g sugars

This sandwich attacks your body from all angles: Three-quarters of a day's calories, more than a day's worth of saturated fat and sodium, and as much sugar as you'd find in 124 Honey Teddy Grahams. If you want any chance of melting fat, stay away from the SuperMelt menu.

OTHER PASSES

Chocolate Fribble Shake
720 calories
20 g fat
(13 g saturated)
94 g sugars

Grilled Chicken Salad
840 calories
54 g fat
(13 g saturated)
1,420 mg sodium

Homestyle Clam Chowder (bowl)
540 calories
36 g fat
(20 g saturated)
1,790 mg sodium

Protein STACKUP

Grilled Chicken Breast
170 calories, 5 g fat
(1 g saturated)

Boca Burger Patty
180 calories, 7 g fat
(2 g saturated)

Big Beef Burger
310 calories 22 g fat
(9 g saturated)

HARDEE'S

C+ While Hardee's earns its reputation as one of the most perilous fast-food chains by continuing to sire one crazily caloric burger after the next (and by failing to offer any impressive breakfast options), this past year has brought encouraging changes to its menu. Most notably, the creation of a trio of lean turkey burgers now provides diners with a way to squash their hunger without breaking the caloric bank.

SURVIVAL STRATEGY

The Sunrise Croissant and the Frisco Breakfast Sandwich are two of your best options in the early hours. For lunch, look to the roast beef, the Big Hot Ham 'N' Cheese, or the BBQ Chicken Wrapper. Or seek salvation in a turkey burger, all of which are under 500 calories.

Eat This

Little Thick Cheeseburger

plus Lettuce and Tomato

436 calories
23 g fat
(9 g saturated)
1,092 mg sodium

Don't be limited by the confines of the drive-thru menu. Fast-food restaurants usually let you alter your burger at no extra cost, and the single best way to exercise your right to customize is to pile on the produce. The simple addition of lettuce and tomato makes a basic burger much more substantial.

OTHER PICKS

Charbroiled BBQ Chicken Sandwich
380 calories
6 g fat
(1 g saturated)
1,220 mg sodium

Hand Breaded Chicken Tenders
(3 pieces)
260 calories
13 g fat
(2.5 g saturated)
770 mg sodium

Ham, Egg & Cheese Biscuit
400 calories
22 g fat
(7 g saturated)
1,400 mg sodium

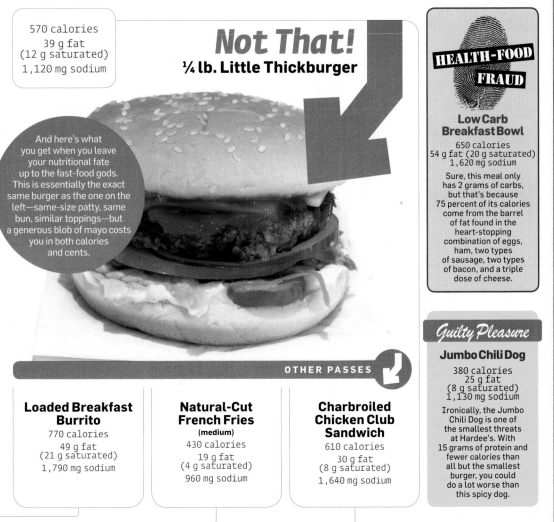

570 calories
39 g fat
(12 g saturated)
1,120 mg sodium

Not That!

¼ lb. Little Thickburger

And here's what you get when you leave your nutritional fate up to the fast-food gods. This is essentially the exact same burger as the one on the left—same-size patty, same bun, similar toppings—but a generous blob of mayo costs you in both calories and cents.

Low Carb Breakfast Bowl

650 calories
54 g fat (20 g saturated)
1,620 mg sodium

Sure, this meal only has 2 grams of carbs, but that's because 75 percent of its calories come from the barrel of fat found in the heart-stopping combination of eggs, ham, two types of sausage, two types of bacon, and a triple dose of cheese.

OTHER PASSES

Loaded Breakfast Burrito

770 calories
49 g fat
(21 g saturated)
1,790 mg sodium

Natural-Cut French Fries (medium)

430 calories
19 g fat
(4 g saturated)
960 mg sodium

Charbroiled Chicken Club Sandwich

610 calories
30 g fat
(8 g saturated)
1,640 mg sodium

Guilty Pleasure

Jumbo Chili Dog

380 calories
25 g fat
(8 g saturated)
1,130 mg sodium

Ironically, the Jumbo Chili Dog is one of the smallest threats at Hardee's. With 15 grams of protein and fewer calories than all but the smallest burger, you could do a lot worse than this spicy dog.

IHOP

D It's hard to give IHOP much credit for finally releasing their nutritional numbers, since it ranks among the last restaurant chains to do so. Factor in the new line of burger patties made out of bacon and the absolute worst breakfast menu in America and it's hard to find much to like about IHOP. The best thing we can say is that lunch and dinner aren't nearly as calamitous as breakfast.

SURVIVAL STRATEGY

You'll have a hard time finding a regular breakfast with fewer than 700 calories and a lunch or dinner with fewer than 1,000 calories. Your only safe bet is to stick to the IHOP for Me menu, where you'll find the nutritional content for a small selection of healthier items.

Eat This

Two × Two × Two

with Bacon

640 calories
37 g fat
(13 g saturated, 0.5 g trans)
1,580 mg sodium

There are two ways to leave IHOP with nutritional dignity: Choose one of the Simple & Fit items, or stick to the basics. This no-frills dish isn't winning any health food awards, but it's a pretty conservative breakfast compared to IHOP's typical 1,000-calorie fare. Just remember to go easy on the syrup.

OTHER PICKS

Chicken Fried Chicken
with Country Gravy, Steamed Broccoli, and Seasoned Red Skin Potatoes
690 calories
33 g fat
(10 g saturated)
2,160 mg sodium

Simple & Fit Whole Wheat French Toast Combo
490 calories
15 g fat
(4 g saturated)
930 mg sodium

Double BLT
650 calories
44 g fat
(10 g saturated)
1,400 mg sodium

1,160 calories
67 g fat
(27 g saturated,
1.5 g trans)
1,880 mg sodium

Not That!

Quick Two-Egg Breakfast
with Bacon

Sounds innocuous enough, yet it packs nearly double the calories and fat of the Two × Two × Two. The principle difference between this plate and the breakfast on the opposite page is the double dose of starch. It's never a good idea to double up on empty carbs, especially when one of them comes in the form of oil-drenched potatoes.

53

The number of breakfast entrées with more than 1,000 calories

Flapjack STACKUP
(per 4 pancakes)

Original Buttermilk
600 calories
17.5 g sugars

Chocolate Chip
720 calorie
32 g sugars

Strawberry Banana
760 calories
41 g sugars

Double Blueberry
800 calories
57 g sugars

Harvest Grain'N Nut
850 calories
22 g sugars

CINN-A-STACK
890 calories
58 g sugars

New York Cheesecake
1,100 calories
53 g sugars

OTHER PASSES

Ham and Egg Melt
1,090 calories
56 g fat
(28 g saturated,
1 g trans)
2,450 mg sodium

Whole Wheat with Banana Slices Viva La French Toast Combo with Bacon
980 calories
51 g fat (13 g saturated,
0.5 g trans)
1,590 mg sodium

Crispy Chicken Strips
with Steamed Broccoli, Mashed Potatoes, and Honey Mustard Sauce
1,010 calories
56 g fat
(14 g saturated,
0.5 g trans)
1,680 mg sodium

IN-N-OUT BURGER

B In-N-Out has the most pared-down menu in America. Wander in to the West Coast powerhouse and you'll find nothing more than burgers, fries, shakes, and sodas. While that's certainly nothing to build a healthy diet on, In-N-Out earns points for offering plenty of calorie-saving menu tweaks, like the Protein-Style Burger, which replaces the bun with lettuce and saves you 150 calories.

SURVIVAL STRATEGY

A single cheeseburger and a glass of iced tea or H_2O make for a reasonable lunch, while the formidable Double-Double should be reserved for an occasional splurge (especially if you use a few of the calorie-lowering secret menu options). But flirt with the fries or the milk shake at your own peril.

Eat This

Double-Single

with Onion, Mustard, and Ketchup

500 calories
24 g fat
(12 g saturated, 0.5 g trans)
1,170 mg sodium

Yet another example of why customization is your friend. A standard Double-Double comes with an extra 170 calories and 6 grams of saturated fat in the form of mayo-based "Spread" and extra cheese. If you ditch these unnecessary toppings, you can get in and out of the drive-thru with a 500-calorie bilevel burger.

OTHER PICKS

Cheeseburger Protein Style
with Onion, Ketchup, and Mustard
250 calories
16 g fat
(8 g saturated, 0.5 g trans)
800 mg sodium

Grilled Cheese
470 calories
28 g fat
(12 g saturated)
1,260 mg sodium

Minute Maid Light Lemonade
(16 fl oz)
8 calories
0 g fat
0 g sugars

MENU MAGIC

Customizing is key in the fast-food world. If you swap Spread for mustard and ketchup, you'll save 80 calories and an impressive 9 grams of fat. Your calorie savings if you opt for a sans-bun Protein Style burger? One hundred and fifty.

875 calories
45 g fat
(15 g saturated, 0.5 g trans)
1,245 mg sodium

Not That!

Cheeseburger

with Onions and French Fries

We're not sure why fries became the gold standard of fast-food sides. The deep-fried potato sticks account for nearly half of this meal's calories, and what do they bring to the plate? Nothing but empty carbs and fat. For 375 fewer calories, you'll be fuller for longer if you opt for the bigger burger on the left.

Guilty Pleasure

Grilled Cheese

470 calories
28 g fat
(12 g saturated)
1,260 mg sodium

You won't find Grilled Cheese on the menu, but it's a custom order worth knowing about, being as how it's one of the lightest things on the menu. If you order it without Spread, you can bring it down to 390 calories. Not bad for a cheesy comfort food.

OTHER PASSES

7Up

(16 fl oz)

200 calories
0 g fat
54 g sugars

Chocolate Shake

590 calories
29 g fat
(19 g saturated, 1 g trans)
320 mg sodium

Hamburger

390 calories
19 g fat
(5 g saturated)
650 mg sodium

19,490

Number of calories in record-setting 100 × 100 burger ordered in 2004

JACK IN THE BOX

C+ Jack in the Box's menu has come a long way in the past few years, but a few major changes still need to be made: banishing anything in a bowl or burrito, offering more than three burgers with less than 500 calories, and eliminating all partially hydrogenated oils once and for all. Jack might have taken the harmful oils out of the fryer, but they still can be found all over the ingredients lists, including in the sirloin beef patty seasoning.

Eat This
Jack's Spicy Chicken

530 calories
21 g fat
(3.5 g saturated)
910 mg sodium

Seems that nearly every major fast-food player needs a spicy chicken sandwich on its menu. Jack's version is surprisingly gentle on the waistline, especially for a place known for producing some of the greasiest grub in the business. Plus, we love that it has fewer than 1,000 milligrams of sodium—a rarity in the realm of fast-food chicken.

Keep your burger small, or order a Whole Grain Chicken Fajita Pita with a fruit cup on the side. For breakfast, order any Breakfast Jack without sausage. Your safest bet is to not touch the fried foods.

OTHER PICKS

Hamburger Deluxe
with Cheese
420 calories
23 g fat
(10 g saturated, 1 g trans)
950 mg sodium

Chicken Fajita Pita
with Fire Roasted Salsa
330 calories
11 g fat
(5 g saturated)
990 mg sodium

Breakfast Jack
with Bacon
310 calories
14 g fat
(5 g saturated)
790 mg sodium

686 calories
35 g fat
(8 g saturated)
1,292 mg sodium

Not That!

Chipotle Chicken Club

The core elements of this recently released specialty sandwich are the same as they are in the sandwich to your left—spicy fried chicken topped with a mayo-based sauce—but the superfluous additions of cheese, bacon, and butter-doused toast result in more than 150 extra calories and double the fat. Not. Worth. It.

ALL THIS

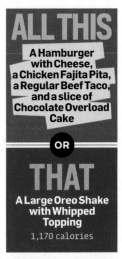

A Hamburger with Cheese, a Chicken Fajita Pita, a Regular Beef Taco, and a slice of Chocolate Overload Cake

OR

THAT

A Large Oreo Shake with Whipped Topping
1,170 calories

Chicken Fajita Pita
(with salsa)

326 calories
10 g fat
(6 g saturated)
987 mg sodium

One of the best entrées in the entire fast-food universe. Low in calories, packed with protein and fiber, this one would be hard to top in your own kitchen.

OTHER PASSES

Meaty Breakfast Burrito
610 calories
37 g fat
(15 g saturated, 0.5 g trans)
1,510 mg sodium

Sourdough Grilled Chicken Club
540 calories
26 g fat
(7 g saturated)
1,490 mg sodium

Sirloin Cheeseburger
900 calories
60 g fat
(19 g saturated, 1.5 g trans)
1,870 mg sodium

JAMBA JUICE

A- Jamba Juice makes more than a few faux-fruit blends, beverages unnecessarily weighed down with sherbet, sorbet, and other added sugars, but their menu has a ton of real-deal smoothies, as well. Jamba's incredible line of Fruit & Veggie smoothies and their low-calorie food menu are unrivaled by other American chains. And as far as dessert goes, the new Whirl'ns Frozen Yogurt is about as good as it gets.

SURVIVAL STRATEGY

For a perfectly guilt-free treat, opt for a Jamba Light or an All Fruit Smoothie in a 16-ounce cup. And unless you're looking to put on weight for your latest movie role, don't touch the Peanut Butter Moo'd or any of the other Creamy Treats.

Eat This

Berry Fulfilling Smoothie

(Original size, 24 fl oz)

230 calories
1 g fat
(0 g saturated)
39 g sugars

Make It Light smoothies, like this berry option, have up to half the sugar of the chain's Classic creations. Consider them the smartest options at the healthiest smoothie shop in the country.

OTHER PICKS

Mango Mantra

(Original size, 24 fl oz)

250 calories
0.5 g fat
51 g sugars

Blueberry & Blackberry Oatmeal

290 calories
3.5 g fat
(1 g saturated)
25 g sugars

Southwestern Chicken Chorizo Breakfast Wrap

310 calories
13 g fat
(3.5 g saturated)
2 g sugars

400 calories
1.5 g fat
(0.5 g saturated)
82 g sugars

Not That!

Banana Berry Smoothie

(Original size, 24 fl oz)

Smoothies have a reputation as a health food, but sugary add-ins turn many frozen-fruit blends into glorified desserts. The fruit in this cup is mixed with frozen yogurt and sherbet—no wonder it has nearly the same sugar count as two McDonald's Hot Fudge Sundaes.

OTHER PASSES

Berry Cherry Pecan Oatmeal

500 calories
14 g fat
(1.5 g saturated)
50 g sugars

Berry Topper Fruit and Yogurt Parfait

(16 fl oz)

460 calories
9 g fat
(1 g saturated)
55 g sugars

Orange Dream Machine

(Original size, 24 fl oz)

470 calories
1.5 g fat
(1 g saturated)
97 g sugars

Baked Good STACKUP

Berry Agave Bar
220 calories
8 g sugars

Cinnamon Swirl
250 calories
15 g sugars

Cranberry Orange Roll
280 calories
22 g sugars

Sweet Belgian Waffle
310 calories
21 g sugars

Blueberry Streusel Muffin
400 calories
20 g sugars

STEALTH HEALTH

Berry UpBEET
(Original size, 24 fl oz)

340 calories
56 g sugars
13 g fiber

True to their name, Jamba's Fruit & Veggie smoothies contain nothing but fruit, fruit juice, and vegetable juice. This berry option packs the most belly-filling fiber, but all three of the flavors are decent—not to mention tasty—ways to meet your veggie quota.

KFC

B+ Hold on a second! KFC gets a B+? Surprisingly enough, KFC has more than a few things going for it. The menu's crispy bird bits are offset by skinless chicken pieces, low-calorie sandwich options, and a host of sides that come from beyond the fryer. Plus, the fact that they've stuck with their grilled chicken line shows that they're determined to cast aside the Kentucky fried nutritional demons of their past.

SURVIVAL STRATEGY

Avoid the bowls, pot pies, and fried chicken combos. Look instead to the grilled chicken, Toasted Wrap, or Snackers. Then adorn your plate with one of the Colonel's healthy sides. If you want fried chicken, make sure you order the strips.

Eat This

Original Recipe Chicken Breast

with Mashed Potatoes and Gravy and Sweet Kernel Corn

580 calories
25.5 g fat
(6 g saturated)
1,610 mg sodium

Fried chicken isn't anyone's idea of a healthy meal, but the Colonel's classic recipe has surprisingly conservative nutrition stats. We defy you to find a fast-food burger meal with two starchy sides for fewer than 600 calories and 6 grams of saturated fat.

OTHER PICKS

Doublicious
with Original Recipe Filet
520 calories
25 g fat
(7 g saturated)
1,180 mg sodium

Hot Wings Value Box
490 calories
27 g fat
(4.5 g saturated)
1,220 mg sodium

Lil' Bucket Strawberry Shortcake Parfait Cup
200 calories
7 g fat (3.5 g saturated)
23 g sugars

790 calories
45 g fat
(37 g saturated)
1,970 mg sodium

Not That!
Chunky Chicken Pot Pie

This is the single worst option on KFC's menu. Chunky Chicken Pot Pie is stuffed with veggies and never touches the deep fryer, but it remains one of the worst chicken dishes of all time. The main calorie culprit is its buttery shell, but the creamy sauce that binds the filling together certainly doesn't help matters.

OTHER PASSES

Lil' Bucket Lemon Crème Parfait Cup
400 calories
13 g fat
(7 g saturated)
50 g sugars

Popcorn Chicken Value Box
680 calories
41 g fat
(8 g saturated)
1,850 mg sodium

Double Down with Original Recipe Filet
610 calories
37 g fat
(11 g saturated, 0.5 g trans)
1,880 mg sodium

KFC Snacker SELECTOR

KFC Honey BBQ Snacker
210 calories
3 g fat (1 g saturated)

KFC Buffalo Crispy Strip Snacker
250 calories
6 g fat (1.5 g saturated)

KFC Ultimate Cheese Crispy Strip Snacker
270 calories
8 g fat (2.5 g saturated)

KFC Crispy Strip Snacker
290 calories
11 g fat (2.5 g saturated)

Chicken STACKUP

Kentucky Grilled Chicken
80 to 220 calories
4 to 10 g fat

Original Recipe
120 to 360 calories
7 to 21 g fat

Spicy Crispy
160 to 420 calories
10 to 27 g fat

Extra Crispy
150 to 510 calories
10 to 33 g fat

KRISPY KREME

C The good news is that Krispy Kreme has finally expanded its food menu beyond doughnuts. The bad news is that the new additions are dominated by bagels, muffins, and sweet rolls—the same type of nutrient-devoid, carb-heavy fare that it's always specialized in. That being said, its bagels are considerably better than most, and combined with a low-calorie coffee drink, make for a stronger beginning to your day than, say, a cream-filled doughnut.

Eat This
Apple Fritter

210 calories
14 g fat
(7 g saturated)
4 g sugars

Amazingly enough, this Apple Fritter is worthy of an *ETNT* All-Star award, not because it's a paradigm of healthy eating, but because we think a doughnut with fewer than 5 grams of sugar deserves some recognition.

OTHER PICKS

Cinnamon Bun Doughnut
260 calories
16 g fat
(8 g saturated)
13 g sugars

Chocolate Kool Kreme Cone
310 calories
9 g fat
(6 g saturated)
33 g sugars

Ice Latte
with 2% milk
(20 fl oz)
150 calories
6 g fat
(4 g saturated)
15 g sugars

SURVIVAL STRATEGY

To stay under 500 calories, you'll need to cap your sweet tooth at one filled or specialty doughnut or, worst-case scenario, two original glazed doughnuts.

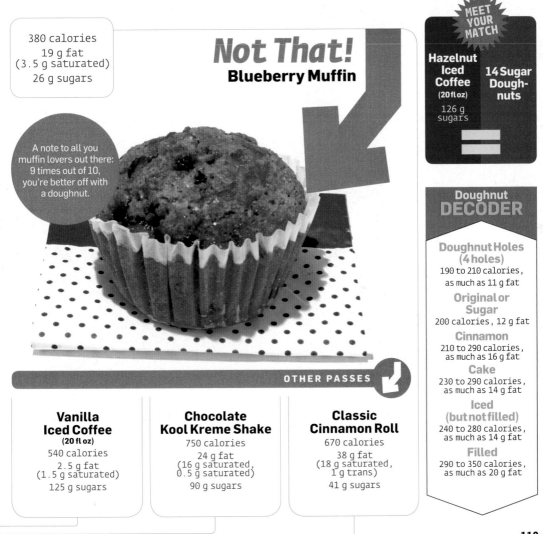

380 calories
19 g fat
(3.5 g saturated)
26 g sugars

Not That!

Blueberry Muffin

A note to all you muffin lovers out there: 9 times out of 10, you're better off with a doughnut.

Doughnut DECODER

Doughnut Holes (4 holes)
190 to 210 calories, as much as 11 g fat

Original or Sugar
200 calories, 12 g fat

Cinnamon
210 to 290 calories, as much as 16 g fat

Cake
230 to 290 calories, as much as 14 g fat

Iced (but not filled)
240 to 280 calories, as much as 14 g fat

Filled
290 to 350 calories, as much as 20 g fat

OTHER PASSES

Vanilla Iced Coffee
(20 fl oz)
540 calories
2.5 g fat
(1.5 g saturated)
125 g sugars

Chocolate Kool Kreme Shake
750 calories
24 g fat
(16 g saturated,
0.5 g saturated)
90 g sugars

Classic Cinnamon Roll
670 calories
38 g fat
(18 g saturated,
1 g trans)
41 g sugars

LONG JOHN SILVER'S

D+ When we first started handing out grades, many major restaurants still featured trans fats prominently on their menus. But as food scientists uncovered healthier alternatives, most of those establishments switched to trans fat-free frying oils. Now, if only LJS would follow suit, it would instantly be one of the healthiest fast-food chains in the country, but until it does, it's one of the absolute worst.

SURVIVAL STRATEGY

The only fish that avoid the trans fat oils are those that are grilled or baked. Beyond that, the commendable Garlic Shrimp Scampi is your safest bet. Pair one of those options with a healthy side. If you need to dip, choose cocktail sauce or malt vinegar instead of tartar sauce.

Eat This

Freshside Grille Shrimp Scampi Entrée
with Rice and Vegetable Medley

330 calories
15 g fat
(3.5 g saturated)
1,230 mg sodium

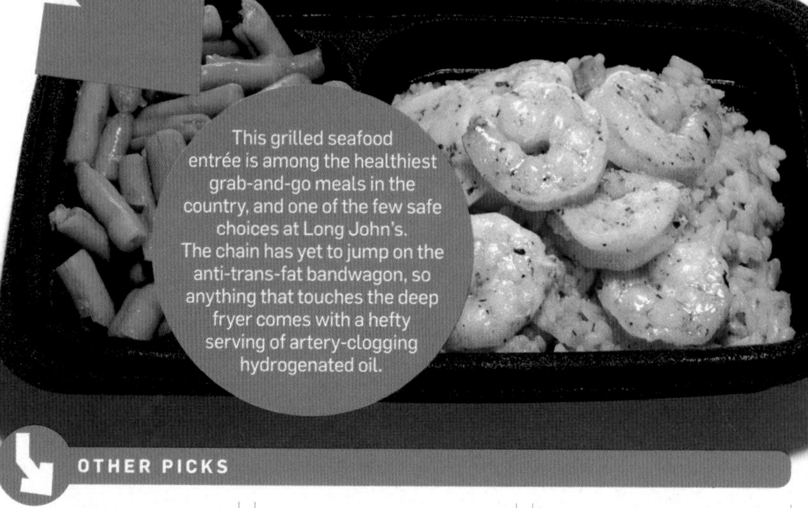

This grilled seafood entrée is among the healthiest grab-and-go meals in the country, and one of the few safe choices at Long John's. The chain has yet to jump on the anti-trans-fat bandwagon, so anything that touches the deep fryer comes with a hefty serving of artery-clogging hydrogenated oil.

OTHER PICKS

Langostino Lobster Stuffed Crab Cakes
(2)
340 calories
18 g fat
(4 g saturated)
780 mg sodium

Freshside Grille Tilapia Entrée
250 calories
4.5 g fat
(2 g saturated)
820 mg sodium

Breaded Mozzarella Sticks
(3) with Marinara Dipping Cup
165 calories
9 g fat
(3.5 g saturated)
475 mg sodium

530 calories
27 g fat
(8 g saturated,
4.5 g trans)
1,500 mg sodium

Not That!
Ultimate Alaskan Pollock Sandwich

Sandwiches with 500 calories and fewer than 10 grams of saturated fat usually find themselves on the Eat This! side of the page, but this fish fiasco packs more trans fats than four Burger King Double Cheeseburgers, making it the trans-fattiest seafood sandwich we've found. Shiver me timbers.

OTHER PASSES

Broccoli Cheese Bites
(5)
230 calories
12 g fat
(4.5 g saturated,
3 g trans)
550 mg sodium

Baja Fish Taco
360 calories
23 g fat
(4.5 g saturated,
3.5 g trans)
810 mg sodium

Breaded Clam Strips Snack Box
320 calories
19 g fat
(4.5 g saturated,
7 g trans)
1,190 mg sodium

DippinSauce STACKUP

Cocktail Sauce
(1 oz)
25 calories, 0 g fat

Sweet & Sour Sauce
(1 dipping cup)
45 calories, 0 g fat

Honey Mustard Sauce
(1 dipping cup)
100 calories, 6 g fat
(1.5 g saturated)

Tartar Sauce
(1 oz)
100 calories, 9 g fat
(1.5 g saturated)

Ranch Sauce
(1 dipping cup)
160 calories,
17 g fat
(2.5 g saturated)

SIDESWIPED

Crumblies
170 calories
12 g fat
(2.5 g saturated,
4 g trans)
410 mg sodium

Crumblies are simply deep-fried bits of batter, and what they lack in calories, they make up for in 2 whole days' worth of trans fats. Calorie for calorie, this are the most dangerous side in America.

McDONALD'S

B+ The world-famous burger baron has come a long way since the publication of *Fast Food Nation*—at least nutritionally speaking. The trans fats are mostly gone, the number of calorie bombs is reduced, and there are more healthy options, such as salads and yogurt parfaits, than ever. Still, too many of the breakfast and lunch items still top the 500-calorie mark, and the dessert menu is a total mess.

SURVIVAL STRATEGY

At breakfast, look no further than the Egg McMuffin—it remains one of the best ways to start your day in the fast-food world. Grilled chicken and Snack Wraps make for a sound lunch. Splurge on a Big Mac or Quarter Pounder, but only if you skip the fries and soda.

Eat This

Premium Grilled Chicken Ranch BLT Sandwich

380 calories
10 g fat
(3 g saturated)
1,000 mg sodium

The beauty of a grilled chicken breast: Its super-low calorie count leaves room for splurge-worthy toppings like bacon and ranch dressing. Just be sure to stay away from the Crispy version of this sandwich. The price you pay for going fried over grilled at Mickey D's is an extra 160 calories and 13 grams of fat.

OTHER PICKS

McDouble
400 calories
19 g fat
(8 g saturated, 1 g trans)
970 mg sodium

Chicken Nuggets
(6) with Chipotle Barbecue Sauce
330 calories
18 g fat
(3 g saturated)
730 mg sodium

Bacon, Egg & Cheese McGriddles
420 calories
18 g fat
(8 g saturated)
1,110 mg sodium

560 calories
37 g fat
(8.5 g saturated)
1,400 mg sodium

Not That!

Premium Bacon Ranch Salad

with Crispy Chicken and Ranch Dressing

Fried chicken and ranch dressing have caused the downfalls of countless fast-food salads. Here, these high-risk toppings result in a bed of greens with more calories and fat than a Quarter Pounder with Cheese. Swap the fried chicken for grilled and the ranch for balsamic vinaigrette, and you'll shave off 295 calories and 25.5 grams of fat.

OTHER PASSES

Bacon, Egg & Cheese Bagel
560 calories
27 g fat
(9 g saturated, 0.5 g trans)
1,300 mg sodium

Chicken Selects Premium Breast Strips
(3) with Creamy Ranch Sauce
490 calories
35 g fat
(5.5 g saturated)
920 mg sodium

Cheeseburger
(2)
620 calories
24 g fat
(12 g saturated, 1 g trans)
1,620 mg sodium

Angus Deluxe Snack Wrap
410 calories
25 g fat
(10 g saturated, 1.5 g trans)
990 mg sodium

A small snack wrap may seem like a smart way to escape the drive-thru with minimal diet damage, but this little steak tortilla houses more calories and saturated fat than a McDouble. If you want a wrap with fewer than 300 calories at McDonald's, grilled chicken's your only option.

Breakfast Sandwich
STACKUP

Egg McMuffin
300 calories
12 g fat

Bacon, Egg & Cheese Biscuit
420 calories
23 g fat

Sausage, Egg & Cheese McGriddles
560 calories
32 g fat

OLIVE GARDEN

D+ Olive Garden is in desperate need of a menu makeover. The chicken and beef entrées are saddled with huge calorie and fat counts, the seafood is swimming in sodium, and the average dinner-size plate of pasta packs a staggering 976 calories. All of this is before you tack on the breadsticks and salad. Olive Garden cooks need to learn to lay off the oil and the salt, then maybe we'll bump them up to a C.

SURVIVAL STRATEGY

Most pasta dishes are burdened with at least a day's worth of sodium and more than 1,000 calories, so stick to the mushroom or cheese ravioli. As for chicken and seafood, stick with the Herb-Grilled Salmon or Parmesan Crusted Tilapia. And lay off the breadsticks!

Eat This

Mediterranean Grilled Chicken

670 calories
22 g fat
(7 g saturated)
1,610 mg sodium

Most of Olive Garden's chicken pastas are doused in heavy sauces, but this dish leans on the bold tastes of lemon-herb vinaigrette, feta cheese, and cherry tomatoes to supply its flavor. The result is one of the few pasta dishes in America with fewer than 700 calories.

OTHER PICKS

Grilled Chicken Caprese Panini

560 calories
23 g fat
(9 g saturated)
1,440 mg sodium

Cheese Ravioli with Marinara Sauce

660 calories
22 g fat
(11 g saturated)
1,440 mg sodium

Stuffed Mushrooms

280 calories
19 g fat
(5 g saturated)
720 mg sodium

1,070 calories
53 g fat
(20 g saturated)
2,220 mg sodium

Not That!
Chicken Scampi

This plate is based on a concept similar to that of the pasta on the left, but the simple addition of garlic cream sauce gives it 60 percent more calories and nearly three times the saturated fat. We've said it before, and we'll say it again: Cream sauce is not your friend.

OTHER PASSES

Hot Artichoke-Spinach Dip
650 calories
31 g fat
(15 g saturated)
1,430 mg sodium

Lasagna Rollata al Forno
1,170 calories
68 g fat
(39 g saturated)
2,510 mg sodium

Grilled Chicken Flatbread
760 calories
44 g fat
(15 g saturated)
1,500 mg sodium

FrankenFood

Lasagna Fritta
1,030 calories
63 g fat
(21 g saturated)
1,590 mg sodium

Olive Garden's battered, deep-fried lasagna invention will set you back half a day's calories and a day's worth of saturated fat, proving that just because you can deep-fry something doesn't mean you should.

Soup STACKUP

Minestrone
100 calories
1 g fat
(0 g saturated)
1,020 mg sodium

Pasta e Fagioli
130 calories
2.5 g fat
(1 g saturated)
680 mg sodium

Zuppa Toscana
170 calories
4 g fat
(2 g saturated)
960 mg sodium

Chicken & Gnocchi
250 calories
8 g fat
(3 g saturated)
1,180 mg sodium

ON THE BORDER

D On the Border continues to make tweaks to their menu, but those tweaks only reinforce what we already know about this place: that its Tex-Mex fare is some of the fattiest, saltiest food in the chain restaurant world. The massive menu suffers from appetizers with 134 grams of fat, salads with a full day's worth of sodium, and fish taco entrées with up to 1,950 calories. À la carte items offer the only real hope here.

SURVIVAL STRATEGY

The Border Smart Menu highlights just three items with fewer than 600 calories and 25 grams of fat each (and an average of 1,490 milligrams of sodium). Create your own combo plate with two individual items, but be sure to pass on the sides.

650 calories
12 g fat
(2 g saturated)
1,690 mg sodium

Cheese and sour cream are the go-to taco toppers at big Tex-Mex chains, but these tortillas replace those fatty fillers with the low-calorie, high-flavor combo of red onion and grilled pineapple. Other than creating your own à la carte meal, this is one of the few ways you'll get a Border entrée with fewer than 700 calories.

OTHER PICKS

Chicken Salsa Fresca
520 calories
9 g fat
(3 g saturated)
2,410 mg sodium

Seasoned Ground Beef Enchiladas
(2) with Chile con Carne
520 calories
30 g fat
(12 g saturated)
1,260 mg sodium

Sundae
with Chocolate Syrup
370 calories
18 g fat
(13 g saturated)
51 g carbs

890 calories
40 g fat
(13 g saturated)
1,990 mg sodium

Not That!

Street-Style Mini Chicken Tacos

with Rice

There are far worse taco options at On the Border—like the 1,950-calorie Dos XX Fish Tacos—but for a few basic chicken tacos accompanied by avocado slices and pico de gallo, this plate's calorie count is unacceptable and far from "mini."

SMART SIDES

Pico de Gallo
15 calories
1 g fat (0 g saturated)
55 mg sodium

Guacamole
50 calories
5 g fat (1 g saturated)
90 mg sodium

Grilled Vegetables
80 calories
1 g fat (0 g saturated)
75 mg sodium

Black Beans
180 calories
3 g fat (1 g saturated)
830 mg sodium

OTHER PASSES

Kahlua Ice Cream Pie
950 calories
50 g fat
(24 g saturated)
111 g carbs

Ground Beef Empanadas
(2) with Chile con Queso
1,240 calories
92 g fat
(32 g saturated)
1,740 mg sodium

Tomatillo Chicken
850 calories
24 g fat
(6 g saturated)
1,650 mg sodium

ALL THIS

1 Chicken Soft Taco, 2 Ground Beef Tostadas, 1 order of Chicken Flautas with Chile con Queso, 1 cup of Chicken Tortilla Soup, 2 Sundaes with Chocolate Syrup, and a side of Guacamole

OR

THAT

Border Sampler
2,060 calories

OUTBACK STEAKHOUS

C Outback has made some respectable strides in recent years, lightening up existing fare (the Alice Springs Chicken Quesadilla shrank from 2,140 calories down to 1,563) and offering a range of items under 500 calories. Still, trouble lurks: Appetizers are deeply flawed, steaks and other cuts of meat routinely carry more than 800 calories, and the average side dish has more than 350 calories.

SURVIVAL STRATEGY

Curb your desire to order the 14-ounce rib eye (1,193 calories) by starting with the Seared Ahi Tuna. Then move on to one of the leaner cuts of meat: the petite fillet, the Outback Special, or the pork tenderloin. If you skip the bread and house salad (590 calories) and choose steamed veggies as your side, you can escape for less than 1,000 calories.

Eat This

Victoria's Filet

(8 oz, without crumb topping) with Baked Potato with Sour Cream and Grilled Asparagus

620 calories
20 g fat
(8 g saturated)
1,200 mg sodium

You're at Outback Steakhouse, so order steak. A lean slab of beef paired with some veggies and a baked potato is one of the safest—not to mention most satisfying—meals on the menu. Just be sure to forgo the crumb topping, or you'll add more than 200 calories to your steak.

OTHER PICKS

Sweet Glazed Pork Tenderloin

with Baked Potato with Sour Cream and Fresh Steamed French Green Beans

625 calories
15 g fat
(7 g saturated)
1,672 mg sodium

Simply Grilled Mahi

(8 oz) with Rice Garnish and Steamed Veggies

472 calories
12 g fat
(6 g saturated)
1,042 mg sodium

California Chicken Salad

with Vinaigrette

690 calories
39 g fat
(9 g saturated)
1,472 mg sodium

1,235 calories
72 g fat
(33 g saturated)
2,007 mg sodium

Not That!

The Outback Burger

with American Cheese and Sweet Potato Fries

Burgers can be a sensible, protein-packed meal, but sit-down chains squash their nutritional potential by serving them up in jumbo portions alongside heaping piles of fried potatoes. All of the burger-and-fry combos at Outback pack more than 1,000 calories.

Wings with Mild Sauce
1,972 calories

16 KFC Original Recipe Chicken Drum-sticks

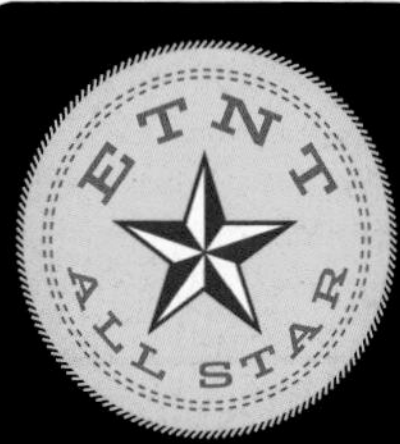

Grilled Shrimp on the Barbie

295 calories
16 g fat
(3 g saturated)
867 mg sodium

On too many chain menus, the word "appetizer" is nothing but a formality—1,000-calorie nachos and plates of french fries smothered in cheese and bacon are hardly a way to warm up the appetite. A true appetizer should be light on fat and low in calories so you're not stuffed when your entrée arrives. This shrimp plate delivers.

OTHER PASSES

Aussie Chicken Cobb Salad

with Crispy Chicken and Thousand Island Dressing

1,298 calories
102 g fat
(33 g saturated)
2,168 mg sodium

Hearts of Gold Mahi

with Fresh Seasonal Mixed Veggies

713 calories
34 g fat
(19 g saturated)
1,600 mg sodium

Baby Back Ribs

(½ order) with Garlic Mashed Potatoes

975 calories
60 g fat
(24 g saturated)
1,988 mg sodium

PANDA EXPRESS

C+ Oddly enough, it's not the wok-fried meat or the viscous sauces that do the most harm on this menu—it's the more than 400 calories of rice and noodles that form the foundation of each meal. Scrape these starches from the plate, and Panda Express starts to look a lot healthier. Only one entrée item has more than 500 calories, and there's hardly a trans fat on the menu. Problems arise when multiple entrées and sides start piling up on one plate, though, so bring some self-restraint to the table.

Eat This

Kung Pao Chicken Entrée

with Steamed Rice and Mixed Veggies

465 calories
14 g fat
(2.5 g saturated)
1,160 mg sodium

All of the nonbreaded chicken entrées at Panda are fair game. Pairing them with a rice-and-vegetable combo makes for a respectable meal, but if you ditch the rice altogether and go straight veggies, you'll save an extra 155 calories.

OTHER PICKS

Peppercorn Shrimp
170 calories
5 g fat
(1 g saturated)
800 mg sodium

Chicken Pot Stickers
(3)
220 calories
11 g fat
(2.5 g saturated)
280 mg sodium

Fortune Cookies
(3)
96 calories
0 g fat
9 g sugars

SURVIVAL STRATEGY

Avoid these entrées: Orange Chicken, Sweet & Sour Chicken, Beijing Beef, and anything with pork. Then swap in Mixed Veggies for the scoop of rice.

910 calories
43 g fat
(8 g saturated)
1,680 mg sodium

Not That!

Orange Chicken Entrée

with Chow Mein

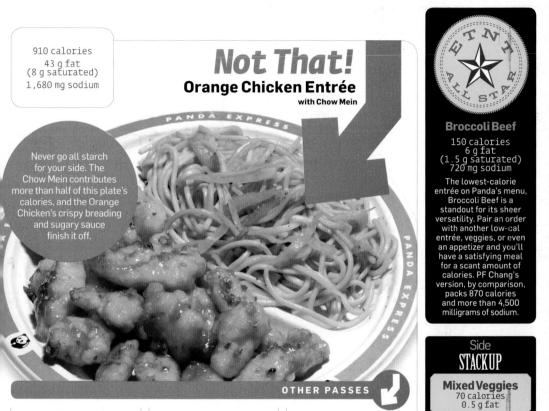

Never go all starch for your side. The Chow Mein contributes more than half of this plate's calories, and the Orange Chicken's crispy breading and sugary sauce finish it off.

Broccoli Beef

150 calories
6 g fat
(1.5 g saturated)
720 mg sodium

The lowest-calorie entrée on Panda's menu, Broccoli Beef is a standout for its sheer versatility. Pair an order with another low-cal entrée, veggies, or even an appetizer and you'll have a satisfying meal for a scant amount of calories. PF Chang's version, by comparison, packs 870 calories and more than 4,500 milligrams of sodium.

OTHER PASSES

Chocolate Chunk Cookie
160 calories
7 g fat
(3 g saturated)
14 g sugars

Chicken Egg Rolls (2)
400 calories
24 g fat
(8 g saturated)
780 mg sodium

Honey Walnut Shrimp
370 calories
23 g fat
(4 g saturated)
470 mg sodium

Side STACKUP

Mixed Veggies
70 calories
0.5 g fat

Steamed Rice
380 calories
0 g fat

Chow Mein
490 calories
22 g fat

Fried Rice
530 calories
16 g fat

PANERA BREAD

B- Panera's menu has barely budged in the past year, and that's not such a bad thing. Its roster of mostly-great salads and soups still stands strong, and between the 340-calorie Power Sandwich and the steel-cut oatmeal, a first-rate breakfast is there for the taking. But only 4 out of 17 sandwiches have 600 calories or fewer and the bakery puts out little not tainted by refined carbs. Until we see real progress, this B- is as good as Panera can hope for.

SURVIVAL STRATEGY

For breakfast, choose between the Egg & Cheese breakfast sandwich and 280-calorie granola parfait. Skip the stand-alone sandwich lunch. Instead, pair soup and a salad, or order the soup and half-sandwich combo.

Eat This

Half Asiago Roast Beef and Half Classic Salad

with Asian Sesame Vinaigrette

475 calories
23 g fat
(8.5 g saturated)
990 mg sodium

At 700 calories, the full version of this sandwich is one of the most caloric on the menu, but when you cut it in half and pair it with a light side salad, you have a balanced lunch on your hands. What's better, this trick works with most every sandwich at Panera.

OTHER PICKS

Smoked Turkey Breast

on Country

420 calories
3 g fat
(0.5 g saturated)
1,650 mg sodium

Full Strawberry Poppyseed & Chicken Signature Salad

340 calories
13 g
(1.5 g saturated)
330 mg sodium

Breakfast Power Sandwich

340 calories
15 g fat (7 g saturated, 0.5 g trans)
820 mg sodium

790 calories
54 g fat
(16 g saturated,
1 g trans)
1,280 mg sodium

Not That!

Steak & Blue Cheese Chopped Salad

The trouble here isn't the steak, it's the high-fat trifecta of blue cheese dressing, fried onions, and Gorgonzola cheese crumbles. You still get plenty of beef and cheese with the meal on the opposite page, and you'll take in half the saturated fat.

OTHER PASSES

Asiago Cheese Bagel with Bacon
610 calories
28 g fat (13 g saturated, 0.5 g trans)
1,350 mg sodium

Full Roasted Turkey Fuji Apple Signature Salad
590 calories
40 g fat (8 g saturated)
920 mg sodium

Sierra Turkey on Asiago Cheese Focaccia
920 calories
49 g fat
(12 g saturated,
1 g trans)
1,900 mg sodium

FrankenFood

Sourdough Bread Bowl
590 calories
2.5 g fat
(0 g saturated)
1,210 mg sodium

Sure, you could eat your lunch out of a bowl made entirely of bread. You could also eat your breakfast off of a pancake plate, but why would you? Bread bowls are just another wacky invention designed to get your novelty neurons firing, and they offer nothing but empty carbs and a boatload—or bowlful—of unnecessary calories.

Guilty Pleasure

Pumpkin Muffie
290 calories
11 g fat
(2 g saturated)
26 g sugars

We've expressed our distaste for muffins in the past—they're glorified cupcakes, people!—but when you chop off their bottoms, they aren't a terrible treat. A regular pumpkin muffin, for example, has double the calories and sugars as this mini muffin. Plus, the top is the tastiest part.

PAPA JOHN'S

C We're glad that Papa John's struck its disastrous pan crust pizza from the menu, but with it also went its whole-wheat crust option. Now, very little separates Papa from the rest of the pizza competition. It still has some high-quality toppings, but they're nothing you can't get elsewhere. What hasn't changed? The breadsticks still deliver far too many calories and the Special Garlic sauce can wreck even the healthiest slice.

Eat This

The Works Original Crust Pizza (1 slice, large pie) and Chickenstrips (3) with Cheese Dipping Sauce

565 calories
24 g fat
(8 g saturated)
1,735 mg sodium

The best defense is a good offense, so start the meal off with a few pieces of belly-filling protein in the form of wings or chicken strips. Consider it insurance against scarfing too many slices later on in the meal.

SURVIVAL STRATEGY

As with any other pizza place, it's best to start with a thin base, ask for light cheese, and cover it with anything other than sausage, pepperoni, or bacon. The Spinach Alfredo remains the pie to pick at Papa John's.

OTHER PICKS

Spinach Alfredo Original Crust Pizza
(2 slices, medium pie)
400 calories
16 g fat
(7 g saturated)
1,000 mg sodium

Sausage Original Crust Pizza
(2 slices, medium pie)
480 calories
22 g fat
(9 g saturated)
1,200 mg sodium

Honey Chipotle Wings
(2)
190 calories
12 g fat
(3 g saturated)
730 mg sodium

715 calories
43 g fat
(13.5 g saturated)
1,720 mg sodium

Not That!

Spicy Italian Original Crust Pizza (1 slice, large pie) and Cheesesticks (2) with Special Garlic Dipping Sauce

Chicken fingers are no health food, but at least they have protein on their side. Cheesesticks, on the other hand, are nothing but empty carbs smothered in saturated fat. And the garlic dip? That little cup supplies 40 percent of this meal's fat count.

OTHER PASSES

Parmesan Breadsticks
(2)
340 calories
10 g fat
(1.5 g saturated)
720 mg sodium

The Meats Thin Crust Pizza
(2 slices, large pie)
620 calories
38 g fat
(14 g saturated)
1,420 mg sodium

Tuscan Six Cheese Thin Crust Pizza
(2 slices, large pie)
520 calories
28 g fat
(12 g saturated)
920 mg sodium

WEAPON OF MASS DESTRUCTION
Cinnapie
(4 sticks))

560 calories
19 g fat
(6 g saturated)
39 g sugars

You've already had a dinner driven by refined carbs, do you really need to follow it up with more of the same? Just four of these cinnamon sticks pretty much guarantee that your delivered dinner will cross the 1,000-calorie mark.

Dipping Sauce STACKUP
(1 cup)

Buffalo Sauce
15 calories
0.5 g fat

Pizza Sauce
20 calories
1 g fat

Cheese Sauce
40 calories
3.5 g fat

Honey Mustard
150 calories
15 g fat

Special Garlic
150 calories
17 g fat

Blue Cheese
150 calories
16 g fat

PERKINS

D Of the more than 90 dishes at Perkins, only five qualify for the Calorie Counter menu. Outside of that you'll find entrées with more than 4,000 milligrams of sodium, pasta plates with more than 100 grams of fat, and an all-day omelet menu that averages more than 1,500 calories per order. Currently the chain has stores in 34 states. Hopefully it cleans up its nutritional act before it hits the other 16.

SURVIVAL STRATEGY

Stick with the sirloin pictured here or choose something off the Calorie Counter menu. Stray from that and your chances of nutritional survival take a nose dive. Even the Grilled Salmon with broccoli, a dish that seems impossible to screw up, packs 1,150 calories.

Eat This

Top Sirloin Steak Dinner

with Baked Potato with Whipped Butter Blend and Butter-Steamed Broccoli

570 calories
22 g fat
(9 g saturated, 0.5 g trans)
280 mg sodium

The fat's a bit high, but this 7-ounce steak dinner is about as good as it gets at problem-riddled Perkins. Scrap the dinner roll, or you'll add on another 120 calories.

OTHER PICKS

French Dip Sandwich

610 calories
31 g fat
(9 g saturated)
2,150 mg sodium

Classic Eggs and Bacon

with Breakfast Potatoes and Seasonal Fresh Fruit

620 calories
37 g fat
(11.5 g saturated)
1,280 mg sodium

White Chocolate Macadamia Nut Cookie

340 calories
19 g fat
(8 g saturated)
14 g sugars

1,000 calories
49 g fat
(19 g saturated)
3,230 mg sodium

Not That!

Butterball Turkey & Dressing

with Mashed Potatoes with Gravy and Broccoli and Cranberry Sauce

White-meat turkey is one of the lightest meats you can have on your plate. Unfortunately, smothering it in gravy and heavy dressing and pairing it with too many starchy extras cancels out any benefit you get from the lean protein. Keep it simple at Perkins.

WEAPON OF MASS DESTRUCTION

Country Sausage Biscuit Platter

1,770 calories
99 g fat
(49 g saturated)
5,080 mg sodium

Two sausage and cheese biscuits, two eggs, a pile of fried potatoes, a stack of bacon, and a smothering of cream gravy combine to give you a plate with 2 days' worth of saturated fat and 3 days' worth of sodium. The scariest part? This isn't the worst breakfast plate on the menu! (See the 1,860-calorie Southern Fried Chicken Biscuit Platter on page TK.)

OTHER PASSES

Banana Nut Mammoth Muffin

with Whipped Butter Blend

700 calories
40 g fat
(9 g saturated)
42 g sugars

Smoked Bacon & Ham Omelette

with Hash Browns and Seasonal Fresh Fruit

1,100 calories
55 g fat
(19 g saturated)
2,960 mg sodium

Triple Decker Club Sandwich

890 calories
55 g fat
(11 g saturated)
2,130 mg sodium

Side STACKUP

Sautéed Spinach
60 calories
3.5 g fat

Buttered Corn
150 calories
8 g fat

Mashed Potatoes
150 calories
7 g fat

Baked Potato
with Lite Sour Cream
210 calories
2.5 g fat

P.F. CHANG'S

C- P.F. Chang's finally crosses the C threshold this year thanks to some significant menu changes, including the introduction of a great new line of salads.It's now considerably easier to put together a nutritionally respectable meal. But noodle dishes and foods from the grill still come with dangerously high fat and calorie counts, while the entire menu continues to suffer from Chang's Achilles' heel: salt overload.

SURVIVAL STRATEGY

Order a lean appetizer like an order of dumplings or the Seared Ahi Tuna for the table, and resolve to split one of the more reasonable entrées between two people. Earn bonus points by tailoring your dish to be light on the oil and sauce.

Eat This
Sichuan Shrimp

360 calories
16 g fat
(2.5 g saturated)
1,200 mg sodium

The Chang's seafood menu ranges from the cream-soaked Shrimp with Candied Walnuts (1,380 calories) all the way down to sensible plates like the 240-calorie Shanghai Shrimp with Garlic Sauce and the lean crustacean creation pictured here. Heavy sauces and crispy breading are the downfall of the higher-cal picks, so beware.

OTHER PICKS

Ginger Chicken with Broccoli
470 calories
11 g fat
(2 g saturated)
2,330 mg sodium

Thai Basil Greens Salad with Chicken
310 calories
9 g fat
(1.5 g saturated)
1,210 mg sodium

Sweet and Sour Pork
710 calories
25 g fat
(6 g saturated)
1,440 mg sodium

A simple way to shave calories off your Chang's plate: Scratch the rice and get a small order of nutrient-packed vegetables instead. Even the highest-calorie veggie—the Lemon Scented Brussels Sprouts—will save you 80 calories over a side of brown rice, and most of the others will save you about 200.

1,000 calories
43 g fat
(7 g saturated)
3,460 mg sodium

Not That!

Hunan-Style Hot Fish

Tilapia is one of the leanest, most nutrient-rich foods around. Unfortunately, deep-fried breading is not. With a variety of tasty grilled options at your disposal, why settle for the deep fryer?

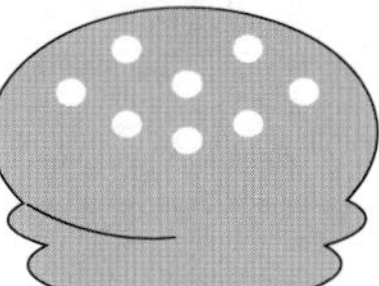

SALT LICK

Hot & Sour Soup (bowl)

7,980 mg sodium
380 calories
11 g fat
(3 g saturated)

Would you like some soup with your salt? There's more than 5 days' worth of sodium in this simple bowl of broth, making it the single saltiest restaurant food we've ever come across—and it's only a side dish!

OTHER PASSES

Pork Fried Rice
1,150 calories
39 g fat
(8 g saturated)
2,110 mg sodium

Thai Chicken Noodle Soup Salad
870 calories
37 g fat
(6 g saturated)
1,390 mg sodium

Kung Pao Chicken
1,110 calories
66 g fat
(10 g saturated)
2,130 mg sodium

PIZZA HUT

C In an attempt to push the menu beyond slices, Pizza Hut expanded into pastas, salads, and something called a P'Zone. Sound like an improvement? Think again. Calzone-like P'Zones all pack more than 1,200 calories each. The salads aren't much better, and the pastas are actually worse. The thin crust and Fit 'N Delicious pizzas offer sub 200-calorie slices and the bone-in wings are a solid start to any meal. Combine those elements and you'll do just fine.

SURVIVAL STRATEGY

Start with a few Baked Hot Wings, then turn to a ham or vegetable Thin 'N Crispy pie or anything on the Fit 'N Delicious menu for slices with as little as 150 calories.

Eat This

All American Traditional Hot Wings
(8)

320 calories
20 g fat
(6 g saturated)
1,160 mg sodium

We know, it's called Pizza Hut. But we have a point here: You could eat an entire plateful of wings and still not reach the calorie count of a single slice of most of the Hut's specialty pies. We'd rather have the wings.

OTHER PICKS

Pepperoni Garlic Parmesan Hand-Tossed Pizza
(2 slices, medium pie)

460 calories
18 g fat
(9 g saturated)
1,280 mg sodium

Pepperoni & Mushroom Personal Pan Pizza

570 calories
23 g fat
(9 g saturated)
1,250 mg sodium

Lemon Pepper Traditional Wings
(2)

150 calories
10 g fat
(2 g saturated)
430 mg sodium

480 calories
28 g fat
(10 g saturated,
0.5 g trans)
1,180 mg sodium

Not That!

Meat Lover's Pizza

(1 slice, 12" large pan pizza)

You can love meat without taking in half a day's saturated fat with one slice of pizza. Specialty pizzas are an excuse to go crazy with a ton of high-fat toppings that do virtually nothing for flavor and increase your calorie load considerably. Get your meat fix from a single source, and top the rest of your pie with veggies.

FrankenFood

Garlic Parmesan Bone-Out Wings

(6)

780 calories
57 g fat
(10.5 g saturated)
2,130 mg sodium

Ever seen a chicken without bones in its wings? Of course not. Mother Nature put them there for a reason, and it wasn't so multinational food corporations could go removing them for their own twisted purposes. Turns out that the freakish "bone-out" wings have twice as many calories as Pizza Hut's traditional wings.

OTHER PASSES

Garlic Parmesan Bone-Out Wings

(2)

260 calories
19 g fat
(3.5 g saturated)
710 mg sodium

Cheese Stuffed Crust Pizza

(2 slices, 14" large pie)

680 calories
28 g fat
(14 g saturated)
1,800 mg sodium

Pepperoni P'Zone Pizza

with Marinara Dipping Sauce

960 calories
30 g fat
(14 g saturated)
2,680 mg sodium

Bread STACKUP

Breadstick

140 calories
5 g fat
(1 g saturated)
260 mg sodium

Cheese Breadstick

170 calories
6 g fat
(2.5 g saturated)
390 mg sodium

Stuffed Pizza Roller

220 calories
10 g fat
(4.5 g saturated)
580 mg sodium

POPEYES

B- Early in 2011, Popeyes introduced the Louisiana Leaux menu, featuring chicken tenders, a wrap, and a po' boy. All three entrées slide in with fewer than 350 calories. We like the direction Popeyes is moving in, but unfortunately the menu is still marred by oversized side dishes, trans fatty flare-ups, and the conspicuous lack of grilled chicken.

SURVIVAL STRATEGY

Skip the chicken-and-biscuit combo meals. Popeyes' chicken harbors more fat than the Original Recipe pieces at KFC, and the biscuit adds an extra 160 calories to your plate. Tenders and nuggets are relatively safe, but when it comes time for sides, settle for nothing less than non-fried foods. A large order of fries, for instance, delivers 3.5 grams of trans fatty acids.

Eat This

Loaded Chicken Wrap

400 calories
17 g fat
(6 g saturated)
1,100 mg sodium

This wrap is the best of both worlds: fried chicken and their signature Red Beans & Rice all rolled into one. Want more? It contains 19 grams of protein and 4 grams of fiber.

OTHER PICKS

Spicy Chicken Leg and Wing
240 calories
14 g fat
(2.5 g saturated)
520 mg sodium

Louisiana Nuggets (6)
230 calories
14 g fat
(6 g saturated, 1 g trans)
350 mg sodium

Bacon Biscuit
400 calories
25 g fat
(12 g saturated)
780 mg sodium

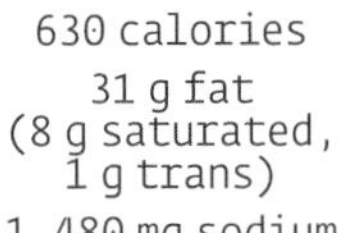

630 calories
31 g fat
(8 g saturated, 1 g trans)
1,480 mg sodium

Not That!
Deluxe Mild Sandwich

Know what you don't need on a piece of crispy fried chicken? Mayo. Trade it for a few shakes of hot sauce and you'll save 150 calories, inching this sandwich back toward the realms of respectability.

The "Naked" chicken dishes at Popeyes may not be breaded, but they're coated with plenty of flavorful seasoning. Choose them over crispy chicken and you save anywhere from 110 to 320 calories.

Chicken STACKUP

Nuggets (4)
150 calories
9 g fat

Mild Leg
160 calories
9 g fat

Naked Tenders (3)
170 calories
2 g fat

Mild Wing
210 calories
14 g fat

Mild Thigh
280 calories
21 g fat

Mild Breast
440 calories
27 g fat

OTHER PASSES

Sausage Biscuit
540 calories
36 g fat
(18 g saturated)
1,100 mg sodium

Louisiana Tenders (mild, 3)
340 calories
14 g fat
(6 g saturated, 1 g trans)
350 mg sodium

Spicy Chicken Breast
360 calories
22 g fat
(8 g saturated, 0.5 g trans)
760 mg sodium

QUIZNOS

C- Submarine sandwiches can only be so bad, right? We thought so, too, until we saw some of the outrageous offerings on the Quiznos menu. The bigger subs and wraps can easily pack 1,000 calories and a full day's worth of saturated fat, and the oversize salads aren't much better. Sammies used to be the easy way out of trouble at Quiznos, but as their calorie counts continue to climb, options for healthy dining grow ever slimmer.

SURVIVAL STRATEGY

Avoid the salads, large subs, and soups that come in bread bowls. Stick with a small sub (at 310 calories, the Honey Bourbon Chicken is easily the best), or pair a Sammie with a cup of soup.

Eat This

Chicken Bacon Ranch Flatbread

(small)

460 calories
23 g fat
(10 g saturated)
1,210 mg sodium

While the recent addition of wraps to the Quiznos menu is a blow to an already-troubled chain, the line of Flatbreads provide some balance to the nutritional force. The thinner vessel is light on carbs, leaving more room for bells and whistles (i.e. bacon and ranch).

OTHER PICKS

Turkey Ranch & Swiss Sub
on Wheat Bread (small)
390 calories
16.5 g fat
(2 g saturated)
1,100 mg sodium

Baja Chicken Sub
(small)
590 calories
29 g fat
(12 g saturated)
1,580 mg sodium

Toasted Roast Beef Sub
(small)
450 calories
23.5 g fat
(4.5 g saturated)
1,080 mg sodium

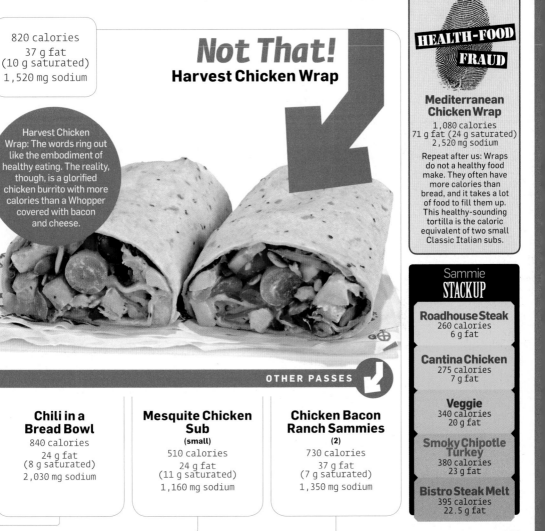

820 calories
37 g fat
(10 g saturated)
1,520 mg sodium

Not That!
Harvest Chicken Wrap

Harvest Chicken Wrap: The words ring out like the embodiment of healthy eating. The reality, though, is a glorified chicken burrito with more calories than a Whopper covered with bacon and cheese.

OTHER PASSES

Chili in a Bread Bowl
840 calories
24 g fat
(8 g saturated)
2,030 mg sodium

Mesquite Chicken Sub
(small)
510 calories
24 g fat
(11 g saturated)
1,160 mg sodium

Chicken Bacon Ranch Sammies
(2)
730 calories
37 g fat
(7 g saturated)
1,350 mg sodium

Mediterranean Chicken Wrap
1,080 calories
71 g fat (24 g saturated)
2,520 mg sodium

Repeat after us: Wraps do not a healthy food make. They often have more calories than bread, and it takes a lot of food to fill them up. This healthy-sounding tortilla is the caloric equivalent of two small Classic Italian subs.

Sammie STACKUP

Roadhouse Steak
260 calories
6 g fat

Cantina Chicken
275 calories
7 g fat

Veggie
340 calories
20 g fat

Smoky Chipotle Turkey
380 calories
23 g fat

Bistro Steak Melt
395 calories
22.5 g fat

RED LOBSTER

A- Compared with the other major sit-down chains and their four-digit fare, Red Lobster looks like a paradigm of sound nutrition. The daily rotating fish specials are the centerpiece of a menu long on low-calorie, high-protein entrées and reasonable vegetable-based sides. That's why Red Lobster is one of America's healthiest chain restaurants. The only flaw you'll find is an overreliance on the deep fryer and the salt shaker.

SURVIVAL STRATEGY

Avoid calorie-heavy Cajun sauces, combo dishes, and anything labeled "crispy." And tell the waiter to keep those biscuits for himself. You'll never go wrong with simple broiled or grilled fish and a vegetable side.

Eat This

Create Your Own Feast

with Peppercorn-Grilled Sirloin, Garlic-Grilled Shrimp, and Baked Potato with Sour Cream

590 calories
14.5 g fat
(5.5 g saturated)
2,170 mg sodium

The Red Lobster menu has a substantial selection of lean protein options, and the Create Your Own Feast menu allows you to mix and match them with health sides. We'd love to see the cooks take it easy with the salt shaker, but for 590 calories, you still end up with a pretty impressive meal.

OTHER PICKS

Crunchy Popcorn Shrimp

560 calories
27 g fat
(2.5 g saturated)
2,100 mg sodium

Clam Strips

370 calories
22 g fat
(2 g saturated)
820 mg sodium

Garden Salad

with Balsamic Vinaigrette (side order)

170 calories
9 g fat
(1 g saturated)
295 mg sodium

1,120 calories
72 g fat
(31 g saturated)
2,670 mg sodium

Not That!

Steak Lobster-and-Shrimp Oscar

with Home-Style Mashed Potatoes

We don't know who Oscar is, but he must love butter. This dish has nearly all the same elements as the steak combo on the left, but a heavy dousing of white wine and lobster butter sauce gives this plate nearly double the calories. Thankfully, it's the only major fail on the Wood-Fire Grill menu.

OTHER PASSES

Caesar Salad
with Caesar Dressing (side order)
550 calories
51 g fat
(9.5 g saturated)
1,120 mg sodium

Crispy Calamari and Vegetables
760 calories
49 g fat
(6 g saturated)
1,530 mg sodium

Parrot Isle Jumbo Coconut Shrimp
880 calories
60 g fat
(15 g saturated)
1,860 mg sodium

Fresh Fish Menu

Red Lobster may have built its name on crustaceans, but it's the daily selection of 25 fresh fish that represents why this is still the best sit-down chain in America. Try any of the fish (minus the cobia) blackened or grilled with a side of mango salsa for an amazing low-cal meal.

ALL THIS

2 Rock Lobster Tails, an order of Garlic-Grilled Jumbo Shrimp, a side of Home-Style Mashed Potatoes, a cup of Creamy Potato Bacon Soup, and a Cheddar Bay biscuit

OR

THAT

Crab Linguini Alfredo
1,120 calories

ROMANO'S MACARONI

C-

In 2010, we commended Macaroni Grill's efforts to revamp a pretty miserable menu by cutting calories and adding menu items such as rosemary spiedinis. This year, we are sad to announce that new leadership at the chain has undone most of the progress from before. Lean proteins and prudent pastas have been traded in for the same cheesy, fatty fare it put out so many years ago. It was great while it lasted.

SURVIVAL STRATEGY

The Pizza, Pasta, and Classics menus are all serious trouble. Instead, opt for a soup-and-salad combo, a spiedini, or a Create Your Own pasta with spaghetti, red sauce, and as many vegetables as you can fit in the bowl. Split a bowl of gelato and call it a day.

Eat This

Pollo Caprese

560 calories
22 g fat
(7 g saturated)
1,530 mg sodium

Crispy breading and creamy sauces cause the undoing of many of this country's chicken-and-pasta combos, but this refreshing entrée contains neither. It's the only way to have pasta and protein on your plate at Romano's for fewer than 700 calories.

OTHER PICKS

Capellini with Arrabbiata Sauce

570 calories
17 g fat
(2.5 g saturated)
1,190 mg sodium

Goat Cheese Peppadew Peppers

360 calories
18 g fat
(7 g saturated)
670 mg sodium

Quattro Cannoli

320 calories
27 g fat
(5 g saturated, 0.5 g trans)
45 g carbs

GRILL

1,440 calories
115 g fat
(23 g saturated, 1 g trans)
3,640 mg sodium

Not That!
Chicken Under a Brick

Romano's doesn't make its ingredients public, so we're not sure how roasted chicken and potatoes can bear such a shameful nutritional profile, but knowing it contains more than half a day's calories and more than a day's saturated fat is reason enough not to order it.

WEAPON OF MASS DESTRUCTION
Chianti BBQ Steak

1,920 calories
121 g fat
(42 g saturated, 0.5 g trans)
3,130 mg sodium

The previous Worst Steak in America was a Ruby Tuesday's rib eye with 912 calories. That means that this Chianti calamity is the worst piece of beef in America by more than 1,000 calories. Scary stuff.

OTHER PASSES

New York Style Cheesecake
760 calories
52 g fat
(32 g saturated, 2 g trans)
61 g carbs

Crispy Artichoke Potato Cakes
820 calories
72 g fat
(12 g saturated)
1,130 mg sodium

Whole Wheat Fettuccine with Basil Pesto Sauce
1,050 calories
66 g fat
(22.5 g saturated)
1,140 mg sodium

SIDESWIPED
Parmesan Fries

700 calories
48 g fat
(12 g saturated, 1 g trans)
1,530 mg sodium

A standard order of restaurant fries packs about 350 calories. A quarter cup of grated Parmesan runs about 100 calories. So where are the rest of these calories (and the trans fats!) coming from? We have no idea, but opt for these fries and you'll blow more than a meal's worth calories on a side order.

RUBY TUESDAY

C- The chain built its reputation on a hearty selection of hamburgers. The problem is, they average 91 grams of fat—about 150 percent of your recommended daily limit. And now that Ruby Tuesday has finally released full sodium counts, it's apparent it's been harboring one of the saltiest menus in America. But with the addition of the Fit & Trim and Petite menus in recent years, Ruby's earns a slight bump up on its report card.

SURVIVAL STRATEGY

Solace lies in the 3 S's: sirloin, salmon, and shrimp all make for relatively innocuous eating, especially when paired with one of Ruby Tuesday's half-dozen healthy sides, such as mashed cauliflower and sautéed portabellas.

Eat This

Barbecue Grilled Chicken

with White Cheddar Mashed Potatoes and Fresh Steamed Broccoli

621 calories
25 g fat
1,402 mg sodium

The Fit & Trim version of this dish comes with a double side of veggies, but a lean slab of protein allows a little room for more substantial sides. Cheddar mashed potatoes sounds like a high-fat comfort food, but other than Brown-Rice Pilaf, it's the healthiest starch at Ruby's.

OTHER PICKS

Asiago Peppercorn Sirloin
401 calories
20 g fat
1,023 mg sodium

Herb-Crusted Tilapia
401 calories
24 g fat
944 mg sodium

Fried Mozzarella (per serving)
101 calories
4 g fat
304 mg sodium

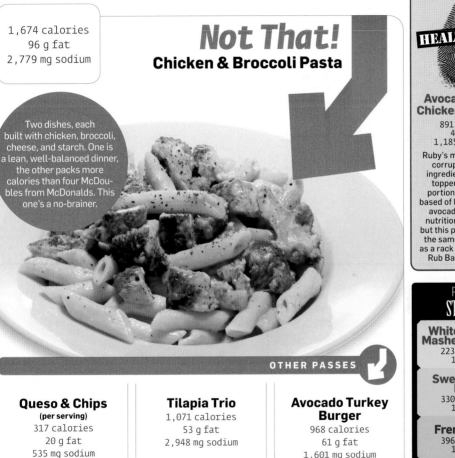

1,674 calories
96 g fat
2,779 mg sodium

Not That!

Chicken & Broccoli Pasta

Two dishes, each built with chicken, broccoli, cheese, and starch. One is a lean, well-balanced dinner, the other packs more calories than four McDoubles from McDonalds. This one's a no-brainer.

OTHER PASSES

Queso & Chips
(per serving)
317 calories
20 g fat
535 mg sodium

Tilapia Trio
1,071 calories
53 g fat
2,948 mg sodium

Avocado Turkey Burger
968 calories
61 g fat
1,601 mg sodium

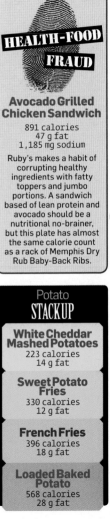

Avocado Grilled Chicken Sandwich
891 calories
47 g fat
1,185 mg sodium

Ruby's makes a habit of corrupting healthy ingredients with fatty toppers and jumbo portions. A sandwich based of lean protein and avocado should be a nutritional no-brainer, but this plate has almost the same calorie count as a rack of Memphis Dry Rub Baby-Back Ribs.

Potato STACKUP

White Cheddar Mashed Potatoes
223 calories
14 g fat

Sweet Potato Fries
330 calories
12 g fat

French Fries
396 calories
18 g fat

Loaded Baked Potato
568 calories
28 g fat

SMOOTHIE KING

B- Smoothie King, the older and smaller of the two smoothie titans, suffers from portion problems. The smallest adult option is 20 ounces, which makes it that much harder to keep the calories from sugar remotely reasonable. Added sugars and honey don't make things any better. (Isn't fruit sweet enough?) Still, the menu boasts some great all-fruit smoothies, light options, and an excellent portfolio of smoothie enhancers.

SURVIVAL STRATEGY

Favor the Stay Healthy and Trim Down portions of the menu, and be sure to stick to 20-ounce smoothies made from nothing but real fruit. No matter what you do, avoid anything listed under the Indulge section—it's pure trouble.

Eat This

Mocha Coffee Smoothie
(20 fl oz)

260 calories
2 g fat
36 g sugars

This blend of coffee, fat-free milk, protein powder, and sugar is one of the best frozen coffee treats in the country. Our advice: Ditch the 100 calories of added sugar by ordering it Skinny, and avoid the other Coffee Smoothie flavors (like Vanilla and Caramel)—they pack an extra 20 to 30 grams of sugar.

OTHER PICKS

Peach Slice Smoothie
(20 fl oz)
251 calories
0 g fat
55 g sugars

Chocolate High Protein Smoothie
(20 fl oz)
366 calories
9 g fat (1 g saturated)
37 g sugars

Blueberry Heave
(20 fl oz)
325 calories
1 g fat (0 g saturated)
64 g sugars

570 calories
12 g fat
(6 g saturated)
88 g sugars

Not That!

Caramel Mo'cuccino Smoothie

(20 fl oz)

The main issue we have with this smoothie? It's not a smoothie at all; it's a milk shake with a few shakes of protein powder.

Strawberry Lemon Twist Smoothie (20 fl oz)
94 g sugars

=

1 full pint of Ben & Jerry's Peanut Butter Cup Ice Cream

776
Average number of calories in a large Snack Right smoothie

OTHER PASSES

Cranberry Supreme
(20 fl oz)
554 calories
1 g fat (0 g saturated)
96 g sugars

Chocolate The Hulk Smoothie
(20 fl oz)
801 calories
31 g fat (12 g saturated)
90 g sugars

Orange Ka-Bam Smoothie
(20 fl oz)
465 calories
0 g fat
108 g sugars

Guilty Pleasure

Yogurt D-Lite Smoothie
(20 fl oz)
275 calories
4 g fat
(2 g saturated)
34 g sugars

This is the only treat on the Indulge menu that's worth, well, indulging in. It's made with frozen yogurt instead of ice cream, which will save you up to 455 calories and 73 grams of sugar.

SONIC

C+ In many respects, the fried-and-fatty pitfalls are more dramatic at Sonic than they are at other chains. You have an oversized selection of deep-fried sides, a tempting lineup of frozen sodas, and an expansive catalogue of shakes, malts, and Sonic Blasts. That said, the chain offers most of its indulgences in small portions, making possible a Jr. Burger with Small Tots and Small Slush for 630 calories—a relative bargain considering what you'd suffer elsewhere.

SURVIVAL STRATEGY

Sounds crazy, but corn dogs, 6-inch hot dogs, and Jr. Burgers are your safest options. Just avoid the shakes. Even a 14-ounce cup can stick you with 600 calories.

Eat This

Chicken Strips (3)
with BBQ Sauce and Tater Tots (small)

555 calories
28 g fat
(5 g saturated)
1,640 mg sodium

Sonic doesn't leave you with many options for a sensible sandwich, so a few chicken fingers is a fair alternative. They're fried, so you still feel like you're indulging, but they're mostly lean protein, leaving space for a pile of crispy tater tots.

OTHER PICKS

Jr. Deluxe Cheeseburger
450 calories
28 g fat
(9 g saturated, 0.5 g trans)
800 mg sodium

Ched 'R' Bites
(12)
280 calories
15 g fat
(6 g saturated)
740 mg sodium

Vanilla Cone
250 calories
13 g fat
(9 g saturated)
24 g sugars

810 calories
46 g fat
(11 g saturated)
1,730 mg sodium

Not That!
Chicken Club Toaster Sandwich

The dangers here are almost too many to count: thick wedges of Texas toast, melted cheese, mayonnaise, bacon, and a greasy breast of batter-fried chicken. This is one of the worst chicken sandwiches in America.

WEAPON OF MASS DESTRUCTION
Ultimate Meat & Cheese Breakfast Burrito

820 calories
60 g fat
(19 g saturated, 1.5 g trans)
2,030 mg sodium

Anytime a breakfast item has both bacon and sausage, you're asking for trouble. Add eggs, cheese, fried potatoes, and a refined-flour tortilla, and you have one shoddy way to start your day. This is the worst item on Sonic's Breakfast menu.

OTHER PASSES

Vanilla Shake
(small)

540 calories
31 g fat
(23 g saturated)
55 g sugars

Mozzarella Sticks
(5)

440 calories
22 g fat
(9 g saturated, 0.5 g trans)
1,050 mg sodium

Sonic Burger
with Mayonnaise

740 calories
48 g fat
(15 g saturated, 1.5 g trans)
760 mg sodium

Guilty Pleasure
Cheese Tots
(small)

290 calories
18 g fat
(5 g saturated)
890 mg sodium

We never thought the day would come when we'd recommend deep-fried potatoes smothered in cheese, but these cheesy tots have fewer calories than any medium fry order we could find in the country, so we thought they deserved a little recognition.

STARBUCKS

B+ Once upon a time, Starbucks was a fine place for coffee, but a dangerous place for fancy drinks and food. But recent years have seen the introduction of a solid line of breakfast and lunch sandwiches, oatmeal, wraps, parfaits, and snack plates, making this coffee shop a reliable place to tame a growling stomach on the go. Just ignore the carb-fueled confections. As for the drinks? Unless you keep it simple, they can do some damage.

SURVIVAL STRATEGY

There's no beating a regular cup of joe or unsweetened tea, but if you need a specialty fix, stick with fat-free milk, sugar-free syrup, and no whipped cream. As for food, go with the Perfect Oatmeal or an Egg White, Spinach, and Feta Wrap.

Eat This

Chicken Sausage Breakfast Wrap

300 calories
10 g fat
(3 g saturated)
700 mg sodium

This is as good as a breakfast wrap gets. The combination of 14 grams of lean protein from the sausage and egg and 5 grams of fiber from the wheat wrap will keep you full and fueled 'til lunch. That's a powerful nutritional punch for a mere 300 calories.

OTHER PICKS

Iced Vanilla Latte

(Grande, 2% milk)
190 calories
4 g fat
(2 g saturated)
28 g sugars

Chicken & Hummus Bistro Box

270 calories
8 g fat
(1 g saturated)
520 mg sodium

Marshmallow Dream Bar

210 calories
4 g fat
(2.5 g saturated)
15 g sugars

Not That!

Bountiful Blueberry Muffin

370 calories
14 g fat
(6 g saturated)
320 mg sodium

It's time you learned the truth: Muffins are icing-less cupcakes. It doesn't matter what healthy ingredients they boast—blueberries, zucchini, carrots, nuts, bran—they're just flour, eggs, butter, and sugar, and they'll leave you hungry shortly after you eat them. How do we know that? Because this muffin has 29 grams of sugar and not even a full gram of fiber.

OTHER PASSES

Old-Fashioned Glazed Doughnut
420 calories
21 g fat
(10 g saturated)
34 g sugars

Cheese & Fruit Bistro Box
480 calories
28 g fat
(10 g saturated, 0.5 g trans)
470 mg sodium

Iced White Chocolate Mocha
(Grande, 2% milk, no whipped cream)
340 calories
9 g fat
(6 g saturated)
52 g sugars

CALORIE-CUTTING LINGO

HOLD THE WHIP
Cuts the cream and saves you up to 110 calories

NONFAT
Uses fat-free milk instead of whole or 2%

SUGAR-FREE SYRUP
Use instead of regular syrup and save up to 150 calories a drink

SKINNY
Your drink will be made with sugar-free syrup and fat-free milk

Espresso
5 calories
0 g sugars

Caffe Americano
15 calories
0 g sugars

Cappuccino
120 calories
10 g sugars

Caffe Latte
190 calories
17 g sugars

Caffe Mocha
260 calories
35 g sugars

STEAK 'N SHAKE

B- For a chain named after two of the most precarious foods on the planet, Steak 'n Shake could be far more dangerous. A single Steakburger with Cheese delivers a modest 330 calories, and not a single salad exceeds 500. Too bad we can't make a similar claim about the shakes. Even the smalls commonly eclipse 600 calories, and at least one—the large M&M shake—has more sugar than 7 Klondike Bars.

SURVIVAL STRATEGY

Go ahead and order a burger, but keep it simple. If you're feeling extra hungry, add a second steak patty for 110 calories. What you want to avoid are the tricked-out chili dishes. Anything entrée-size will saddle you with 830 to 1,220 calories.

Eat This

Double Steakburger

with Cheese

460 calories
25 g fat
(11 g saturated, 1 g trans)
720 mg sodium

This is one of the only drive-thrus in the country where a substantial double-stacked cheeseburger weighs in at under 500 calories. Just be sure to stick to the Original Steakburger menu. The specialty burgers at Steak 'n Shake are less impressive.

OTHER PICKS

Cheesy Cheddar Steakburger
480 calories
27 g fat
(12 g saturated, 1 g trans)
630 mg sodium

Apple Pecan Grilled Chicken Salad
with Reduced Fat Berry Balsamic Vinaigrette
380 calories
9.5 g fat
(1 g saturated)
800 mg sodium

Oreo Ice Cream Sandwich
270 calories
12 g fat
(5 g saturated)
20 g sugars

860 calories
57 g fat
(19 g saturated,
4.5 g trans)
1,390 mg sodium

Not That!

A.1. Peppercorn Melt

"Melt" is code for extra cheese and butter-drenched bread, and when you're already dealing with ground beef and cheese, that kind of excess is just plain unnecessary.

WEAPON OF MASS DESTRUCTION
Chili Deluxe
(bowl)

74 g fat
(39 g saturated,
1.5 g trans)
2,560 mg sodium

At its best, chili is a lean protein- and fiber-packed respite from the fatty offerings on most American menus. But chili is only as lean as the meat that goes into it. Steak 'n Shake must use some ridiculously high-fat beef to produce a cheese-topped chili bowl with the same number of calories and more saturated fat than two (!) Triple Steakburgers with Cheese. Beware: Six of the eight offerings on Steak 'n Shake's chili menu pack 830 calories or more.

OTHER PASSES

Cookies 'n Cream Milk Shake
(small)
700 calories
25 g fat
(16 g saturated)
88 g sugars

Southwest Grilled Chicken Salad
with Ranch Dressing
640 calories
42 g fat
(8.5 g saturated)
1,040 mg sodium

Wisconsin Buttery Steakburger
710 calories
49 g fat
(21 g saturated,
1.5 g trans)
760 mg sodium

MEET YOUR MATCH

Chocolate Chip Pancakes
105 g sugars

19 Chips Ahoy! Original cookies

SUBWAY

A Subway is the first major fast-food chain to carry avocado (now available at breakfast, too), and all the heart-healthy fats found within, in every one of its 24,200 US stores. That's huge, but not nearly as huge as the chain's other initiative. Last year, Subway cut sodium by 15 percent in its regular sandwiches and 28 percent in its Fresh Fit sandwiches. If the chain weren't already America's healthiest chain, it certainly is now.

SURVIVAL STRATEGY

Trouble lurks in three areas at Subway: 1) hot subs, 2) foot-longs, 3) chips and soda. Stick to 6-inch cold subs made with ham, turkey, roast beef, or chicken. Load up on veggies, and be extra careful about your condiment choices.

Eat This

Steak and Cheese Toasted Sandwich (6")

and Veggie Delite Salad with Fat-Free Italian Dressing

465 calories
11 g fat
(4.5 g saturated)
1,845 mg sodium

Nearly identical sandwiches with one critical difference: The Philly on the opposite page has 120 extra calories and double the saturated fat. The choice is yours.

OTHER PICKS

Turkey Breast and Ham
(6" with double meat)
340 calories
4 g fat
(1 g saturated)
1,320 mg sodium

Buffalo Chicken Toasted Sandwich
(6")
420 calories
15 g fat
(3 g saturated)
1,130 mg sodium

Steak, Egg & Cheese Muffin Melts
(2)
400 calories
12 g fat
(5 g saturated)
1,180 mg sodium

870 calories
53 g fat
(15 g saturated, 1.5 g trans)
1,935 mg sodium

Not That!

The Big Philly Cheesesteak Toasted Sandwich (6")
and Veggie Delite Salad with Ranch Dressing

Subway does a lot of things better than other sandwich shops, but ranch dressing ain't one of 'em. The salad dressing alone accounts for more than 30 percent of this meal's calories.

OTHER PASSES

Breakfast B.M.T. Melt Omelet Sandwich
(6")
490 calories
22 g fat
(8 g saturated)
1,630 mg sodium

Chicken & Bacon Ranch Melt
570 calories
28 g fat (10 g saturated, 0.5 g trans)
1,080 mg sodium

Cold Cut Combo
(6")
430 calories
20 g fat
(7 g saturated)
920 mg sodium

STEALTH HEALTH

Ordering 9-Grain Wheat or Honey Oat bread instead of a white roll will increase your fiber load by four or five times, respectively. Fiber-rich foods take your body a while to digest, so they keep you fuller longer, and an *American Journal of Clinical Nutrition* study found that eating more fiber-packed whole grains resulted in less belly fat compared to a diet high in refined grains.

(14)
The number of 6-inch subs with fewer than 350 calories

CONDIMENT CATASTROPHE

All Sandwiches

Subway's numbers are good, but they're not *that* good. That's because the calorie counts don't include condiments. Sandwich Sauce, mayo, and ranch will each cost you 110 calories and up to 12 grams of fat. Tack on cheese and suddenly all of those 350-calorie subs have inched above 500 calories. Stick to veggies, mustard, and light mayonnaise.

T.G.I. FRIDAY'S

D It's been a year of ups and downs for Friday's. On one hand, they became one of the last chain's in America to release full nutritional info. On the other hand, they did away with our favorite part of the menu, the small portions option they provided for many of their most popular dishes. Now it's back to the same atrocious appetizers, frightening salads, and disastrous entrées they've been serving forever. But at least we know exactly how bad it all is now.

SURVIVAL STRATEGY

Danger is waiting in every crack and corner of Friday's menu. Your best bets? The grilled salmon, the 670-calorie Dragonfire Chicken, a Black Angus steak (either the Petite Sirloin or the FlatIron).

Balsamic-Glazed Chicken Caesar Salad

500 calories
28 g fat
(7 g saturated)
1,870 mg sodium

"Caesar" is usually a nutritional red flag, but the dressing here is a Caesar vinaigrette, a less creamy take on the classic. Other than the Low-Fat Balsamic Vinaigrette it's one of the only Friday's dressings with fewer than 300 calories, and the lightest of all Friday's entrée salads.

OTHER PICKS

Petite Sirloin and Langostino Lobster

460 calories
24 g fat
(13 g saturated)
1,710 mg sodium

Dragonfire Salmon

with Ginger-Lime Slaw and Fresh Steamed Broccoli

760 calories
33.5 g fat
(5 g saturated)
2,720 mg sodium

Spinach Florentine Flatbread

440 calories
27 g fat
(13 g saturated)
1,210 mg sodium

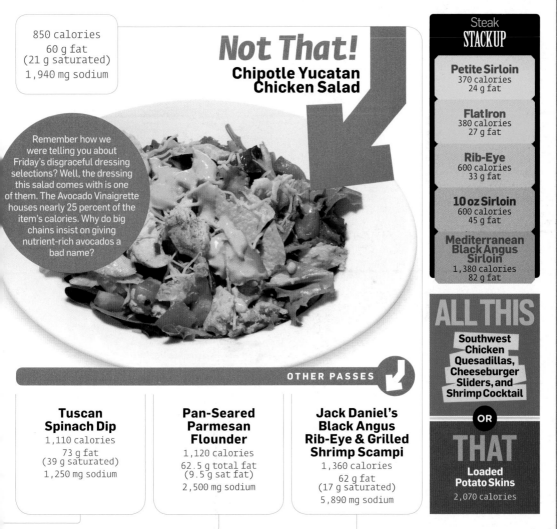

850 calories
60 g fat
(21 g saturated)
1,940 mg sodium

Not That!

Chipotle Yucatan Chicken Salad

Remember how we were telling you about Friday's disgraceful dressing selections? Well, the dressing this salad comes with is one of them. The Avocado Vinaigrette houses nearly 25 percent of the item's calories. Why do big chains insist on giving nutrient-rich avocados a bad name?

OTHER PASSES

Tuscan Spinach Dip
1,110 calories
73 g fat
(39 g saturated)
1,250 mg sodium

Pan-Seared Parmesan Flounder
1,120 calories
62.5 g total fat
(9.5 g sat fat)
2,500 mg sodium

Jack Daniel's Black Angus Rib-Eye & Grilled Shrimp Scampi
1,360 calories
62 g fat
(17 g saturated)
5,890 mg sodium

Steak STACKUP

Petite Sirloin
370 calories
24 g fat

Flat Iron
380 calories
27 g fat

Rib-Eye
600 calories
33 g fat

10 oz Sirloin
600 calories
45 g fat

Mediterranean Black Angus Sirloin
1,380 calories
82 g fat

ALL THIS

Southwest Chicken Quesadillas, Cheeseburger Sliders, and Shrimp Cocktail

OR

THAT

Loaded Potato Skins
2,070 calories

TACO BELL

B The Bell made a bold play in 2010 when they began to play up their menu as a potentially healthy dieting option. A bit far-fetched, but can you blame them? Taco Bell combines two things with bad nutritional reputations—Mexican food and fast food—but provides dozens of ways for you to keep your meal under 500 calories. Stick to the Fresco Menu, where no single item exceeds 350 calories. Not a diet, but close.

SURVIVAL STRATEGY

Stay away from Grilled Stuft Burritos, food served in a bowl, and anything prepared with multiple "layers"—they're all trouble. Instead, order any two of the following: crunchy tacos, bean burritos, or anything on the Fresco menu.

Eat This

Beef Gordita Supreme and Fresco Chicken Soft Taco

450 calories
17.5 g fat
(6 g saturated)
1,030 mg sodium

More substantial than a taco and lower in calories than a burrito, the Gordita is the perfect compromise at Taco Bell, and with just 150 calories each, a steak or chicken Fresco taco makes a solid sidekick. Just don't substitute the Cheesy Gordita Crunch for the Beef Supreme, or you'll add an extra 190 calories to your meal.

OTHER PICKS

Chili Cheese Burrito
380 calories
17 g fat
(8 g saturated, 0.5 g trans)
930 mg sodium

Chicken Enchirito
340 calories
14 g fat
(7 g saturated)
1,080 mg sodium

Cinnamon Twists
170 calories
7 g fat
(0 g saturated)
10 g sugars

580 calories
29 g fat
(9 g saturated, 0.5 g trans)
1,280 mg sodium

Not That!

Express Taco Salad

with Chips

None of Taco Bell's salads are good for you. Why? Because they're not really salads; they're giant tacos. This is the lightest salad on the menu, and it has the same amount of saturated fat as the chain's worst item—the 990-calorie Volcano Nachos.

Caramel Apple Empanada

310 calories
15 g fat
(2.5 g saturated)
13 g sugars

Chicken Quesadilla

530 calories
28 g fat
(12 g saturated, 0.5 g trans)
1,210 mg sodium

Beefy 5-Layer Burrito

550 calories
22 g fat
(8 g saturated)
1,280 mg sodium

Doritos Locos Tacos

200 calories
11 g fat
(4.5 g saturated)
370 mg sodium

What do you get when you swap out a regular corn taco shell for one made entirely of Doritos? Twenty-five additional ingredients, apparently. Taco Bell's Doritos Locos tacos have the same number of calories as their standard counterparts, but they pack 33 ingredients, including six different artificial colors. Sadly, this is also Taco Bells' most successful product launch ever.

ALL THIS

1 Beef Soft Taco Supreme, 1 Chicken Soft Taco, 1 Cheese Roll-Up, and an order of Cheesy Nachos

OR

THAT

Beef XXL Grilled Stuft Burrito

880 calories

TIM HORTONS

B+ When it comes to sandwiches, Tim Hortons trumps the competition. Not a single lunch sandwich tops 500 calories, and its worst breakfast item is a 550-calorie sausage, egg, and cheese bagel. Supplement a lighter sandwich with Tim's oatmeal, yogurt, or soup, and you're golden. The menu still houses a variety of confections and empty carbohydrates, though, so don't let your guard down.

SURVIVAL STRATEGY

More than ever, it's about the quality of your calories instead of quantity. Your best bet at breakfast is the fruit-topped yogurt or brown sugar oatmeal. For lunch, choose either two wraps or one sandwich and a zero-calorie beverage, and you'll be on solid ground.

Eat This

Turkey Caesar Sandwich

and Creamy Vanilla Yogurt with Berries

530 calories
13.5 g fat
(3.5 g saturated)
1,400 mg sodium

This combo is a perfect example of why we dig Tim Hortons: It has turkey, creamy yogurt, fresh fruit, and yes, even bacon, all for the low, low price of 530 calories. Pretty incredible stuff.

OTHER PICKS

Chocolate Dip Donut
210 calories
8 g fat
(3.5 g saturated)
7 g sugars

BBQ Chicken Wrap Snacker and Chicken Noodle Soup
(small)
290 calories
8.5 g fat
(3 g saturated)
1,250 mg sodium

Iced Coffee
with Cream and Sugar (medium)
130 calories
8 g fat
(4.5 g saturated)
14 g sugars

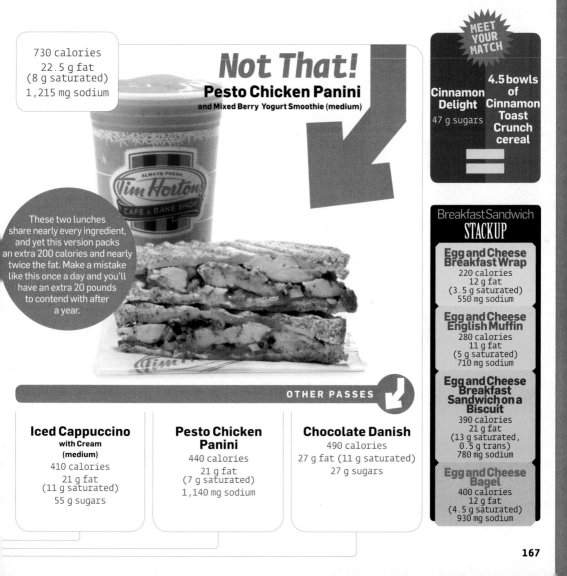

730 calories
22.5 g fat
(8 g saturated)
1,215 mg sodium

Not That!

Pesto Chicken Panini

and Mixed Berry Yogurt Smoothie (medium)

These two lunches share nearly every ingredient, and yet this version packs an extra 200 calories and nearly twice the fat. Make a mistake like this once a day and you'll have an extra 20 pounds to contend with after a year.

OTHER PASSES

Iced Cappuccino
with Cream (medium)
410 calories
21 g fat
(11 g saturated)
55 g sugars

Pesto Chicken Panini
440 calories
21 g fat
(7 g saturated)
1,140 mg sodium

Chocolate Danish
490 calories
27 g fat (11 g saturated)
27 g sugars

Breakfast Sandwich
STACKUP

Egg and Cheese Breakfast Wrap
220 calories
12 g fat
(3.5 g saturated)
550 mg sodium

Egg and Cheese English Muffin
280 calories
11 g fat
(5 g saturated)
710 mg sodium

Egg and Cheese Breakfast Sandwich on a Biscuit
390 calories
21 g fat
(13 g saturated, 0.5 g trans)
780 mg sodium

Egg and Cheese Bagel
400 calories
12 g fat
(4.5 g saturated)
930 mg sodium

UNO CHICAGO GRILL

D+ Uno strikes a curious (if not altogether healthy) balance between oversized sandwiches and burgers, lean grilled steaks and fish entrées, and one of the world's most calorie-dense foods, deep dish pizza, which Uno's invented. It may pride itself on its nutrition transparency, but the only thing that's truly transparent is that there are far too many dishes here that pack 1,000 calories or more.

Eat This

Pepperoni Thin Crust Pizza

with Traditional Crust (½ pie)

495 calories
23 g fat
(10 g saturated)
1,165 mg sodium

The only way to get your pizza fix at Uno without ingesting 1,000 or more calories in one sitting is to eat half of a thin-crust pizza. Surprisingly, the Pepperoni pie is the lightest meat-topped option.

SURVIVAL STRATEGY

Stick with flatbread instead of deep-dish pizzas—this one move could save you more than 1,000 calories at a sitting. Beyond that, turn to the Smoke, Sizzle & Splash section of the menu for nutrition salvation.

OTHER PICKS

Roasted Eggplant, Spinach & Feta
Traditional Thin Crust Pizza (½ pie)
440 calories
16 g fat
(5.5 g saturated)
815 mg sodium

Baked Stuffed Chicken
360 calories
14 g fat
(7 g saturated)
1,420 mg sodium

Red Bliss Mashed Potatoes
270 calories
14 g fat
(3.5 g saturated)
650 mg sodium

1,810 calories
125 g fat
(36 g saturated)
3,030 mg sodium

Not That!

Prima Pepperoni Individual Deep Dish Pizza

with Traditional Crust

An average "individual" pizza at Uno houses an astonishing 1,800 calories. The thick, oily crust is obviously the culprit, but we're still baffled as to how the chain manages to fit that much fat into a small circle of dough. It's impressive—in the worst possible way.

ATTACK OF THE APPETIZER

Pizza Skins

2,070 calories
140 g fat
(48 g saturated, 1 g trans)
3,050 mg sodium

Uno's pizza crust is already the worst in the country, so we're not surprised that filling it with potatoes, bacon, cheese, and sour cream results in a catastrophe.

OTHER PASSES

French Fries
450 calories
33 g fat
(4.5 g saturated)
1,290 mg sodium

Chicken Milanese
850 calories
56 g fat
(12 g saturated)
2,370 mg sodium

Fig, Goat Cheese & Broccoli
Traditional Thin Crust Pizza
(½ pie)
610 calories
26 g fat (10 g saturated)
925 mg sodium

Farmer's Market Individual Pizza
with Nine Grain Crust
1,490 calories
91 g fat
(25 g saturated)
1,950 mg sodium

This is the lightest individual pizza on Uno's menu, which is like being the least wealthy Kardashian sister. The Nine Grain dough has nearly the same amounts of calories and fat as the Traditional deep dish crust. Stay away.

WENDY'S

B+ Scoring a decent meal at Wendy's is just about as easy as scoring a bad one, and that's a big compliment to pay a burger joint. Options such as chili and mandarin oranges offer the side-order variety that's missing from less-evolved fast-food chains. Plus, Wendy's offers a handful of Jr. Burgers that don't stray far above 300 calories. Where Wendy's errs is in the expanded line of desserts and the roster of double- and triple-patty burgers. The new bacon obsession doesn't help either.

SURVIVAL STRATEGY

Choose a grilled chicken sandwich or a wrap—they don't exceed 320 calories. Or opt for a small burger and pair it with chili or a side salad.

Eat This

Chicken Nuggets (10)

with Barbecue Sauce

490 calories
29 g fat
(6 g saturated)
1,050 mg sodium

QUALITY
NATURAL-CUT
FRIES
WITH SEA SALT
IS OUR RECIPE

Chicken nuggets remain one of the safest options at the drive-thru. You get a higher protein-to-bread ratio compared with a sandwich, and you avoid the need for high-calorie toppings. This is the largest order of Nuggets Wendy's offers, and it still has fewer calories than the majority of sandwiches on the menu.

OTHER PICKS

Double Stack

400 calories
21 g fat
(9 g saturated, 1.5 g trans)
1,080 mg sodium

Ultimate Chicken Grill

390 calories
10 g fat
(3.5 g saturated)
880 mg sodium

Chocolate Frosty

(small)

300 calories
8 g fat
(5 g saturated)
42 g sugars

740 calories
38 g fat
(12 g saturated)
1,780 mg sodium

Not That!
Asiago Ranch Chicken Club

Be wary of specialty sandwiches; they're usually tricked out with tons of unnecessary extras. In this case, bacon, cheese, ranch sauce, and a buttered bun combine to make a chicken sandwich with more calories than a Baconator. Order it with grilled chicken to bring it down to a much more reasonable 580 calories.

OTHER PASSES

Chocolate Frosty Shake (small)
580 calories
13 g fat
(8 g saturated, 0.5 g trans)
93 g sugars

BLT Cobb Salad
660 calories
46 g fat
(15 g saturated, 0.5 g trans)
1,840 mg sodium

Dave's Hot 'N Juicy Quarter Pound Single
580 calories
33 g fat
(14 g saturated, 1.5 g trans)
1,240 mg sodium

Bacon Burger DECODER

Baconator Single
A ¼-pound beef patty with cheese, bacon, mayo, and ketchup. Packs 620 calories.

Bacon Deluxe
The Baconator with lettuce, onion, pickles, and tomatoes. Comes as a single or an 850-calorie double.

Junior Bacon Cheeseburger
A smaller beef patty on a smaller bun with produce—at a full 290 fewer calories than the Single Bacon Deluxe, it's your best option.

HIDDEN DANGER

Trans Fats
Most processed beef contains trace amounts of natural trans fats, but Wendy's beef is loaded with the stuff. Even a basic ¼-Pound Cheeseburger has 1.5 grams of trans fats, nearly as much as the American Heart Association recommends be our upper limit for an entire day.

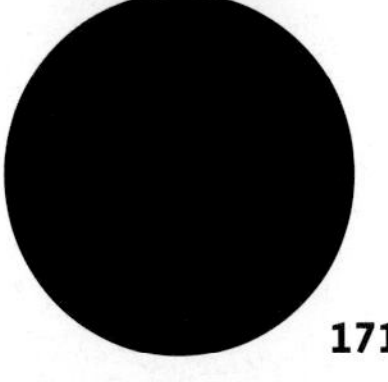

4

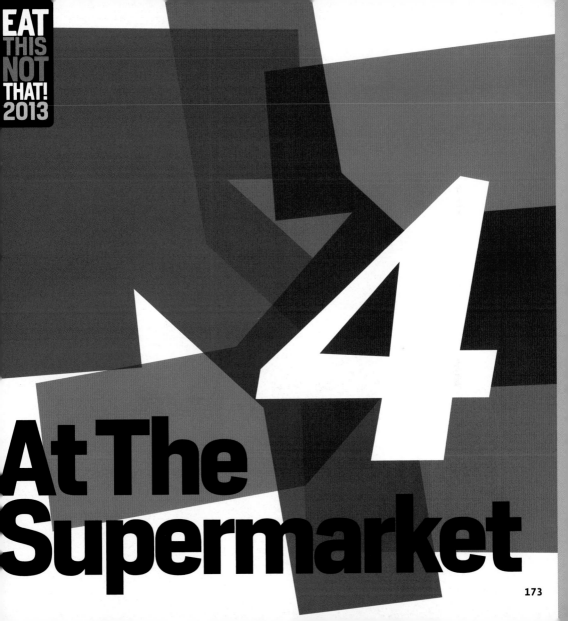

At The Supermarket

Who Likes Food? All of Us!

Who Likes Shopping? All of Us! Who Likes Food Shopping? Hands? Anyone? Hello...?

The answer is, almost nobody likes food shopping. A trip to the grocery store means spending an hour or so parsing specious nutritional claims and confusing price schemes and annoying, cloying packaging tricks, and then doling out more money than you ever imagined you'd have to under soul-sucking florescent lighting that could make Brooklyn Decker look like the Crypt Keeper.

All those mendacious marketing techniques in the supermarket are designed to populate your cart with foodlike substances that trick your taste buds while doing maximum damage to your waistline. It doesn't matter how thorough your command of the English language is; Eminem couldn't pronounce half of what's on an ingredients list, and only Don Draper could make sense of marketing gobbledygook like "Part of a Well-Balanced Diet" and "Loaded with Nine Essential Nutrients." There are about 40,000 products in your average supermarket, and unless you're swooping through the aisles with a math whiz (to calculate what the real calorie counts are), a dietician (to explain what all those crazy words on the ingredients lists mean), and a marketing expert (to decode phrases like "all natural" and "heart healthy"), chances are you're going to make a few mistakes.

Make the same mistake over and over, and you could be shelling out extra money and gaining extra pounds. What you need is a cheat sheet that will lead you away from the worst offenders and toward the nutritionally safe options. Fortunately, you've got one in your hands.

For sure, shopping smart is harder than ever, in part because food is more expensive than ever. This past February, for example, wholesale food prices shot up by 3.9 percent on a year-over-year basis, the largest 1-month price increase since 1974. And a recent survey by the International Food Information Council Foundation found that 79 percent of consumers say that price impacts their decisions about what foods and drinks to buy, up from 64 percent back in 2006. Only 66 percent consider "healthfulness" an important aspect.

But in reality, over the long haul, healthy food is cheaper—because the less nutrition you get from the food you eat, the more you have to eat to satisfy your body. That means you're spending more money on junk—and gaining more fat. Fortunately, there's an answer: The foods in this chapter are the very best in class—the ultimate tickets to a leaner belly, a fatter wallet, and a happier image looking back at you from the mirror. But before you fire up your food cart, lock and load your coupons, and head down to the grocery store, remember these essential tips on how to buy more nutrition for less money.

Demand to see a birth certificate!

That whole wacky controversy over the presidency may be over (it's over, okay?), but that doesn't mean there aren't plenty of imposters still lurking out there. And they're not in the White House—they're in your house! I'm talking about food imposters—things that are sold like food, but are only partially food. The supermarket is filled with mini Manchurian candidates, products that started out as innocents but were corrupted along the way. Consider that container of applesauce, for example: When apples are turned into applesauce, manufacturers can double their caloric load by adding high-fructose corn syrup (HFCS) while also stripping off the peel, which is where much of the fiber and other nutrients are found. So which will help your health more: an apple, or a mash of apple, water, and HFCS? Bottom line: The closer to the food's original form you can get, the better.

Buy nutrition, not calories.

Which is the better yogurt buy: 5.3 ounces of Fage Total 2% with Peach for $2.08, or 6 ounces of Yoplait Original 99% Fat Free Harvest Peach for exactly half that amount—$1.04? No-brainer, right? But think again: By paying half the price for the Yoplait, you're getting less than half the protein (5 grams versus 12), one-third more sugar, and 30 additional calories. Since protein is the stuff that makes you feel full, and sugar is the stuff that leads to up-and-down food cravings, that sounds like a bad investment: Over time, you're likely to wind up buying, and eating, and smuggling along your waistline more of the sugary Yoplait than you should. Or consider the choice of Kashi TLC Honey Toasted 7 Grain Crunchy granola bars ($4.19 for a box of 12) versus Nature Valley Crunchy Oats 'n Honey granola bars ($3.59 for a box of 12). Pretty equal in size, and they both sound pretty healthy. Another no-brainer, right? But shell out the additional 60 cents for the Kashi—that's about 17 percent more money—and you're buying double the fiber, 50 percent more protein, and one-third less sugar.

Don't plan a quickie.

Planning a shopping trip is a chore, what with the list and the unpacking all the bags and the kids hanging out of the cart trying to snag a box of anything decorated with Dora, Diego, SpongeBob, Jillian Michaels, or other characters. It's tempting to make a bunch of short, quick trips instead. But a recent study found that shoppers who stopped by for quickies ended up spending an average of 54 percent more on groceries than they had planned. You're not sneaking into Pakistan to pop Bin Laden, after all; you're implementing your family's long-term health and nutrition strategy. A quick exit isn't your primary goal. A well-stocked fridge is. (Hint: Few people know this, but supermarket shopping is the reason God invented MP3 players. The aisles are a lot less intimidating when Lady Gaga is singing "Born This Way" into your ears.)

Focus on the top dog.

By law, ingredients have to be listed by weight, so whatever's at the top of the list is what's most prevalent in the food. The top two or three ingredients are all you really need to focus on; they'll tell you all you need to know about the relative healthfulness of a product. A package of Oreos, for example, has 20 ingredients on its side. The very first ingredient? Sugar.

Sweet Cereals

Eat This

Kellogg's Froot Loops

(1 cup)

110 calories, 1 g fat (0.5 g saturated)
135 mg sodium, 3 g fiber, 12 g sugars

It's still far from a healthy choice, but the denigrated Froot Loops actually have more fiber than the Kashi

Kellogg's Special K Red Berries (1 cup)

110 calories
0 g fat
190 mg sodium
3 g fiber
9 g sugars

This cereal employs wheat bran to up the fiber count and dried strawberries for sweetness.

General Mills Cinnamon Burst Cheerios (1 cup)

110 calories
2 g fat
(0 g saturated)
125 mg sodium
5 g fiber
9 g sugars

As fiber rich as sweet cereal gets.

General Mills Kix (1 cup)

88 calories
1 g fat
(0 g saturated)
144 mg sodium
2.5 g fiber
2.5 g sugars

Kix just might be the safest of all the sweetened kids' cereals. Try it with blueberries.

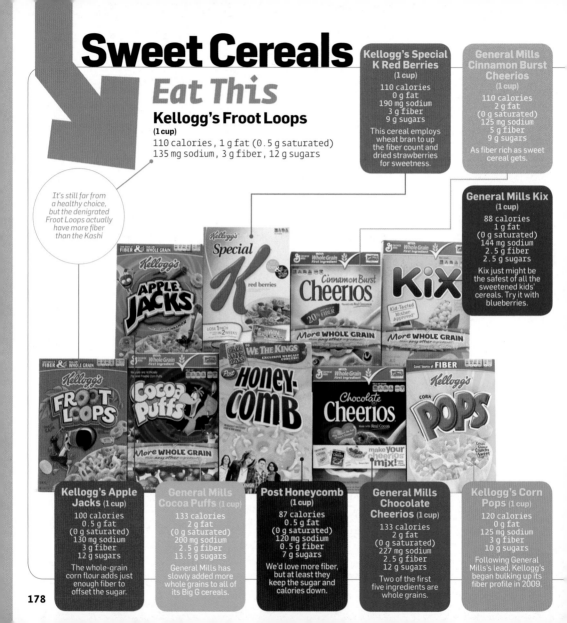

Kellogg's Apple Jacks (1 cup)

100 calories
0.5 g fat
(0 g saturated)
130 mg sodium
3 g fiber
12 g sugars

The whole-grain corn flour adds just enough fiber to offset the sugar.

General Mills Cocoa Puffs (1 cup)

133 calories
2 g fat
(0 g saturated)
200 mg sodium
2.5 g fiber
13.5 g sugars

General Mills has slowly added more whole grains to all of its Big G cereals.

Post Honeycomb (1 cup)

87 calories
0.5 g fat
(0 g saturated)
120 mg sodium
0.5 g fiber
7 g sugars

We'd love more fiber, but at least they keep the sugar and calories down.

General Mills Chocolate Cheerios (1 cup)

133 calories
2 g fat
(0 g saturated)
227 mg sodium
2.5 g fiber
12 g sugars

Two of the first five ingredients are whole grains.

Kellogg's Corn Pops (1 cup)

120 calories
0 g fat
125 mg sodium
3 g fiber
10 g sugars

Following General Mills's lead, Kellogg's began bulking up its fiber profile in 2009.

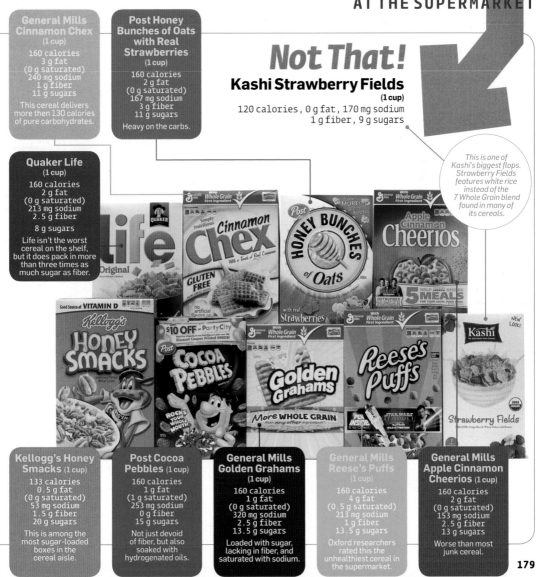

General Mills Cinnamon Chex (1 cup)
160 calories
3 g fat
(0 g saturated)
240 mg sodium
1 g fiber
11 g sugars
This cereal delivers more then 130 calories of pure carbohydrates.

Post Honey Bunches of Oats with Real Strawberries (1 cup)
160 calories
2 g fat
(0 g saturated)
167 mg sodium
3 g fiber
11 g sugars
Heavy on the carbs.

Not That!

Kashi Strawberry Fields
(1 cup)
120 calories, 0 g fat, 170 mg sodium
1 g fiber, 9 g sugars

This is one of Kashi's biggest flops. Strawberry Fields features white rice instead of the 7 Whole Grain blend found in many of its cereals.

Quaker Life (1 cup)
160 calories
2 g fat
(0 g saturated)
213 mg sodium
2.5 g fiber
8 g sugars
Life isn't the worst cereal on the shelf, but it does pack in more than three times as much sugar as fiber.

Kellogg's Honey Smacks (1 cup)
133 calories
0.5 g fat
(0 g saturated)
53 mg sodium
1.5 g fiber
20 g sugars
This is among the most sugar-loaded boxes in the cereal aisle.

Post Cocoa Pebbles (1 cup)
160 calories
1 g fat
(1 g saturated)
253 mg sodium
0 g fiber
15 g sugars
Not just devoid of fiber, but also soaked with hydrogenated oils.

General Mills Golden Grahams (1 cup)
160 calories
1 g fat
(0 g saturated)
320 mg sodium
2.5 g fiber
13.5 g sugars
Loaded with sugar, lacking in fiber, and saturated with sodium.

General Mills Reese's Puffs (1 cup)
160 calories
4 g fat
(0.5 g saturated)
213 mg sodium
1 g fiber
13.5 g sugars
Oxford researchers rated this the unhealthiest cereal in the supermarket.

General Mills Apple Cinnamon Cheerios (1 cup)
160 calories
2 g fat
(0 g saturated)
153 mg sodium
2.5 g fiber
13 g sugars
Worse than most junk cereal.

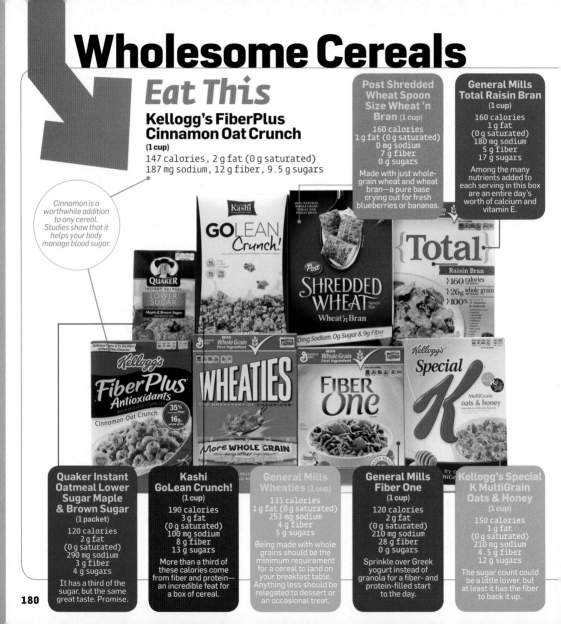

Wholesome Cereals

Eat This

Kellogg's FiberPlus Cinnamon Oat Crunch

(1 cup)

147 calories, 2 g fat (0 g saturated)
187 mg sodium, 12 g fiber, 9.5 g sugars

Cinnamon is a worthwhile addition to any cereal. Studies show that it helps your body manage blood sugar.

Post Shredded Wheat Spoon Size Wheat 'n Bran (1 cup)

160 calories
1 g fat (0 g saturated)
0 mg sodium
7 g fiber
0 g sugars

Made with just whole-grain wheat and wheat bran—a pure base crying out for fresh blueberries or bananas.

General Mills Total Raisin Bran

(1 cup)

160 calories
1 g fat
(0 g saturated)
180 mg sodium
5 g fiber
17 g sugars

Among the many nutrients added to each serving in this box are an entire day's worth of calcium and vitamin E.

Quaker Instant Oatmeal Lower Sugar Maple & Brown Sugar

(1 packet)

120 calories
2 g fat
(0 g saturated)
290 mg sodium
3 g fiber
4 g sugars

It has a third of the sugar, but the same great taste. Promise.

Kashi GoLean Crunch!

(1 cup)

190 calories
3 g fat
(0 g saturated)
100 mg sodium
8 g fiber
13 g sugars

More than a third of these calories come from fiber and protein—an incredible feat for a box of cereal.

General Mills Wheaties (1 cup)

133 calories
1 g fat (0 g saturated)
253 mg sodium
4 g fiber
5 g sugars

Being made with whole grains should be the minimum requirement for a cereal to land on your breakfast table. Anything less should be relegated to dessert or an occasional treat.

General Mills Fiber One

(1 cup)

120 calories
2 g fat
(0 g saturated)
210 mg sodium
28 g fiber
0 g sugars

Sprinkle over Greek yogurt instead of granola for a fiber- and protein-filled start to the day.

Kellogg's Special K MultiGrain Oats & Honey

(1 cup)

150 calories
1 g fat
(0 g saturated)
210 mg sodium
4.5 g fiber
12 g sugars

The sugar count could be a little lower, but at least it has the fiber to back it up.

Quaker Cinnamon Oatmeal Squares (1 cup)
210 calories
2.5 g fat
(0.5 g saturated)
190 mg sodium
5 g fiber
9 g sugars

Overloaded with sugar and cheap refined carbs like maltodextrin.

General Mills Oatmeal Crisp Hearty Raisin
(1 cup)
230 calories
2.5 g fat
(0.5 g saturated)
120 mg sodium
5 g fiber
19 g sugars

Each bowl before adding milk has just 10 calories fewer than a McDonald's hamburger.

Not That!

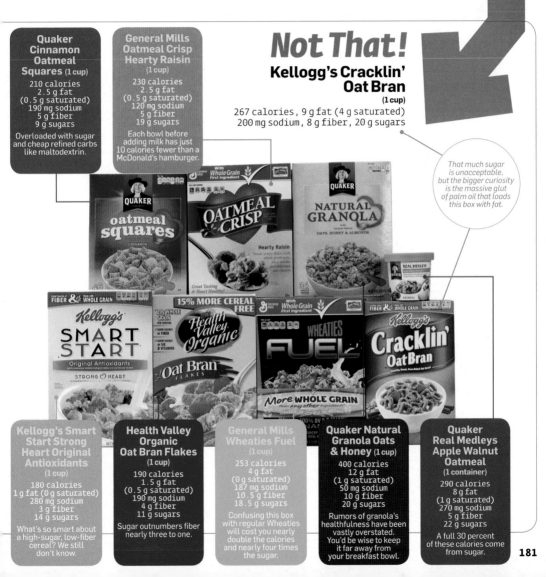

Kellogg's Cracklin' Oat Bran

(1 cup)
267 calories, 9 g fat (4 g saturated)
200 mg sodium, 8 g fiber, 20 g sugars

That much sugar is unacceptable, but the bigger curiosity is the massive glut of palm oil that loads this box with fat.

Kellogg's Smart Start Strong Heart Original Antioxidants
(1 cup)
180 calories
1 g fat (0 g saturated)
280 mg sodium
3 g fiber
14 g sugars

What's so smart about a high-sugar, low-fiber cereal? We still don't know.

Health Valley Organic Oat Bran Flakes
(1 cup)
190 calories
1.5 g fat
(0.5 g saturated)
190 mg sodium
4 g fiber
11 g sugars

Sugar outnumbers fiber nearly three to one.

General Mills Wheaties Fuel
(1 cup)
253 calories
4 g fat
(0 g saturated)
187 mg sodium
10.5 g fiber
18.5 g sugars

Confusing this box with regular Wheaties will cost you nearly double the calories and nearly four times the sugar.

Quaker Natural Granola Oats & Honey (1 cup)
400 calories
12 g fat
(1 g saturated)
50 mg sodium
10 g fiber
20 g sugars

Rumors of granola's healthfulness have been vastly overstated. You'd be wise to keep it far away from your breakfast bowl.

Quaker Real Medleys Apple Walnut Oatmeal
(1 container)
290 calories
8 g fat
(1 g saturated)
270 mg sodium
5 g fiber
22 g sugars

A full 30 percent of these calories come from sugar.

Breakfast Breads

Eat This

Outside of green vegetables, you'll find very few foods that pack 8 grams of fiber into 100 calories. That makes this an unbeatable foundation for breakfast sandwiches.

Thomas' Light Multi-Grain English Muffins (1 muffin, 57 g)

100 calories, 1 g fat (0 g saturated)
160 mg sodium, 26 g carbohydrates, 8 g fiber

Food for Life Ezekiel 4:9 Sprouted 100% Whole Grain Cinnamon Raisin Bread (1 slice, 34 g)

80 calories
0 g fat
65 mg sodium
18 g carbohydrates
2 g fiber

Barley, millet, and spelt help boost fiber.

Thomas' Hearty Grains 100% Whole Wheat Bagels (1 bagel, 95 g)

240 calories
2 g fat
(0.5 g saturated)
400 mg sodium
49 g carbohydrates
7 g fiber

One of the best bagels we've seen. Tons of fiber, plus 10 grams of protein in each serving.

Oroweat Health-Full Nutty Grain Bread (1 slice, 38 g)

80 calories
1 g fat (0 g saturated)
150 mg sodium
17 g carbohydrates
5 g fiber

This bread is studded with sesame seeds, a great source of the mood-improving amino acid tryptophan.

Thomas' Bagel Thins Cinnamon Raisin (1 bagel, 46 g)

110 calories
1 g fat (0 g saturated)
160 mg sodium
25 g carbohydrates
5 g fiber

Switching to these is the best way to wean yourself off bagels. Try a swipe of peanut butter instead of cream cheese for a near-perfect snack.

Pepperidge Farm Whole Grain Mini Bagels 100% Whole Wheat (1 bagel, 40 g)

100 calories
0.5 g fat
(0 g saturated)
120 mg sodium
20 g carbohydrates
3 g fiber

The perfect base for a ham and egg breakfast sandwich.

Not That!

Sara Lee Original Made with Whole Grain English Muffins

(1 muffin, 66 g)

140 calories, 1 g fat (0 g saturated)
210 mg sodium, 27 g carbohydrates, 2 g fiber

The more fiber you work into your breakfast, the more likely you'll be to make it to lunch without experiencing hunger pains. That means this muffin is a recipe for midmorning cravings.

Thomas' Plain Mini Bagels

(1 bagel, 43 g)

120 calories
1 g fat (0 g saturated)
240 mg sodium
24 g carbohydrates
<1 g fiber

Once your palate is accustomed to whole grains, flavorless, nutritionless lumps of refined carbs like this will taste boring.

Pepperidge Farm Bagels Cinnamon Raisin

(1 bagel, 99 g)

270 calories
1 g fat
(0 g saturated)
250 mg sodium
57 g carbohydrates
3 g fiber

This bagel belongs on a dessert menu, not a breakfast table.

Nature's Pride 100% Natural Nutty Oat Bread

(1 slice, 43 g)

120 calories
2 g fat
(0 g saturated)
150 mg sodium
20 g carbohydrates
3 g fiber

You should demand far more fiber than this from a 120-calorie slice of bread.

Sara Lee Deluxe Bagels Plain

(1 bagel, 95 g)

260 calories
1 g fat (0 g saturated)
400 mg sodium
50 g carbohydrates
2 g fiber

This is a wedge of refined carbohydrates, and as such, it will induce a blood sugar roller coaster that will wreak havoc on your energy reserves.

Pepperidge Farm Brown Sugar Cinnamon Swirl Bread

(1 slice, 38 g)

110 calories
2 g fat
(0 g saturated)
140 mg sodium
21 g carbohydrates
<1 g fiber

This bread contains five different forms of sugar.

Yogurts

Eat This

Fage Total 2% with Peach

(1 container, 5.3 oz)

140 calories, 2.5 g fat (1.5 g saturated)
0 g fiber, 16 g sugars, 12 g protein

It takes Fage more than a pound of raw milk to make one container of this yogurt, which is why it's so thick and loaded with protein. Equally as commendable is the fact that Fage eschews preservatives and artificial thickeners.

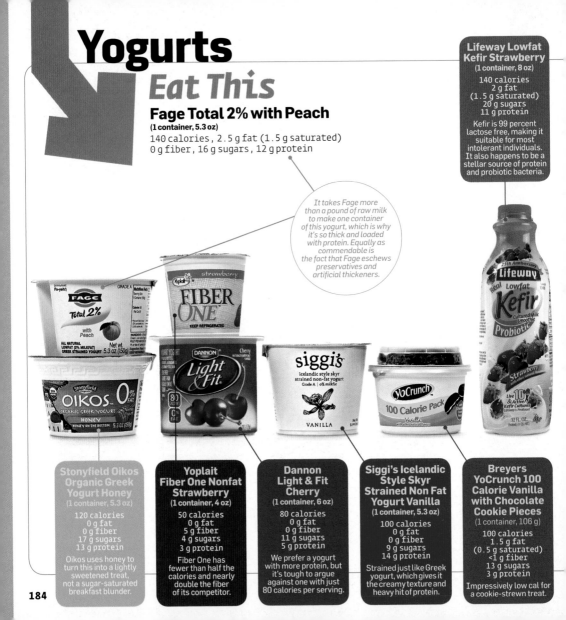

Lifeway Lowfat Kefir Strawberry
(1 container, 8 oz)

140 calories
2 g fat
(1.5 g saturated)
20 g sugars
11 g protein

Kefir is 99 percent lactose free, making it suitable for most intolerant individuals. It also happens to be a stellar source of protein and probiotic bacteria.

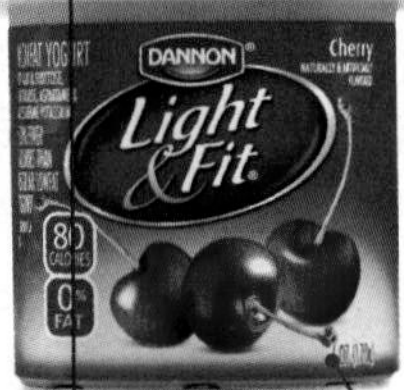

Stonyfield Oikos Organic Greek Yogurt Honey
(1 container, 5.3 oz)

120 calories
0 g fat
0 g fiber
17 g sugars
13 g protein

Oikos uses honey to turn this into a lightly sweetened treat, not a sugar-saturated breakfast blunder.

Yoplait Fiber One Nonfat Strawberry
(1 container, 4 oz)

50 calories
0 g fat
5 g fiber
4 g sugars
3 g protein

Fiber One has fewer than half the calories and nearly double the fiber of its competitor.

Dannon Light & Fit Cherry
(1 container, 6 oz)

80 calories
0 g fat
0 g fiber
11 g sugars
5 g protein

We prefer a yogurt with more protein, but it's tough to argue against one with just 80 calories per serving.

Siggi's Icelandic Style Skyr Strained Non Fat Yogurt Vanilla
(1 container, 5.3 oz)

100 calories
0 g fat
0 g fiber
9 g sugars
14 g protein

Strained just like Greek yogurt, which gives it the creamy texture and heavy hit of protein.

Breyers YoCrunch 100 Calorie Vanilla with Chocolate Cookie Pieces
(1 container, 106 g)

100 calories
1.5 g fat
(0.5 g saturated)
<1 g fiber
13 g sugars
3 g protein

Impressively low cal for a cookie-strewn treat.

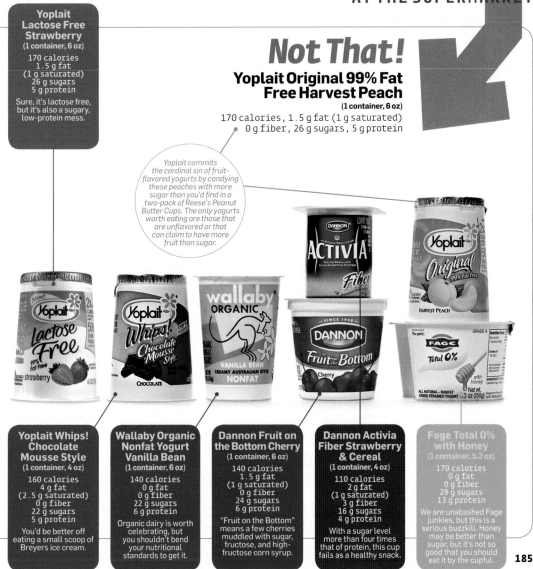

Yoplait Lactose Free Strawberry
(1 container, 6 oz)

170 calories
1.5 g fat
(1 g saturated)
26 g sugars
5 g protein

Sure, it's lactose free, but it's also a sugary, low-protein mess.

Not That!

Yoplait Original 99% Fat Free Harvest Peach

(1 container, 6 oz)

170 calories, 1.5 g fat (1 g saturated)
0 g fiber, 26 g sugars, 5 g protein

Yoplait commits the cardinal sin of fruit-flavored yogurts by candying these peaches with more sugar than you'd find in a two-pack of Reese's Peanut Butter Cups. The only yogurts worth eating are those that are unflavored or that can claim to have more fruit than sugar.

Yoplait Whips! Chocolate Mousse Style
(1 container, 4 oz)

160 calories
4 g fat
(2.5 g saturated)
0 g fiber
22 g sugars
5 g protein

You'd be better off eating a small scoop of Breyers ice cream.

Wallaby Organic Nonfat Yogurt Vanilla Bean
(1 container, 6 oz)

140 calories
0 g fat
0 g fiber
22 g sugars
6 g protein

Organic dairy is worth celebrating, but you shouldn't bend your nutritional standards to get it.

Dannon Fruit on the Bottom Cherry
(1 container, 6 oz)

140 calories
1.5 g fat
(1 g saturated)
0 g fiber
24 g sugars
6 g protein

"Fruit on the Bottom" means a few cherries muddled with sugar, fructose, and high-fructose corn syrup.

Dannon Activia Fiber Strawberry & Cereal
(1 container, 4 oz)

110 calories
2 g fat
(1 g saturated)
3 g fiber
16 g sugars
4 g protein

With a sugar level more than four times that of protein, this cup fails as a healthy snack.

Fage Total 0% with Honey
(1 container, 5.3 oz)

170 calories
0 g fat
0 g fiber
29 g sugars
13 g protein

We are unabashed Fage junkies, but this is a serious buzzkill. Honey may be better than sugar, but it's not so good that you should eat it by the cupful.

Cheeses

Eat This

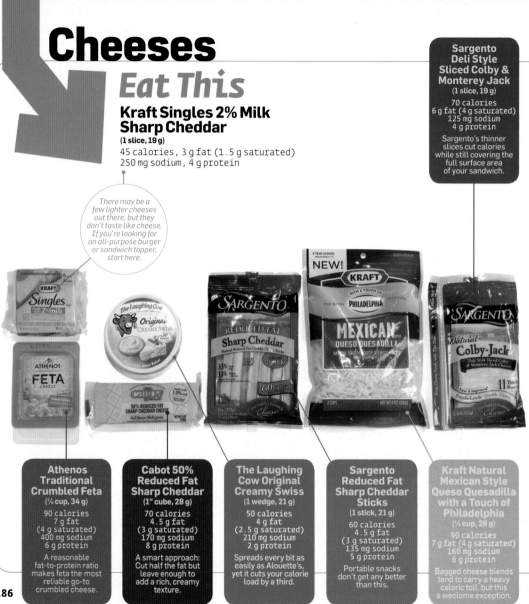

Kraft Singles 2% Milk Sharp Cheddar

(1 slice, 19 g)

45 calories, 3 g fat (1.5 g saturated)
250 mg sodium, 4 g protein

There may be a few lighter cheeses out there, but they don't taste like cheese. If you're looking for an all-purpose burger or sandwich topper, start here.

Sargento Deli Style Sliced Colby & Monterey Jack

(1 slice, 19 g)

70 calories
6 g fat (4 g saturated)
125 mg sodium
4 g protein

Sargento's thinner slices cut calories while still covering the full surface area of your sandwich.

Athenos Traditional Crumbled Feta

(¼ cup, 34 g)

90 calories
7 g fat
(4 g saturated)
400 mg sodium
6 g protein

A reasonable fat-to-protein ratio makes feta the most reliable go-to crumbled cheese.

Cabot 50% Reduced Fat Sharp Cheddar

(1" cube, 28 g)

70 calories
4.5 g fat
(3 g saturated)
170 mg sodium
8 g protein

A smart approach: Cut half the fat but leave enough to add a rich, creamy texture.

The Laughing Cow Original Creamy Swiss

(1 wedge, 21 g)

50 calories
4 g fat
(2.5 g saturated)
210 mg sodium
2 g protein

Spreads every bit as easily as Alouette's, yet it cuts your calorie load by a third.

Sargento Reduced Fat Sharp Cheddar Sticks

(1 stick, 21 g)

60 calories
4.5 g fat
(3 g saturated)
135 mg sodium
5 g protein

Portable snacks don't get any better than this.

Kraft Natural Mexican Style Queso Quesadilla with a Touch of Philadelphia

(¼ cup, 28 g)

90 calories
7 g fat (4 g saturated)
160 mg sodium
6 g protein

Bagged cheese blends tend to carry a heavy caloric toll, but this a weclome exception.

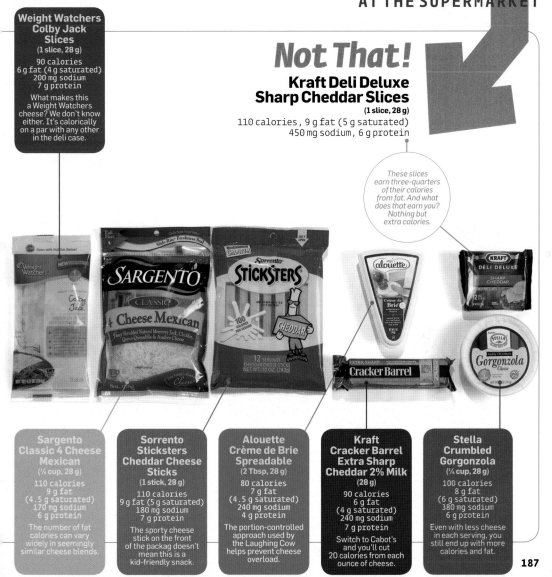

Weight Watchers Colby Jack Slices
(1 slice, 28 g)

90 calories
6 g fat (4 g saturated)
200 mg sodium
7 g protein

What makes this a Weight Watchers cheese? We don't know either. It's calorically on a par with any other in the deli case.

Not That!

Kraft Deli Deluxe Sharp Cheddar Slices
(1 slice, 28 g)

110 calories, 9 g fat (5 g saturated)
450 mg sodium, 6 g protein

These slices earn three-quarters of their calories from fat. And what does that earn you? Nothing but extra calories.

Sargento Classic 4 Cheese Mexican
(¼ cup, 28 g)

110 calories
9 g fat
(4.5 g saturated)
170 mg sodium
6 g protein

The number of fat calories can vary widely in seemingly similar cheese blends.

Sorrento Sticksters Cheddar Cheese Sticks
(1 stick, 28 g)

110 calories
9 g fat (5 g saturated)
180 mg sodium
7 g protein

The sporty cheese stick on the front of the packag doesn't mean this is a kid-friendly snack.

Alouette Crème de Brie Spreadable
(2 Tbsp, 28 g)

80 calories
7 g fat
(4.5 g saturated)
240 mg sodium
4 g protein

The portion-controlled approach used by the Laughing Cow helps prevent cheese overload.

Kraft Cracker Barrel Extra Sharp Cheddar 2% Milk
(28 g)

90 calories
6 g fat
(4 g saturated)
240 mg sodium
7 g protein

Switch to Cabot's and you'll cut 20 calories from each ounce of cheese.

Stella Crumbled Gorgonzola
(¼ cup, 28 g)

100 calories
8 g fat
(6 g saturated)
380 mg sodium
6 g protein

Even with less cheese in each serving, you still end up with more calories and fat.

Deli Meats

Eat This

Applegate Organics Smoked Turkey Breast
(56 g)
50 calories, 0 g fat
360 mg sodium, 12 g protein

Applegate Farms eschews antibiotics, producing some of the most pristine, natural meats in the supermarket.

Hormel Natural Choice Deli Roast Beef
(56 g)
60 calories
2 g fat
(1 g saturated)
520 mg sodium
11 g protein

One of the few deli brands to forgo all nitrites, nitrates, and other preservatives.

Oscar Mayer Turkey Bologna
(1 slice, 28 g)
50 calories
4 g fat
(1 g saturated)
270 mg sodium
3 g protein

Turkey doesn't always mean healthier. This time it does.

Jones Naturally Hickory Smoked Canadian Bacon
(51 g)
60 calories
1.5 g fat
(0.5 g saturated)
460 mg sodium
11 g protein

The easiest swap in the supermarket; you get twice as much food for half the calories.

Hormel Natural Choice Oven Roasted Carved Chicken Breast
(56 g)
60 calories
1.5 g fat
(0.5 g saturated)
340 mg sodium
12 g protein

This chicken is almost pure protein.

Oscar Mayer Center Cut Bacon
(2 slices)
70 calories
4.5 g fat
(1.5 g saturated)
270 mg sodium
7 g protein

If you want bacon, eat bacon. You won't take in any extra calories and you'll actually cut fat and sodium.

Not That!

Land O'Frost competes with Buddig for the most calorie-dense lunch meat around.

Land O'Frost Premium Honey Smoked Turkey Breast

(52 g)

80 calories, 3 g fat (1 g saturated)
540 mg sodium, 9 g protein

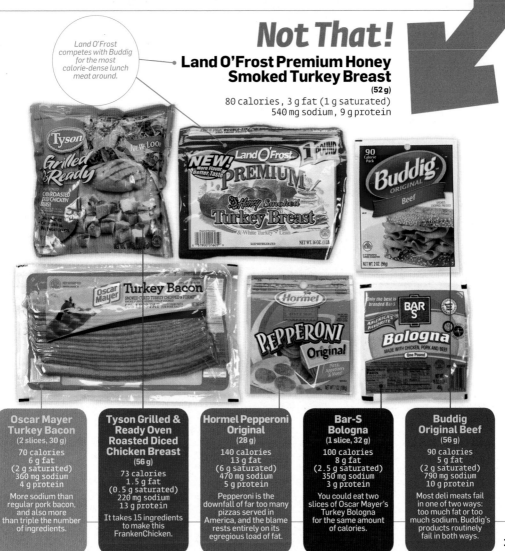

Oscar Mayer Turkey Bacon
(2 slices, 30 g)
70 calories
6 g fat
(2 g saturated)
360 mg sodium
4 g protein

More sodium than regular pork bacon, and also more than triple the number of ingredients.

Tyson Grilled & Ready Oven Roasted Diced Chicken Breast
(56 g)
73 calories
1.5 g fat
(0.5 g saturated)
220 mg sodium
13 g protein

It takes 15 ingredients to make this FrankenChicken.

Hormel Pepperoni Original
(28 g)
140 calories
13 g fat
(6 g saturated)
470 mg sodium
5 g protein

Pepperoni is the downfall of far too many pizzas served in America, and the blame rests entirely on its egregious load of fat.

Bar-S Bologna
(1 slice, 32 g)
100 calories
8 g fat
(2.5 g saturated)
350 mg sodium
3 g protein

You could eat two slices of Oscar Mayer's Turkey Bologna for the same amount of calories.

Buddig Original Beef
(56 g)
90 calories
5 g fat
(2 g saturated)
790 mg sodium
10 g protein

Most deli meats fail in one of two ways: too much fat or too much sodium. Buddig's products routinely fail in both ways.

Hot Dogs and Sausages

Eat This

Hebrew National 97% Fat Free Beef Franks

(1 frank, 45 g)

40 calories, 1 g fat (0 g saturated), 520 mg sodium, 6 g protein

There's no reason to fear hot dogs. A recent study from Kansas State University found that microwave-cooked hot dogs have fewer cancer-causing compounds than even rotisserie chicken. Stick with low-calorie brands and you're never far from a quick, healthy, and protein-packed meal.

Johnsonville Chicken Sausage Chipotle Monterey Jack Cheese (1 link, 85 g)

170 calories
12 g fat
(4 g saturated)
770 mg sodium
13 g protein

We're glad to see the sausage behemoth get on board with the chicken variety.

Applegate Farms The Great Organic Uncured Beef Hot Dog (1 frank, 56 g)

110 calories
8 g fat (3 g saturated)
330 mg sodium
7 g protein

It looks and tastes like a classic ballpark frank, but without the dubious waste cuts or antibiotic-heavy meat.

Aidells Cajun Style Andouille (1 link, 85 g)

160 calories
11 g fat
(4 g saturated)
600 mg sodium
15 g protein

Remember Aidells. It's one of the most reliable purveyors in the deli fridge.

Al Fresco Chipotle Chorizo Chicken Sausage (1 link, 85 g)

140 calories
7 g fat
(2 g saturated)
420 mg sodium
15 g protein

Our love for Al Fresco runs deep. No company offers a wider variety of bold-flavored, low-calorie sausages.

Jennie-O Turkey Breakfast Sausage Links Lean (2 links, 56 g)

90 calories
5 g fat
(1.5 g saturated)
370 mg sodium
10 g protein

Cutting fat doesn't just drop the calorie count, it also makes more space for protein.

Not That!

Oscar Mayer Classic Light Beef Franks

(1 frank, 45 g)

90 calories, 7 g fat (3 g saturated), 380 mg sodium, 5 g protein

Hot dogs vary widely in terms of fat content, so it's important to flip the package and scan the ingredient statement. Case in point: You could eat half a dozen of the Hebrew National dogs on the opposite page and still not reach the fat load of these "light" franks.

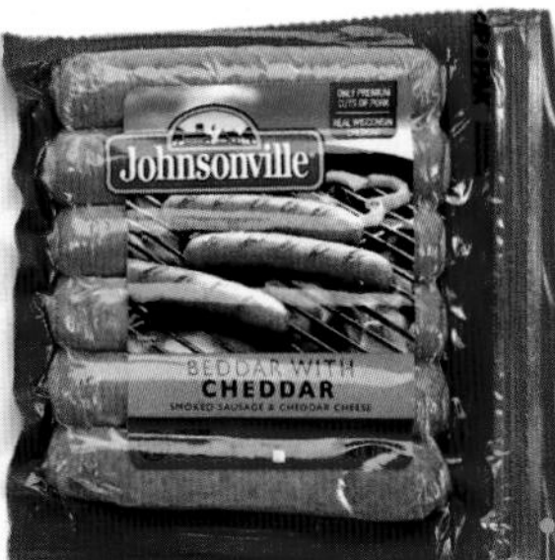

Johnsonville
BEDDAR WITH CHEDDAR
SMOKED SAUSAGE & CHEDDAR CHEESE

Jennie-O Breakfast Lover's Turkey Sausage
(56 g)

125 calories
10 g fat
(3 g saturated)
310 mg sodium
8 g protein

With "turkey" on the label you should expect more from your breakfast sausage.

Hillshire Farm Polska Kielbasa
(56 g)

180 calories
16 g fat
(5 g saturated)
510 mg sodium
7 g protein

Both kielbasa and chorizo are spicy ethnic sausages, but opt for Al Fresco and you double up on protein while cutting calories, fat, and sodium.

Hillshire Farm Smoked Bratwurst
(1 link, 76 g)

240 calories
22 g fat
(8 g saturated)
780 mg sodium
8 g protein

More than 80 percent of this brat's calories come from fat.

Oscar Mayer Selects Angus Beef Franks
(1 frank, 57 g)

180 calories
17 g fat
(7 g saturated)
420 mg sodium
6 g protein

Applegate provides a more protein-packed dog for fewer calories and less sodium and fat. This is an easy choice.

Johnsonville Beddar with Cheddar
(1 link, 66 g)

210 calories
18 g fat
(7 g saturated)
630 mg sodium
8 g protein

More calories, less protein, and a hearty dose of MSG.

Condiments

Eat This

Kraft Mayo with Olive Oil

(1 Tbsp, 15 g)

45 calories, 4 g fat (0 g saturated)
95 mg sodium, <1 g sugars

A study published in the British Journal of Nutrition *suggests that monounsaturated fatty acids might actually facilitate the breakdown of fat. The olive oil used in this jar has more than three times as many monounsaturates as the soybean oil used in regular mayo.*

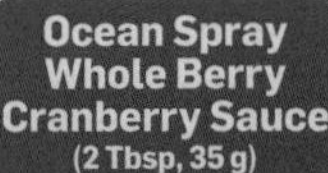

Ocean Spray Whole Berry Cranberry Sauce
(2 Tbsp, 35 g)

55 calories
0 g fat
5 mg sodium
11 g sugars

Not just for Thanksgiving anymore. Turn to cranberry sauce for a low-calorie, high-antioxidant sandwich companion.

The Rib House Medium BBQ Sauce (2 Tbsp, 31 g)

25 calories
0 g fat
240 mg sodium
6 g sugars

The Rib House's sauce earns a touch of sweetness from brown sugar, but its primary ingredients are tomato paste and vinegar. This is as good as barbecue sauce gets.

Annie's Naturals Organic Horseradish Mustard
(2 tsp, 10 g)

10 calories
0 g fat
120 mg sodium
0 g sugars

This bottle contains no ingredients that you wouldn't have in your kitchen.

Annie's Naturals Organic Ketchup
(1 Tbsp, 17 g)

15 calories
0 g fat
170 mg sodium
4 g sugars

Go ahead and spring for organic. Research shows that organically raised tomatoes produce nearly twice as much cancer-fighting lycopene.

Grey Poupon Savory Honey Mustard
(1 Tbsp, 15 g)

30 calories
0 g fat
15 mg sodium
3 g sugars

Made mostly from mustard seeds, which are loaded with omega-3 fatty acids.

McCormick Fat Free Tartar Sauce
(2 Tbsp, 32 g)

30 calories
0 g fat
250 mg sodium
5 g sugars

Although by no means a nutritious condiment, this light take on tartar does eliminate more than 100 calories per serving.

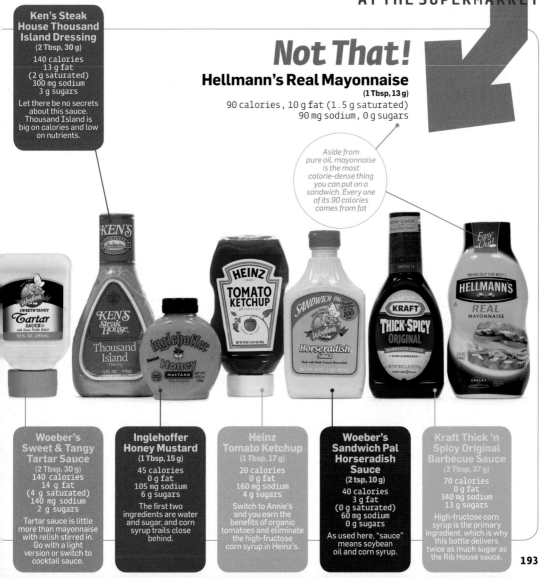

Ken's Steak House Thousand Island Dressing
(2 Tbsp, 30 g)

140 calories
13 g fat
(2 g saturated)
300 mg sodium
3 g sugars

Let there be no secrets about this sauce. Thousand Island is big on calories and low on nutrients.

Not That!

Hellmann's Real Mayonnaise

(1 Tbsp, 13 g)

90 calories, 10 g fat (1.5 g saturated)
90 mg sodium, 0 g sugars

Aside from pure oil, mayonnaise is the most calorie-dense thing you can put on a sandwich. Every one of its 90 calories comes from fat

Woeber's Sweet & Tangy Tartar Sauce
(2 Tbsp, 30 g)

140 calories
14 g fat
(4 g saturated)
140 mg sodium
2 g sugars

Tartar sauce is little more than mayonnaise with relish stirred in. Go with a light version or switch to cocktail sauce.

Inglehoffer Honey Mustard
(1 Tbsp, 15 g)

45 calories
0 g fat
105 mg sodium
6 g sugars

The first two ingredients are water and sugar, and corn syrup trails close behind.

Heinz Tomato Ketchup
(1 Tbsp, 17 g)

20 calories
0 g fat
160 mg sodium
4 g sugars

Switch to Annie's and you earn the benefits of organic tomatoes and eliminate the high-fructose corn syrup in Heinz's.

Woeber's Sandwich Pal Horseradish Sauce
(2 tsp, 10 g)

40 calories
3 g fat
(0 g saturated)
60 mg sodium
0 g sugars

As used here, "sauce" means soybean oil and corn syrup.

Kraft Thick 'n Spicy Original Barbecue Sauce
(2 Tbsp, 37 g)

70 calories
0 g fat
340 mg sodium
13 g sugars

High-fructose corn syrup is the primary ingredient, which is why this bottle delivers twice as much sugar as the Rib House sauce.

Breads

Eat This

Arnold Health-Full Flax & Fiber

(2 slices, 76 g)

160 calories, 2 g fat (0 g saturated), 280 mg sodium
32 g carbohydrates, 8 g fiber, 10 g protein

This loaf is loaded with beta-glucan, a type of soluble fiber found naturally in oats. Studies indicate that beta-glucan may work better than other fibers at reducing cholesterol level and heart disease risk.

Martin's Famous Long Potato Rolls
(1 roll, 53 g)

130 calories
1.5 g fat
(0 g saturated)
200 mg sodium
26 g carbohydrates
4 g fiber
6 g protein

A perfect hot dog vessel. Potato flour packs a potent fiber punch.

Alexia Whole Grain Hearty Rolls
(1 roll, 43 g)

90 calories
1 g fat (0 g saturated)
190 mg sodium
17 g carbohydrates
2 g fiber
4 g protein

Unless your roll has 100 calories or fewer, it has no place on the dinner table.

Mission Yellow Extra Thin Corn Tortillas
(2 tortillas, 37 g)

80 calories
1 g fat (0 g saturated)
10 mg sodium
18 g carbohydrates
3 g fiber
2 g protein

Fiber-rich corn trumps flour every time in the tortilla battle.

Pepperidge Farm Whole Grain 15 Grain
(2 slices, 86 g)

200 calories
4 g fat
(1 g saturated)
230 mg sodium
40 g carbohydrates
8 g fiber
10 g protein

Five grams of protein and 4 grams of fiber per slice? Yes, please!

Arnold Sandwich Thins White
(1 roll, 43 g)

100 calories
1 g fat
(0 g saturated)
170 mg sodium
23 g carbohydrates
5 g fiber
4 g protein

Protein and fiber supply more than a third of these calories.

Flatout Original Flatbread
(1 piece, 57 g)

130 calories
2 g fat
(0 g saturated)
310 mg sodium
24 g carbohydrates
3 g fiber
7 g protein

Not one of Flatout's flatbreads has fewer than 3 grams of fiber.

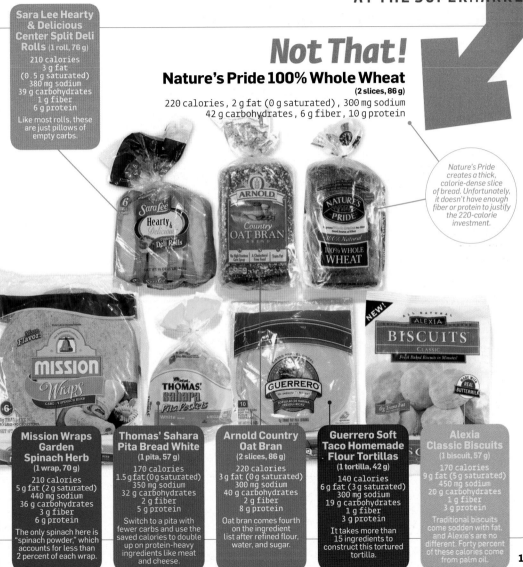

Sara Lee Hearty & Delicious Center Split Deli Rolls (1 roll, 76 g)

210 calories
3 g fat
(0.5 g saturated)
380 mg sodium
39 g carbohydrates
1 g fiber
6 g protein

Like most rolls, these are just pillows of empty carbs.

Not That!

Nature's Pride 100% Whole Wheat

(2 slices, 86 g)

220 calories, 2 g fat (0 g saturated), 300 mg sodium
42 g carbohydrates, 6 g fiber, 10 g protein

Nature's Pride creates a thick, calorie-dense slice of bread. Unfortunately, it doesn't have enough fiber or protein to justify the 220-calorie investment.

Mission Wraps Garden Spinach Herb (1 wrap, 70 g)

210 calories
5 g fat (2 g saturated)
440 mg sodium
36 g carbohydrates
3 g fiber
6 g protein

The only spinach here is "spinach powder," which accounts for less than 2 percent of each wrap.

Thomas' Sahara Pita Bread White (1 pita, 57 g)

170 calories
1.5 g fat (0 g saturated)
350 mg sodium
32 g carbohydrates
2 g fiber
5 g protein

Switch to a pita with fewer carbs and use the saved calories to double up on protein-heavy ingredients like meat and cheese.

Arnold Country Oat Bran (2 slices, 86 g)

220 calories
3 g fat (0 g saturated)
300 mg sodium
40 g carbohydrates
2 g fiber
8 g protein

Oat bran comes fourth on the ingredient list after refined flour, water, and sugar.

Guerrero Soft Taco Homemade Flour Tortillas (1 tortilla, 42 g)

140 calories
6 g fat (3 g saturated)
300 mg sodium
19 g carbohydrates
1 g fiber
3 g protein

It takes more than 15 ingredients to construct this tortured tortilla.

Alexia Classic Biscuits (1 biscuit, 57 g)

170 calories
9 g fat (5 g saturated)
450 mg sodium
20 g carbohydrates
1 g fiber
3 g protein

Traditional biscuits come sodden with fat, and Alexia's are no different. Forty percent of these calories come from palm oil.

Grains & Noodles

Eat This

Ronzoni Healthy Harvest Whole Grain Spaghetti

(2 oz, 56 g dry)

180 calories, 1 g fat (0 g saturated)
41 g carbohydrates, 6 g fiber

Whole-grain pastas are loaded with fiber, and diets rich in fiber are shown to decrease your odds of developing either diabetes or heart disease. You want about 20 grams per day, and this spaghetti has 30 percent of that.

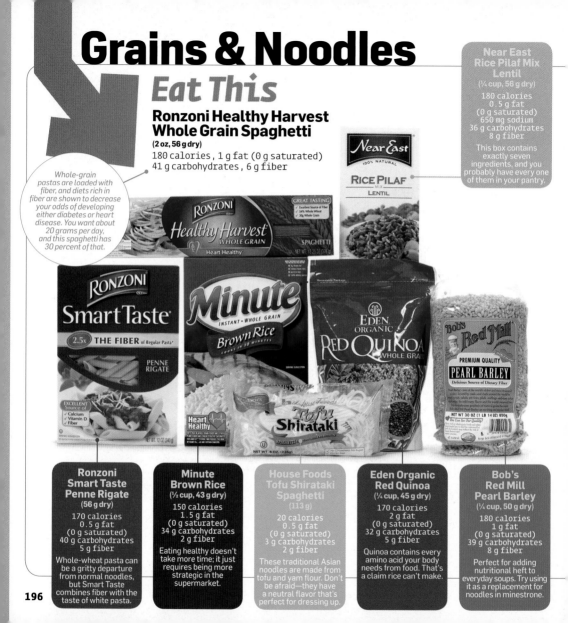

Near East Rice Pilaf Mix Lentil

(¼ cup, 56 g dry)

180 calories
0.5 g fat
(0 g saturated)
650 mg sodium
36 g carbohydrates
8 g fiber

This box contains exactly seven ingredients, and you probably have every one of them in your pantry.

Ronzoni Smart Taste Penne Rigate

(56 g dry)

170 calories
0.5 g fat
(0 g saturated)
40 g carbohydrates
5 g fiber

Whole-wheat pasta can be a gritty departure from normal noodles, but Smart Taste combines fiber with the taste of white pasta.

Minute Brown Rice

(½ cup, 43 g dry)

150 calories
1.5 g fat
(0 g saturated)
34 g carbohydrates
2 g fiber

Eating healthy doesn't take more time; it just requires being more strategic in the supermarket.

House Foods Tofu Shirataki Spaghetti

(113 g)

20 calories
0.5 g fat
(0 g saturated)
3 g carbohydrates
2 g fiber

These traditional Asian noodles are made from tofu and yam flour. Don't be afraid—they have a neutral flavor that's perfect for dressing up.

Eden Organic Red Quinoa

(¼ cup, 45 g dry)

170 calories
2 g fat
(0 g saturated)
32 g carbohydrates
5 g fiber

Quinoa contains every amino acid your body needs from food. That's a claim rice can't make.

Bob's Red Mill Pearl Barley

(¼ cup, 50 g dry)

180 calories
1 g fat
(0 g saturated)
39 g carbohydrates
8 g fiber

Perfect for adding nutritional heft to everyday soups. Try using it as a replacement for noodles in minestrone.

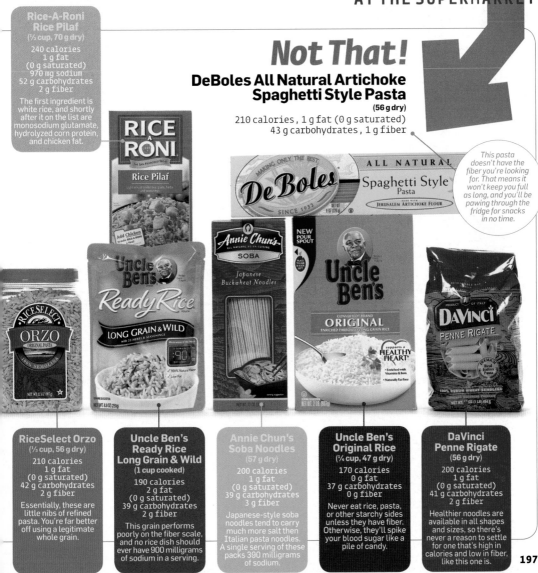

Rice-A-Roni Rice Pilaf
(⅓ cup, 70 g dry)
240 calories
1 g fat
(0 g saturated)
970 mg sodium
52 g carbohydrates
2 g fiber

The first ingredient is white rice, and shortly after it on the list are monosodium glutamate, hydrolyzed corn protein, and chicken fat.

Not That!

DeBoles All Natural Artichoke Spaghetti Style Pasta

(56 g dry)
210 calories, 1 g fat (0 g saturated)
43 g carbohydrates, 1 g fiber

This pasta doesn't have the fiber you're looking for. That means it won't keep you full as long, and you'll be pawing through the fridge for snacks in no time.

RiceSelect Orzo
(⅓ cup, 56 g dry)
210 calories
1 g fat
(0 g saturated)
42 g carbohydrates
2 g fiber

Essentially, these are little nibs of refined pasta. You're far better off using a legitimate whole grain.

Uncle Ben's Ready Rice Long Grain & Wild
(1 cup cooked)
190 calories
2 g fat
(0 g saturated)
39 g carbohydrates
2 g fiber

This grain performs poorly on the fiber scale, and no rice dish should ever have 900 milligrams of sodium in a serving.

Annie Chun's Soba Noodles
(57 g dry)
200 calories
1 g fat
(0 g saturated)
39 g carbohydrates
3 g fiber

Japanese-style soba noodles tend to carry much more salt then Italian pasta noodles. A single serving of these packs 390 milligrams of sodium.

Uncle Ben's Original Rice
(¼ cup, 47 g dry)
170 calories
0 g fat
37 g carbohydrates
0 g fiber

Never eat rice, pasta, or other starchy sides unless they have fiber. Otherwise, they'll spike your blood sugar like a pile of candy.

DaVinci Penne Rigate
(56 g dry)
200 calories
1 g fat
(0 g saturated)
41 g carbohydrates
2 g fiber

Healthier noodles are available in all shapes and sizes, so there's never a reason to settle for one that's high in calories and low in fiber, like this one is.

Sauces

Eat This

The typical teriyaki sauce suffers from two blights: too much sodium and too much sugar. This one avoids both, which makes it by far the best teriyaki in the supermarket.

La Choy Teriyaki Stir Fry Sauce & Marinade
(1 Tbsp)
10 calories, 0 g fat
105 mg sodium, 1 g sugars

Huy Fong Chili Garlic Sauce
(1 tsp)
0 calories
0 g fat
115 mg sodium
<1 g sugars

Chili pepper is the primary ingredient, and it contains not a single gram of added sugar.

Amy's Light in Sodium Organic Family Marinara
(½ cup)
80 calories
4.5 g fat
(0.5 g saturated)
290 mg sodium
5 g sugars

Stick with the low-sodium version. Amy's regular marinara has 290 milligrams more sodium.

Ragú Light No Sugar Added Tomato & Basil
(½ cup)
60 calories
1 g fat (0 g saturated)
320 mg sodium
6 g sugars

Think Italians add sugar to their marinara? Of course not—added sugars mask the naturally sweet flavor of cooked tomatoes.

Classico Roasted Red Pepper Alfredo
(½ cup)
120 calories
10 g fat
(6 g saturated)
620 mg sodium
2 g sugars

Smart move: The roasted red peppers in this jar displace a heavy load of fatty cream and cheese calories.

Cucina Antica La Vodka
(½ cup)
62 calories
4 g fat
(1 g saturated)
241 mg sodium
1 g sugars

Cucina Antica gets the tomato-to-cream ratio right with this superlative sauce.

La Choy Teriyaki Marinade and Sauce

(1 Tbsp)

40 calories, 0 g fat
570 mg sodium, 8 g sugars

If you end up with 2 tablespoons of this stuff on your plate, you'll be about to take in almost half your day's sodium and more sugar than you'd find in a scoop of Edy's Slow Churned Double Fudge Brownie Ice Cream.

Bertolli Vodka Sauce (½ cup)

150 calories
9 g fat
(4.5 g saturated)
730 mg sodium
9 g sugars

It's not the vodka you have to worry about, it's the belt-buckling triad of cream, oil, and sugar.

Newman's Own Alfredo (½ cup)

180 calories
16 g fat
(9 g saturated)
820 mg sodium
2 g sugars

Worse Alfredo sauces exist, but that doesn't make Newman's a winner. One serving packs nearly half a day's sodium and saturated fat.

Prego Veggie Smart Smooth and Simple (½ cup)

90 calories
1.5 g fat
(0 g saturated)
410 mg sodium
11 g sugars

Nice try, Prego, but the vegetable juice concentrates in this jar do more harm than good. Rule of marinara: Keep it simple.

Amy's Organic Tomato Basil (½ cup)

110 calories
6 g fat
(1 g saturated)
580 mg sodium
6 g sugars

We applaud Amy's use of organic tomatoes, but 110 calories is just far too much for a tomato-based pasta sauce.

Maggi Sweet Chili Sauce (1 Tbsp)

35 calories
0 g fat
250 mg sodium
8 g sugars

The first two ingredients are sugar and water. That not only adds unnecessary calories, but also makes this sauce seem less spicy, meaning you'll need more to achieve the desired effect.

Soups

Eat This

V8 Tomato Herb

(1 cup)

90 calories, 0 g fat
480 mg sodium, 19 g carbohydrates
3 g fiber, 3 g protein

Carrots and red peppers are among the primary ingredients in this carton. That's how each serving earns you nearly half of your daily vitamin A requirement.

Progresso Light Zesty! Santa Fe Style Chicken (1 cup)

80 calories
1 g fat (0 g saturated)
460 mg sodium
12 g carbohydrates
2 g fiber
5 g protein

The black beans in this soup bolster the fiber content, plus add a shot of brain-boosting antioxidants.

Campbell's Healthy Request Condensed Homestyle Chicken Noodle (1 cup prepared)

60 calories
1.5 g fat
(0.5 g saturated)
410 mg sodium
10 g carbohydrates
1 g fiber
3 g protein

Low cal, light sodium.

Progresso Light Beef Pot Roast (1 cup)

80 calories
2 g fat (1 g saturated)
470 mg sodium
10 g carbohydrates
2 g fiber
7 g protein

There's a bounty of vegetation in this can, and it includes carrots, green beans, potatoes, tomatoes, celery, and peas.

Campbell's Select Harvest Light Southwestern-Style Vegetable (1 cup)

50 calories
0 g fat
650 mg sodium
13 g carbohydrates
4 g fiber
2 g protein

One third of the calories come from fiber.

Campbell's Chunky Grilled Steak Chili with Beans (1 cup)

200 calories
3 g fat (1 g saturated)
870 mg sodium
27 g carbohydrates
7 g fiber
16 g protein

Campbell's Chunky Chili line is surprisingly lean—not one can tops 240 calories per serving.

Not That!

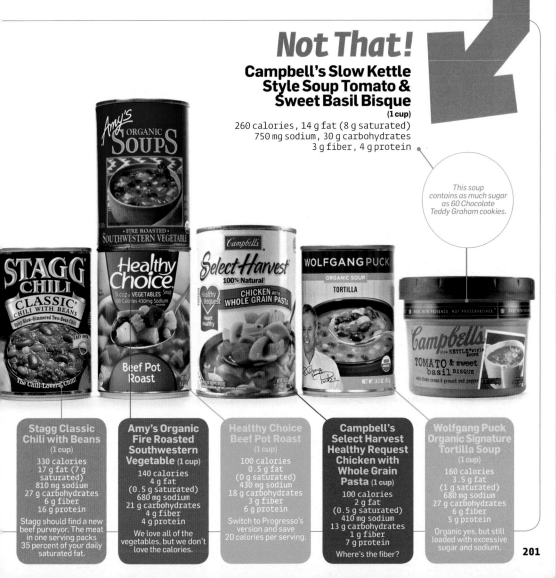

Campbell's Slow Kettle Style Soup Tomato & Sweet Basil Bisque

(1 cup)

260 calories, 14 g fat (8 g saturated)
750 mg sodium, 30 g carbohydrates
3 g fiber, 4 g protein

This soup contains as much sugar as 60 Chocolate Teddy Graham cookies.

Stagg Classic Chili with Beans

(1 cup)

330 calories
17 g fat (7 g saturated)
810 mg sodium
27 g carbohydrates
6 g fiber
16 g protein

Stagg should find a new beef purveyor. The meat in one serving packs 35 percent of your daily saturated fat.

Amy's Organic Fire Roasted Southwestern Vegetable (1 cup)

140 calories
4 g fat
(0.5 g saturated)
680 mg sodium
21 g carbohydrates
4 g fiber
4 g protein

We love all of the vegetables, but we don't love the calories.

Healthy Choice Beef Pot Roast

(1 cup)

100 calories
0.5 g fat
(0 g saturated)
430 mg sodium
18 g carbohydrates
3 g fiber
6 g protein

Switch to Progresso's version and save 20 calories per serving.

Campbell's Select Harvest Healthy Request Chicken with Whole Grain Pasta (1 cup)

100 calories
2 g fat
(0.5 g saturated)
410 mg sodium
13 g carbohydrates
1 g fiber
7 g protein

Where's the fiber?

Wolfgang Puck Organic Signature Tortilla Soup

(1 cup)

160 calories
3.5 g fat
(1 g saturated)
680 mg sodium
27 g carbohydrates
6 g fiber
5 g protein

Organic yes, but still loaded with excessive sugar and sodium.

Bars

Eat This

Kashi TLC Honey Toasted 7 Grain Crunchy
(2 bars, 40 g)
170 calories, 5 g fat (0.5 g saturated)
26 g carbohydrates
4 g fiber, 8 g sugars, 6 g protein

The objective with granola and snack bars is simple: Maximize fiber and protein and minimize sugar. This bar accomplishes the goal by holding tight to Kashi's commitment to whole grains.

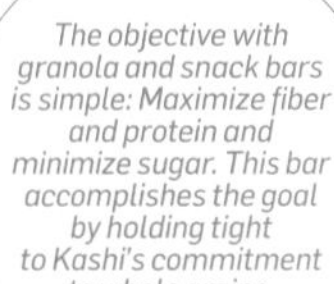

Kashi GoLean Roll! Caramel Peanut (1 bar, 55 g)
190 calories
5 g fat
(1.5 g saturated)
27 g carbohydrates
6 g fiber
14 g sugars
12 g protein

Keep this bar in mind next time you're craving a candy bar. It's rich with fiber and protein, yet still decadent.

Kellogg's FiberPlus Antioxidants Caramel Coconut Fudge (1 bar, 36 g)
130 calories
4 g fat (3 g saturated)
26 g carbohydrates
9 g fiber
7 g sugars
2 g protein

The heft of fiber in this bar will put a dent in your hunger.

Lärabar Apple Pie (1 bar, 45 g)
190 calories
10 g fat
(1 g saturated)
5 mg sodium
24 g carbohydrates
5 g fiber
18 g sugars
4 g protein

Ordinarily 18 grams is too much sugar, but in Lärabar's case, every single gram comes directly from real fruit.

Gnu Foods Flavor & Fiber Banana Walnut Bar (1 bar, 45 g)
140 calories
4 g fat (0 g saturated)
30 g carbohydrates
12 g fiber
8 g sugars
4 g protein

Gnu builds its bars on a base of fiber-rich grains, then adds fruits and nuts for a truly substantial snack.

Pure Protein Blueberry Crumb Cake (1 bar, 50 g)
190 calories
6 g fat
(3.5 g saturated)
19 g carbohydrates
1 g fiber
2 g sugars
18 g protein

This bar's ratio of protein to sugar is as good as you'll find anywhere in the supermarket.

Not That!

Nature Valley Crunchy Oats 'n Honey

(2 bars, 42 g)

190 calories, 6 g fat (0.5 g saturated)
29 g carbohydrates, 2 g fiber, 12 g sugars, 4 g protein

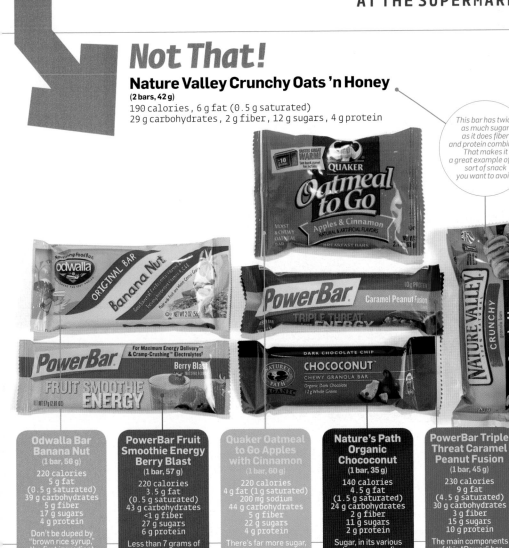

This bar has twice as much sugar as it does fiber and protein combined. That makes it a great example of the sort of snack you want to avoid.

Odwalla Bar Banana Nut

(1 bar, 56 g)

220 calories
5 g fat
(0.5 g saturated)
39 g carbohydrates
5 g fiber
17 g sugars
4 g protein

Don't be duped by "brown rice syrup," the first ingredient in this bar. It's a euphemism for sugar.

PowerBar Fruit Smoothie Energy Berry Blast

(1 bar, 57 g)

220 calories
3.5 g fat
(0.5 g saturated)
43 g carbohydrates
<1 g fiber
27 g sugars
6 g protein

Less than 7 grams of protein and fiber combined and more sugar than a Kit Kat bar.

Quaker Oatmeal to Go Apples with Cinnamon

(1 bar, 60 g)

220 calories
4 g fat (1 g saturated)
200 mg sodium
44 g carbohydrates
5 g fiber
22 g sugars
4 g protein

There's far more sugar, brown sugar, and high-fructose corn syrup than apple.

Nature's Path Organic Chococonut

(1 bar, 35 g)

140 calories
4.5 g fat
(1.5 g saturated)
24 g carbohydrates
2 g fiber
11 g sugars
2 g protein

Sugar, in its various guises, appears five times in this ingredient statement.

PowerBar Triple Threat Caramel Peanut Fusion

(1 bar, 45 g)

230 calories
9 g fat
(4.5 g saturated)
30 g carbohydrates
3 g fiber
15 g sugars
10 g protein

The main components of this "Power" bar are caramel and "chocolatey coating."

Crackers

Eat This

Wheat Thins Fiber Selects Garden Vegetable

(15 crackers, 30 g)

120 calories, 4 g fat (0.5 g saturated)
240 mg sodium, 22 g carbohydrates, 5 g fiber

The primary ingredient here is whole-wheat flour, which is precisely what you want. The extra fiber—a form of oat fiber that Nabisco adds to this Fiber Selects line—is just a bonus.

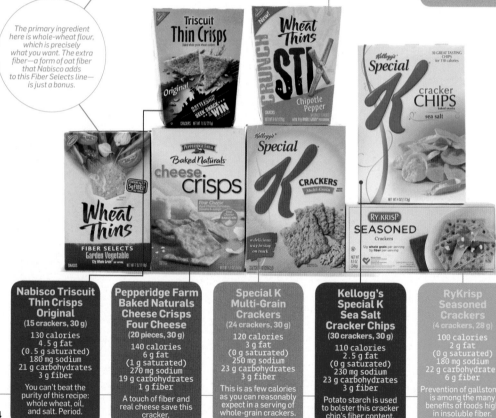

Nabisco Wheat Thins Crunch Stix Chipotle Pepper
(14 pieces, 29 g)

130 calories
4 g fat
(0.5 g saturated)
170 mg sodium
22 g carbohydrates
2 g fiber

Whole-grain flour is the first ingredient, a rarity with novelty crackers.

Nabisco Triscuit Thin Crisps Original
(15 crackers, 30 g)

130 calories
4.5 g fat
(0.5 g saturated)
180 mg sodium
21 g carbohydrates
3 g fiber

You can't beat the purity of this recipe: whole wheat, oil, and salt. Period.

Pepperidge Farm Baked Naturals Cheese Crisps Four Cheese
(20 pieces, 30 g)

140 calories
6 g fat
(1 g saturated)
270 mg sodium
19 g carbohydrates
1 g fiber

A touch of fiber and real cheese save this cracker.

Special K Multi-Grain Crackers
(24 crackers, 30 g)

120 calories
3 g fat
(0 g saturated)
250 mg sodium
23 g carbohydrates
3 g fiber

This is as few calories as you can reasonably expect in a serving of whole-grain crackers.

Kellogg's Special K Sea Salt Cracker Chips
(30 crackers, 30 g)

110 calories
2.5 g fat
(0 g saturated)
230 mg sodium
23 g carbohydrates
3 g fiber

Potato starch is used to bolster this cracker chip's fiber content.

RyKrisp Seasoned Crackers
(4 crackers, 28 g)

100 calories
2 g fat
(0 g saturated)
180 mg sodium
22 g carbohydrates
6 g fiber

Prevention of gallstones is among the many benefits of foods high in insoluble fiber.

Keebler Club Crackers Multi-Grain
(8 crackers, 28 g)
140 calories
6 g fat
(0 g saturated)
240 mg sodium
18 g carbohydrates
<1 g fiber

The "multiple" grains in this box amount to a lot of refined wheat with a scant amount of oat.

Not That!

Ritz Roasted Vegetable

(10 crackers, 32 g)
160 calories, 7 g fat (2 g saturated)
300 mg sodium, 20 g carbohydrates, 0 g fiber

As the name suggests, this box contains a handful of dehydrated vegetables. The problem is, the main ingredient is still refined flour, and it's bogged down with hydrogenated oils and high-fructose corn syrup.

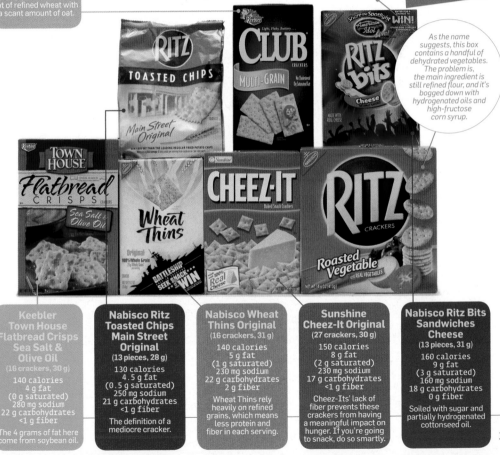

Keebler Town House Flatbread Crisps Sea Salt & Olive Oil
(16 crackers, 30 g)
140 calories
4 g fat
(0 g saturated)
280 mg sodium
22 g carbohydrates
<1 g fiber

The 4 grams of fat here come from soybean oil.

Nabisco Ritz Toasted Chips Main Street Original
(13 pieces, 28 g)
130 calories
4.5 g fat
(0.5 g saturated)
250 mg sodium
21 g carbohydrates
<1 g fiber

The definition of a mediocre cracker.

Nabisco Wheat Thins Original
(16 crackers, 31 g)
140 calories
5 g fat
(1 g saturated)
230 mg sodium
22 g carbohydrates
2 g fiber

Wheat Thins rely heavily on refined grains, which means less protein and fiber in each serving.

Sunshine Cheez-It Original
(27 crackers, 30 g)
150 calories
8 g fat
(2 g saturated)
230 mg sodium
17 g carbohydrates
<1 g fiber

Cheez-Its' lack of fiber prevents these crackers from having a meaningful impact on hunger. If you're going to snack, do so smartly.

Nabisco Ritz Bits Sandwiches Cheese
(13 pieces, 31 g)
160 calories
9 g fat
(3 g saturated)
160 mg sodium
18 g carbohydrates
0 g fiber

Soiled with sugar and partially hydrogenated cottonseed oil.

Chips

Eat This

Lay's Baked! Original Potato Crisps

(15 crisps, 1 oz)

120 calories, 2 g fat (0 g saturated)
135 mg sodium

Baked chips don't rely on oil to crisp up, which means they can get by with far less fat. If you eat just one 1-ounce bag a week, you'll shed more than 2 pounds this year by choosing Lay's Baked! instead of Ruffles Reduced Fat.

Snyder's of Hanover Braided Twists Multigrain
(9 twists, 30 g)

120 calories
2 g fat
(0 g saturated)
160 mg sodium

The 3 grams of fiber in each serving make this a respectable snack.

Popchips Barbeque Potato
(20 chips, 1 oz)

120 calories
4 g fat
(0 g saturated)
190 mg sodium

More crunch than a baked chip, yet less fat than a fried chip.

Stacy's Pita Chips Garden Veggie Medley
(9 chips, 1 oz)

130 calories
5 g fat
(0.5 g saturated)
270 mg sodium

Delivers a respectable 3 grams of protein per serving.

Funyuns Flamin' Hot Onion Flavored Rings
(13 rings, 1 oz)

130 calories
7 g fat
(1 g saturated)
300 mg sodium

Funyuns inflict surprisingly little damage by novelty snack standards.

Chex Mix Bold Party Blend
(½ cup, 29 g)

120 calories
4 g fat
(1 g saturated)
190 mg sodium

The "bold" blend, surprisingly, is lower in sodium than some of the other Chex mixes.

Rold Gold Cheesy Garlic Pretzel Nuggets
(17 pretzels, 1 oz)

110 calories
2 g fat
(0 g saturated)
390 mg sodium

We wish Rold Gold would take it easy with the salt, but you won't find a lower-calorie cheese snack in the snack aisle.

Tostitos Baked! Scoops! Tortilla Chips
(14 chips, 1 oz)

120 calories
3 g fat
(0.5 g saturated)
140 mg sodium

This is the healthiest salsa-shoveling device on the shelf.

Wise BBQ Flavored Potato Chips
(15 chips, 1 oz)
150 calories
10 g fat
(3 g saturated)
210 mg sodium

This bag contains a bunch of processing junk like monosodium glutamate and artificial colors.

Snyder's of Hanover Pretzel Pieces Sea Salt & Cracked Pepper
(⅓ cup, 31 g)
140 calories
6 g fat
(3 g saturated)
370 mg sodium

More sodium than a large order of McDonald's fries.

Not That!

Ruffles Reduced Fat Potato Chips

(13 chips, 1 oz)
140 calories, 7 g fat (1 g saturated)
180 mg sodium

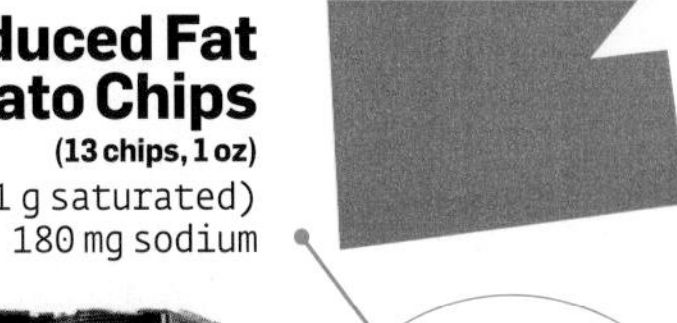

If you could stick Ruffles and its ilk under a hot iron to smooth out the ridges, you'd realize that each chip is actually much bigger than it seems. Avoid the portion distortion by sticking to chips that are already flat.

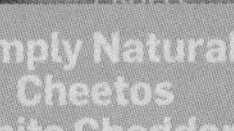

Tostitos Multigrain Tortilla Chips
(8 chips, 1 oz)
150 calories
7 g fat
(1 g saturated)
110 mg sodium

The "multiple" grains in this bag consist almost entirely of corn.

Simply Natural Cheetos White Cheddar Puffs
(32 pieces, 1 oz)
150 calories
9 g fat
(1.5 g saturated)
290 mg sodium

Contains maltodextrin and disodium phosphate—not exactly "natural."

Gardetto's Original Recipe Snack Mix
(½ cup, 30 g)
150 calories
7 g fat
(1.5 g saturated, 1.5 g trans)
260 mg sodium

The trans fats in this mix are simply unacceptable.

Cheetos Flamin' Hot Crunchy
(21 pieces, 1 oz)
170 calories
11 g fat
(1.5 g saturated)
250 mg sodium

The seasoning contains partially hydrogenated oils.

Lay's Garden Tomato & Basil Flavored Potato Chips
(15 chips, 1 oz)
160 calories
10 g fat
(1 g saturated)
170 mg sodium

"Garden" here means little more than tomato powder.

Dips and Spreads

Eat This

On the Border Salsa con Queso

(2 Tbsp, 34 g)

45 calories, 3 g fat (0.5 g saturated), 260 mg sodium

Cheese dips, by nature, tend to be heavy with calories, but On the Border lightens the load by blending in tomatoes, peppers, water, and fat-free milk.

Athenos Hummus Original
(2 Tbsp, 27 g)

50 calories
3 g fat
(0 g saturated)
160 mg sodium

Made with real olive oil, which lends an authentic flavor and more heart-healthy fats.

Newman's Own Mild Salsa
(2 Tbsp, 32 g)

10 calories
0 g fat
65 mg sodium

We balked when Ronald Reagan tried to turn ketchup into a vegetable, but if someone did the same for salsa, a legitimate nutritional superpower, we'd throw our support behind it.

Wholly Guacamole Guaca Salsa
(2 Tbsp, 30 g)

35 calories
3 g fat
(0 g saturated)
110 mg sodium

Avocados are the first of only seven ingredients, all of which you likely keep stocked in your kitchen.

Tribe Hummus Sweet Roasted Red Peppers
(2 Tbsp, 28 g)

45 calories
2.5 g fat
(0 g saturated)
125 mg sodium

Based on chickpeas and tahini, hummus makes for an incredible vegetable dip and sandwich spread.

Desert Pepper Black Bean Dip Spicy
(2 Tbsp, 31 g)

25 calories
0 g fat
240 mg sodium

This jar contains a trio of nutritional A-listers: black beans, tomatoes, and green bell peppers.

Sabra Caponata
(2 Tbsp, 28 g)

25 calories
2 g fat
(0 g saturated)
90 mg sodium

Built from potent Mediterranean produce like eggplants and tomatoes, this dip is perfect for dressing up chicken or fish or spreading on a pita.

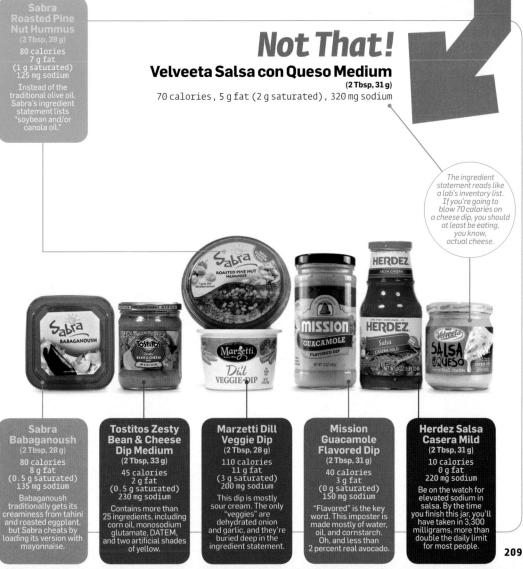

Sabra Roasted Pine Nut Hummus
(2 Tbsp, 28 g)
80 calories
7 g fat
(1 g saturated)
125 mg sodium

Instead of the traditional olive oil, Sabra's ingredient statement lists "soybean and/or canola oil."

Not That!

Velveeta Salsa con Queso Medium

(2 Tbsp, 31 g)
70 calories, 5 g fat (2 g saturated), 320 mg sodium

The ingredient statement reads like a lab's inventory list. If you're going to blow 70 calories on a cheese dip, you should at least be eating, you know, actual cheese.

Sabra Babaganoush
(2 Tbsp, 28 g)
80 calories
8 g fat
(0.5 g saturated)
135 mg sodium

Babaganoush traditionally gets its creaminess from tahini and roasted eggplant, but Sabra cheats by loading its version with mayonnaise.

Tostitos Zesty Bean & Cheese Dip Medium
(2 Tbsp, 33 g)
45 calories
2 g fat
(0.5 g saturated)
230 mg sodium

Contains more than 25 ingredients, including corn oil, monosodium glutamate, DATEM, and two artificial shades of yellow.

Marzetti Dill Veggie Dip
(2 Tbsp, 28 g)
110 calories
11 g fat
(3 g saturated)
200 mg sodium

This dip is mostly sour cream. The only "veggies" are dehydrated onion and garlic, and they're buried deep in the ingredient statement.

Mission Guacamole Flavored Dip
(2 Tbsp, 31 g)
40 calories
3 g fat
(0 g saturated)
150 mg sodium

"Flavored" is the key word. This imposter is made mostly of water, oil, and cornstarch. Oh, and less than 2 percent real avocado.

Herdez Salsa Casera Mild
(2 Tbsp, 31 g)
10 calories
0 g fat
220 mg sodium

Be on the watch for elevated sodium in salsa. By the time you finish this jar, you'll have taken in 3,300 milligrams, more than double the daily limit for most people.

Dressings

Eat This

Bolthouse Farms Yogurt Dressing Chunky Blue Cheese

(2 Tbsp, 30 g)

35 calories, 2.5 g fat (1 g saturated), 135 mg sodium

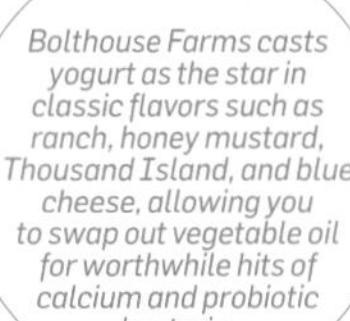

Bolthouse Farms casts yogurt as the star in classic flavors such as ranch, honey mustard, Thousand Island, and blue cheese, allowing you to swap out vegetable oil for worthwhile hits of calcium and probiotic bacteria.

Annie's Naturals Lite Honey Mustard Vinaigrette
(2 Tbsp, 31 g)

40 calories
3 g fat (0 g saturated)
125 mg sodium

After water, mustard is the main ingredient, a surprising rarity among honey mustard dressings.

Newman's Own Lite Low Fat Sesame Ginger
(2 Tbsp, 30 g)

35 calories
1.5 g fat
(0 g saturated)
330 mg sodium

Relegates oil to a supporting role so that vinegar, soy sauce, and ginger can drive the flavor.

Cucina Antica Organic Caesar Dressing
(2 Tbsp, 30 g)

50 calories
5 g fat (1 g saturated)
390 mg sodium

A touch of Romano cheese, not an excess of cheap oil, supplies rich flavor for a fraction of the fat.

Bolthouse Farms Classic Balsamic Olive Oil Vinaigrette
(2 Tbsp, 30 g)

30 calories
0 g fat
150 mg sodium

The lightest vinaigrette we've ever come across. Just another reason why Bolthouse is one of our favorite producers.

Kraft Roasted Red Pepper Italian with Parmesan
(2 Tbsp, 32 g)

40 calories
2 g fat (0 g saturated)
440 mg sodium

The bulk of this bottle is filled with vinegar and tomato puree, a huge improvement over the typical oil-based formula.

Not That!

Kraft Roka Blue Cheese

(2 Tbsp, 29 g)
120 calories, 13 g fat (2 g saturated)
290 mg sodium

Virtually every calorie in this bottle comes from soybean oil, which is a common theme in the dressing aisle. Consider them wasted calories; soybean oil doesn't have the same heart-healthy cachet as olive or canola oil.

Wish-Bone Bruschetta Italian

(2 Tbsp, 30 ml)
60 calories
5 g fat
(1 g saturated)
340 mg sodium

The front label boasts about olive oil, but the ingredient statement reveals that it accounts for less than 2 percent of the recipe.

Newman's Own Balsamic Vinaigrette

(2 Tbsp, 30 g)
90 calories
9 g fat
(1 g saturated)
290 mg sodium

Save cash and calories by making your own vinaigrette at home: Mix two parts olive oil with one part balsamic, plus salt and pepper.

Hidden Valley Farmhouse Originals Caesar

(2 Tbsp, 30 g)
120 calories
11 g fat
(1.5 g saturated)
220 mg sodium

When you purchase a 24-ounce bottle of this dressing, you're committing yourself to nearly 3,000 calories.

Ken's Steak House Lite Asian Sesame with Ginger and Soy

(2 Tbsp, 30 g)
70 calories
4 g fat
(0.5 g saturated)
440 mg sodium

After water, sugar is the first ingredient in this bottle, which is why each serving packs 7 grams of the sweet stuff.

Newman's Own Lite Honey Mustard Dressing

(2 Tbsp, 30 g)
70 calories
4 g fat
(0.5 g saturated)
280 mg sodium

Keep in mind that "light" is a relative term.

Cookies

Eat This

Chips Ahoy! Chewy

(2 cookies, 27 g)
120 calories, 5 g fat (2.5 g saturated)
85 mg sodium, 10 g sugars

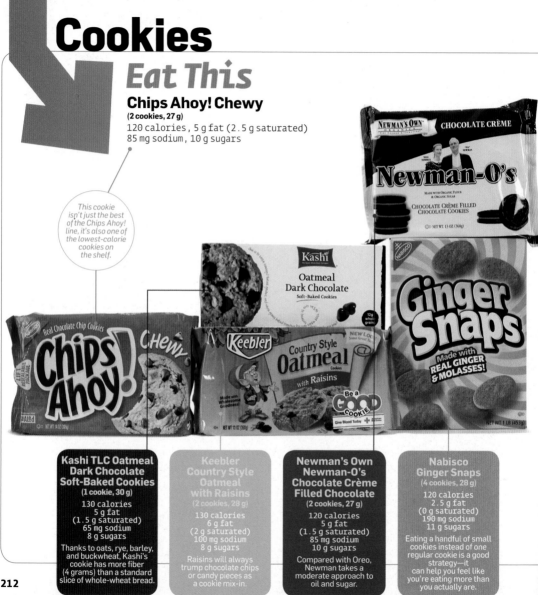

This cookie isn't just the best of the Chips Ahoy! line, it's also one of the lowest-calorie cookies on the shelf.

Kashi TLC Oatmeal Dark Chocolate Soft-Baked Cookies
(1 cookie, 30 g)
130 calories
5 g fat
(1.5 g saturated)
65 mg sodium
8 g sugars

Thanks to oats, rye, barley, and buckwheat, Kashi's cookie has more fiber (4 grams) than a standard slice of whole-wheat bread.

Keebler Country Style Oatmeal with Raisins
(2 cookies, 28 g)
130 calories
6 g fat
(2 g saturated)
100 mg sodium
8 g sugars

Raisins will always trump chocolate chips or candy pieces as a cookie mix-in.

Newman's Own Newman-O's Chocolate Crème Filled Chocolate
(2 cookies, 27 g)
120 calories
5 g fat
(1.5 g saturated)
85 mg sodium
10 g sugars

Compared with Oreo, Newman takes a moderate approach to oil and sugar.

Nabisco Ginger Snaps
(4 cookies, 28 g)
120 calories
2.5 g fat
(0 g saturated)
190 mg sodium
11 g sugars

Eating a handful of small cookies instead of one regular cookie is a good strategy—it can help you feel like you're eating more than you actually are.

Not That!

Keebler Soft Batch Chocolate Chip

(2 cookies, 32 g)

150 calories, 7 g fat (3 g saturated)
110 mg sodium, 12 g sugars

This cookie has more fat, more sodium, and more sugar than the same cookie from Chips Ahoy!

Keebler Sandies Simply Shortbread
(2 cookies, 31 g)

160 calories
9 g fat
(4 g saturated)
90 mg sodium
7 g sugars

We love the low sugar count, but not the heavy deposits of soybean and palm oils.

Nabisco Chocolate Crème Oreo
(2 cookies, 30 g)

150 calories
7 g fat
(2.5 g saturated)
110 mg sodium
13 g sugars

Regular Oreos are even worse—they deliver an extra gram of sugar and 10 extra calories per serving.

Keebler Chips Deluxe Oatmeal Chocolate Chip
(2 cookies, 31 g)

150 calories
7 g fat
(3 g saturated)
105 mg sodium
10 g sugars

Add just one of these 75-calorie Keebler cookies to your daily diet and you'll gain nearly 8 pounds this year.

Mrs. Fields Milk Chocolate Chip
(1 cookie, 32 g)

140 calories
7 g fat
(3.5 g saturated)
125 mg sodium
12 g sugars

The dearth of fiber ensures that this will pass straight through your belly, spike your blood sugar, and convert quickly to flab.

Candy Bars

Eat This

Pretzel M&M's

(1 bag, 32 g)
150 calories, 5 g fat (3 g saturated)
16 g sugars

The latest spin on M&M's trounces everything else in the candy co.'s sugary arsenal. The original milk chocolate core has been replaced with pretzel, which is low in calories by confectionary standards. As a result, you trade in a boatload of sugar for a satisfying cookie-like crunch.

York Peppermint Pattie
(1 patty, 39 g)
140 calories
2.5 g fat
(1.5 g saturated)
25 g sugars

For a smaller treat, go with York Miniatures. You can have three for about the same number of calories.

Life Savers Gummies
(10 pieces, 40 g)
130 calories
0 g fat
25 g sugars

The secret to the chew: gelatin. Starburst uses the same trick, but spoils it with a strange mix of oils.

Hershey's Kit Kat
(1 package, 42 g)
210 calories
11 g fat
(7 g saturated)
21 g sugars

The wafer core is light and porous, which saves you calories over the denser bars.

Nestlé 100 Grand
(1 package, 43 g)
190 calories
8 g fat
(5 g saturated)
22 g sugars

This is an *Eat This, Not That*! Hall of Famer, routinely beating out more common chocolate bars by 80 or more calories.

Hershey's Take 5
(1 package, 42 g)
200 calories
11 g fat
(5 g saturated)
18 g sugars

The pretzel core saves you a boatload of calories.

Not That!

Milk Chocolate M&M's

(1 bag, 48 g)

240 calories, 10 g fat (6 g saturated)
31 g sugars

M&M's pack in a lot of sugar even by candy-bar standards. This little bag is loaded with more sweetness than two Little Debbie Chocolate Marshmallow Pies.

Nestlé Baby Ruth
(1 bar, 60 g)
280 calories
14 g fat
(8 g saturated)
33 g sugars

Together, saturated fat and sugar account for more than 200 of the calories in this package.

Mars Twix Caramel
(1 package, 51 g)
250 calories
12 g fat
(9 g saturated)
24 g sugars

This package contains nearly as much saturated fat as two Snickers bars.

Nestlé Butterfinger
(1 bar, 60 g)
270 calories
11 g fat
(6 g saturated)
28 g sugars

Nobody better lay a finger on this Butterfinger.

Twizzlers Twists Strawberry
(4 pieces, 45 g)
160 calories
0.5 g fat
(0 g saturated)
19 g sugars

You could have 40 real strawberries for the same number of calories.

Andes Thins Crème de Menthe
(8 pieces, 38 g)
200 calories
13 g fat
(11 g saturated)
22 g sugars

This is one of the worst candies in the supermarket. The first two ingredients are sugar and partially hydrogenated oil.

Frozen Breakfast Entrées

Eat This

Jimmy Dean Delights Turkey Sausage Breakfast Bowl

(1 bowl, 198 g)

240 calories, 8 g fat (3.5 g saturated), 720 mg sodium
19 g carbohydrates, 2 g fiber, 22 g protein

An ideal breakfast includes a substantial load of protein, and this bowl has that nailed. Protein accounts for 40 percent of the calories, which increases your odds of making it to lunch without snacking.

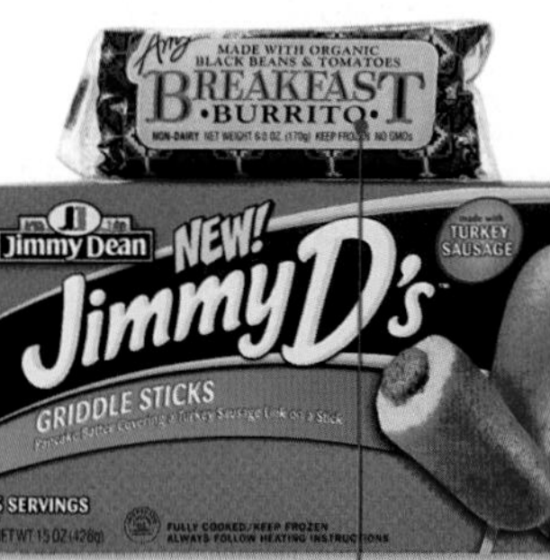

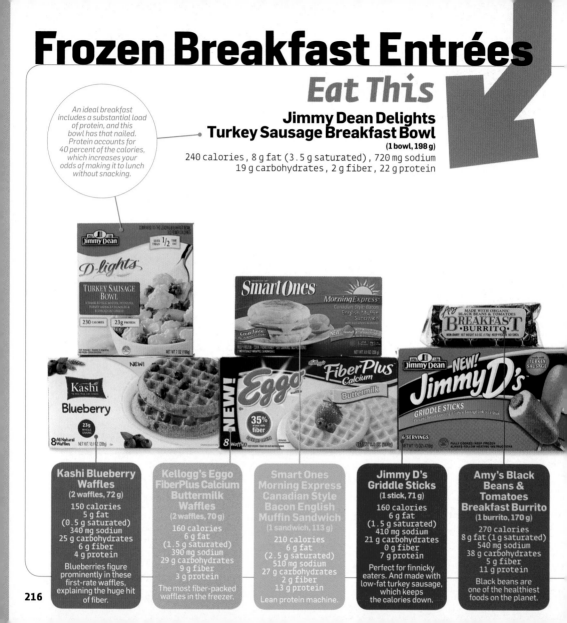

Kashi Blueberry Waffles
(2 waffles, 72 g)

150 calories
5 g fat
(0.5 g saturated)
340 mg sodium
25 g carbohydrates
6 g fiber
4 g protein

Blueberries figure prominently in these first-rate waffles, explaining the huge hit of fiber.

Kellogg's Eggo FiberPlus Calcium Buttermilk Waffles
(2 waffles, 70 g)

160 calories
6 g fat
(1.5 g saturated)
390 mg sodium
29 g carbohydrates
9 g fiber
3 g protein

The most fiber-packed waffles in the freezer.

Smart Ones Morning Express Canadian Style Bacon English Muffin Sandwich
(1 sandwich, 113 g)

210 calories
6 g fat
(2.5 g saturated)
510 mg sodium
27 g carbohydrates
2 g fiber
13 g protein

Lean protein machine.

Jimmy D's Griddle Sticks
(1 stick, 71 g)

160 calories
6 g fat
(1.5 g saturated)
410 mg sodium
21 g carbohydrates
0 g fiber
7 g protein

Perfect for finnicky eaters. And made with low-fat turkey sausage, which keeps the calories down.

Amy's Black Beans & Tomatoes Breakfast Burrito
(1 burrito, 170 g)

270 calories
8 g fat (1 g saturated)
540 mg sodium
38 g carbohydrates
5 g fiber
11 g protein

Black beans are one of the healthiest foods on the planet.

Not That!

Lean Pockets Sausage, Egg & Cheese

(1 piece, 127 g)

270 calories, 9 g fat (4 g saturated), 480 mg sodium
38 g carbohydrates, 3 g fiber, 10 g protein

More than 150 of these calories are carbohydrates, which is not how you want to start your day.

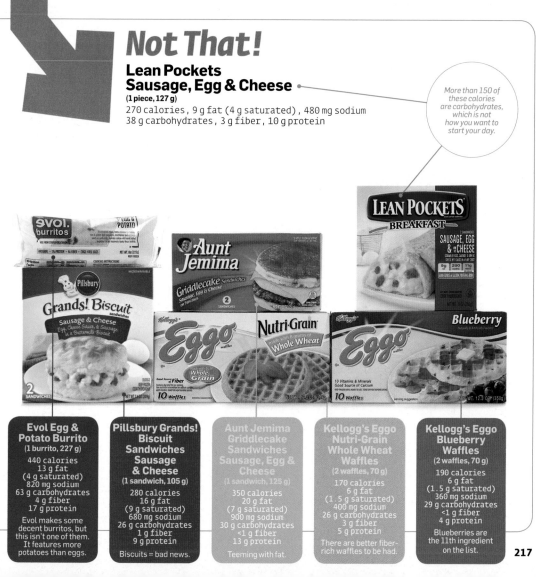

Evol Egg & Potato Burrito
(1 burrito, 227 g)
440 calories
13 g fat
(4 g saturated)
820 mg sodium
63 g carbohydrates
4 g fiber
17 g protein

Evol makes some decent burritos, but this isn't one of them. It features more potatoes than eggs.

Pillsbury Grands! Biscuit Sandwiches Sausage & Cheese
(1 sandwich, 105 g)
280 calories
16 g fat
(9 g saturated)
680 mg sodium
26 g carbohydrates
1 g fiber
9 g protein

Biscuits = bad news.

Aunt Jemima Griddlecake Sandwiches Sausage, Egg & Cheese
(1 sandwich, 125 g)
350 calories
20 g fat
(7 g saturated)
900 mg sodium
30 g carbohydrates
<1 g fiber
13 g protein

Teeming with fat.

Kellogg's Eggo Nutri-Grain Whole Wheat Waffles
(2 waffles, 70 g)
170 calories
6 g fat
(1.5 g saturated)
400 mg sodium
26 g carbohydrates
3 g fiber
5 g protein

There are better fiber-rich waffles to be had.

Kellogg's Eggo Blueberry Waffles
(2 waffles, 70 g)
190 calories
6 g fat
(1.5 g saturated)
360 mg sodium
29 g carbohydrates
<1 g fiber
4 g protein

Blueberries are the 11th ingredient on the list.

Frozen Pizzas

Eat This

Kashi Basil Pesto Stone-Fired Thin Crust

(⅓ pie, 113 g)

240 calories, 9 g fat (3.5 g saturated)
590 mg sodium, 27 g carbohydrates
4 g fiber, 14 g protein

This pie features more pesto than cheese, which means you end up with more monounsaturated fat from olive oil than saturated fat from dairy. That's a healthy swap.

Lean Cuisine French Bread Pepperoni

(1 pie, 170 g)

310 calories
9 g fat (3 g saturated)
610 mg sodium
55 g carbohydrates
3 g fiber
20 g protein

Cut out 100 empty calories without sacrificing protein with this first-rate pizza package.

Amy's Cheese

(1 pie, 167 g)

420 calories
17 g fat (6 g saturated)
720 mg sodium
49 g carbohydrates
3 g fiber
18 g protein

For the rare times when you allow yourself the privilege of eating a whole pizza, this is exactly where you should turn.

Newman's Own Thin & Crispy Uncured Pepperoni

(⅓ pie, 125 g)

320 calories
16 g fat (6 g saturated)
800 mg sodium
31 g carbohydrates
1 g fiber
15 g protein

Newman's skips the nitrates and nitrites with its pepperoni.

Bagel Bites Cheese & Pepperoni

(4 pieces, 88 g)

190 calories
6 g fat
(2.5 g saturated)
380 mg sodium
29 g carbohydrates
2 g fiber
8 g protein

Each mini-bagel contains fewer than 50 calories.

Tofurky Vegan Cheese (⅓ pie, 113 g)

240 calories
8 g fat
(2.5 g saturated)
350 mg sodium
39 g carbohydrates
4 g fiber
6 g protein

Tofurky's "cheese" is made using a combination of protein, flour, and oils. It's a great alternative for those who are lactose intolerant.

Evol Flatbreads Meatballs & Mozzarella

(½ pie, 113 g)

330 calories
13 g fat
(5 g saturated)
790 mg sodium
34 g carbohydrates
2 g fiber
18 g protein

You won't find a more decadent pie for fewer calories in the freezer.

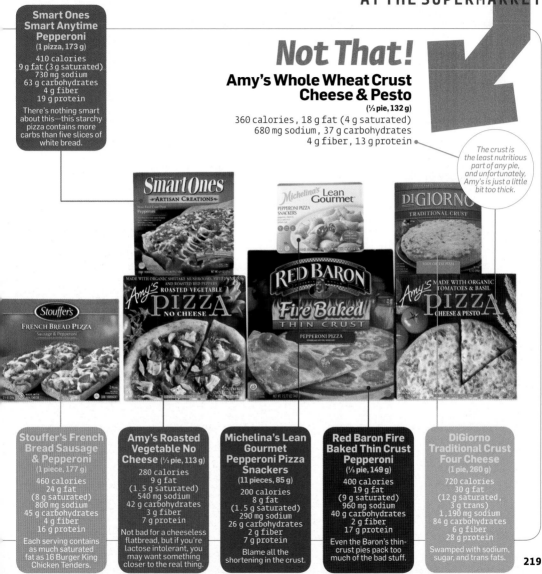

Smart Ones Smart Anytime Pepperoni
(1 pizza, 173 g)

410 calories
9 g fat (3 g saturated)
730 mg sodium
63 g carbohydrates
4 g fiber
19 g protein

There's nothing smart about this—this starchy pizza contains more carbs than five slices of white bread.

Not That!

Amy's Whole Wheat Crust Cheese & Pesto

(⅓ pie, 132 g)

360 calories, 18 g fat (4 g saturated)
680 mg sodium, 37 g carbohydrates
4 g fiber, 13 g protein

The crust is the least nutritious part of any pie, and unfortunately, Amy's is just a little bit too thick.

Stouffer's French Bread Sausage & Pepperoni
(1 piece, 177 g)

460 calories
24 g fat
(8 g saturated)
800 mg sodium
45 g carbohydrates
4 g fiber
16 g protein

Each serving contains as much saturated fat as 16 Burger King Chicken Tenders.

Amy's Roasted Vegetable No Cheese (⅓ pie, 113 g)

280 calories
9 g fat
(1.5 g saturated)
540 mg sodium
42 g carbohydrates
3 g fiber
7 g protein

Not bad for a cheeseless flatbread, but if you're lactose intolerant, you may want something closer to the real thing.

Michelina's Lean Gourmet Pepperoni Pizza Snackers
(11 pieces, 85 g)

200 calories
8 g fat
(1.5 g saturated)
290 mg sodium
26 g carbohydrates
2 g fiber
7 g protein

Blame all the shortening in the crust.

Red Baron Fire Baked Thin Crust Pepperoni
(⅓ pie, 149 g)

400 calories
19 g fat
(9 g saturated)
960 mg sodium
40 g carbohydrates
2 g fiber
17 g protein

Even the Baron's thin-crust pies pack too much of the bad stuff.

DiGiorno Traditional Crust Four Cheese
(1 pie, 260 g)

720 calories
30 g fat
(12 g saturated,
3 g trans)
1,190 mg sodium
84 g carbohydrates
6 g fiber
28 g protein

Swamped with sodium, sugar, and trans fats.

Frozen Pasta Entrées

Eat This

If you do it daily, the 40 calories you save by eating Kashi's Chicken Pasta Pomodoro instead of Smart Ones' Three Cheese Ziti will help you shed more than 4 pounds in a year. And you'll be less hungry while you do it, too, because Kashi's meal provides more protein and fiber.

Kashi Chicken Pasta Pomodoro

(1 entrée, 283 g)

280 calories, 6 g fat (1.5 g saturated)
470 mg sodium, 38 g carbohydrates
6 g fiber, 19 g protein

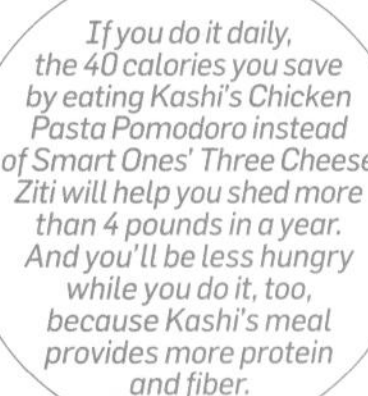

Michelina's Zap'ems Gourmet Macaroni & Cheese with Cheddar and Romano

(1 package, 213 g)

260 calories
6 g fat (2.5 g saturated)
500 mg sodium
39 g carbohydrates
2 g fiber
10 g protein

Diffuse the comfort food's flab-producing potential by opting for this light rendition.

Stouffer's Easy Express Garlic Chicken Skillet

(326 g, ½ package)

330 calories
6 g fat
(2.5 g saturated)
990 mg sodium
45 g carbohydrates
5 g fiber
24 g protein

Budding chefs, take note: The more vegetables you use, the less sauce and pasta you'll need.

Lean Cuisine Four Cheese Cannelloni

(1 package, 258 g)

240 calories
6 g fat (3 g saturated)
690 mg sodium
30 g carbohydrates
3 g fiber
17 g protein

Swap out white sauce for red sauce and you'll save a few hundred calories per serving every time.

Bertolli Mediterranean Style Chicken, Rigatoni & Broccoli

(½ package, 340 g)

390 calories
15 g fat (4 g saturated)
990 mg sodium
38 g carbohydrates
4 g fiber
22 g protein

After pasta, the first two ingredients are broccoli and chicken.

Not That!

Smart Ones Three Cheese Ziti Marinara

(1 entrée, 255 g)
300 calories, 8 g fat (3.5 g saturated)
580 mg sodium, 44 g carbohydrates
4 g fiber, 14 g protein

Marinara is typically the safest of the pasta sauces, but that rule fails to hold as soon as Smart Ones buries the plate under a rubbery quilt of cheese.

Romano's Macaroni Grill Creamy Basil Parmesan Chicken & Pasta (½ package, 340 g)

470 calories
21 g fat (12 g saturated)
1,040 mg sodium
42 g carbohydrates
4 g fiber
29 g protein

Romano takes a heavy-handed approach with cream, as demonstrated by the exorbitant glut of saturated fat in this dish.

Bertolli Oven Bake Meals Roasted Chicken Cannelloni (½ package, 298 g)

480 calories
26 g fat (11 g saturated)
870 mg sodium
40 g carbohydrates
6 g fiber
22 g protein

These noodles are stuffed with cheese and covered with cream. A little dairy fat isn't so bad, but this is overload.

Stouffer's Signature Classics Chicken Fettuccini Alfredo (1 package, 297 g)

570 calories
27 g fat (7 g saturated)
850 mg sodium
55 g carbohydrates
5 g fiber
26 g protein

Alfredo sauce contains any of the following: oil, butter, cheese, cream, and egg yolk. In other words, it's a full-fat assault.

Amy's Light in Sodium Macaroni & Cheese (1 entrée, 255 g)

400 calories
16 g fat (10 g saturated)
290 mg sodium
47 g carbohydrates
3 g fiber
16 g protein

We've seen worse mac out there, but Amy's packages its pasta as a healthy alternative to the normal stuff, and we're just not buying it.

Frozen Fish Entrées

Eat This

Gorton's Grilled Fillets Cajun Blackened

(1 fillet, 108 g)

90 calories, 3 g fat (0.5 g saturated), 400 mg sodium, 16 g protein

The smoky, spicy finesse of a blackening rub can imbue any fillet with massive flavor at no caloric cost. It's easily one of the healthiest ways to prepare meat and fish.

Margaritaville Island Lime Shrimp
(6 shrimp, 4 oz)
240 calories
11 g fat
(3 g saturated)
330 mg sodium
12 g protein
These shrimp have also been tossed in butter. The difference is quantity; here it's a light bath, but in SeaPak's scampi it's a tidal wave.

Cape Gourmet Cooked Shrimp
(3 oz)
50 calories
0.5 g fat
330 mg sodium
10 g protein
Unadulterated shrimp are one of the leanest sources of protein on the planet.

SeaPak Salmon Burgers
(1 burger, 91 g)
110 calories
5 g fat (1 g saturated)
340 mg sodium
16 g protein
Toss this on the grill, then sandwich it between a toasted bun with arugula, grilled onions, and Greek yogurt spiked with olive oil, garlic, and fresh dill.

Atlantic Capes Bay Scallops
(4 oz)
150 calories
1 g fat (0 g saturated)
155 mg sodium
29 g protein
Scallops are teeming with the amino acid tryptophan, which bolsters feelings of well-being and helps regulate the sleep cycle.

Gourmet Dining Shrimp Stir Fry
(¼ package, 198 g)
200 calories
1 g fat (0 g saturated)
640 mg sodium
12 g protein
American interpretations of Asian cuisine tend to be high in sodium, but this solid blend of fiber and protein more than makes up for it.

Not That!

Van de Kamp's Crunchy Fish Fillets

(2 fillets, 99 g)

230 calories, 13 g fat (4.5 g saturated), 440 mg sodium, 8 g protein

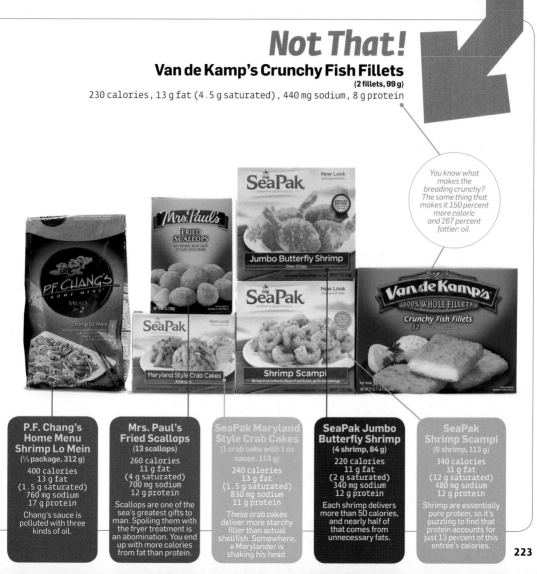

You know what makes the breading crunchy? The same thing that makes it 150 percent more caloric and 267 percent fattier: oil.

P.F. Chang's Home Menu Shrimp Lo Mein

(½ package, 312 g)

400 calories
13 g fat
(1.5 g saturated)
760 mg sodium
17 g protein

Chang's sauce is polluted with three kinds of oil.

Mrs. Paul's Fried Scallops

(13 scallops)

260 calories
11 g fat
(4 g saturated)
700 mg sodium
12 g protein

Scallops are one of the sea's greatest gifts to man. Spoiling them with the fryer treatment is an abomination. You end up with more calories from fat than protein.

SeaPak Maryland Style Crab Cakes

(1 crab cake with 1 oz sauce, 113 g)

240 calories
13 g fat
(1.5 g saturated)
830 mg sodium
11 g protein

These crab cakes deliver more starchy filler than actual shellfish. Somewhere, a Marylander is shaking his head.

SeaPak Jumbo Butterfly Shrimp

(4 shrimp, 84 g)

220 calories
11 g fat
(2 g saturated)
340 mg sodium
12 g protein

Each shrimp delivers more than 50 calories, and nearly half of that comes from unnecessary fats.

SeaPak Shrimp Scampi

(6 shrimp, 113 g)

340 calories
31 g fat
(12 g saturated)
480 mg sodium
12 g protein

Shrimp are essentially pure protein, so it's puzzling to find that protein accounts for just 13 percent of this entrée's calories.

Frozen Chicken Entrées

Eat This

Evol Bowls Teriyaki Chicken

(1 bowl, 255 g)

250 calories, 6 g fat (1 g saturated), 490 mg sodium
34 g carbohydrates, 4 g fiber, 14 g protein

Evol's teriyaki bowl is made with brown rice, free-range chicken, and enough produce to meet 90 percent of your day's vitamin A needs.

Banquet Chicken Fried Chicken Meal (1 entrée, 286 g)

350 calories
17 g fat
(4 g saturated)
930 mg sodium
35 g carbohydrates
5 g fiber
12 g protein

Thinner breading and a heavier reliance on sides saves you 90 calories over Banquet's "premium" version.

Ethnic Gourmet Chicken Tikka Masala (1 package, 283 g)

260 calories
6 g fat (2 g saturated)
680 mg sodium
32 g carbohydrates
3 g fiber
19 g protein

The sauce is created with fat-free yogurt, which provides the thick heft of cream without all the calories.

Marie Callender's Fresh Flavor Steamer Chicken Teriyaki (1 meal, 283 g)

280 calories
3.5 g fat
(1 g saturated)
890 mg sodium
44 g carbohydrates
3 g fiber
17 g protein

The wealth of veggies keeps the calories low.

Kashi Lemongrass Coconut Chicken (1 entrée, 283 g)

300 calories
8 g fat (4 g saturated)
680 mg sodium
38 g carbohydrates
7 g fiber
18 g protein

Instead of the standard white rice, this meal rests on a whole-grain blend of oats, red winter wheat, and quinoa.

Smart Ones Smart Anytime Grilled Flatbread Chicken Marinara with Mozzarella Cheese (1 flatbread, 170 g)

290 calories
6 g fat
(1.5 g saturated)
640 mg sodium
41 g carbohydrates
3 g fiber
18 g protein

Not That!

Healthy Choice Pineapple Chicken

(1 entrée, 255 g)

380 calories, 7 g fat (1 g saturated), 190 mg sodium
70 g carbohydrates, 4 g fiber, 9 g protein

Another Healthy Choice dessert masquerading as dinner. This bowl contains 29 grams of sugar, as much as you'd find in two scoops of Breyers Chocolate Ice Cream.

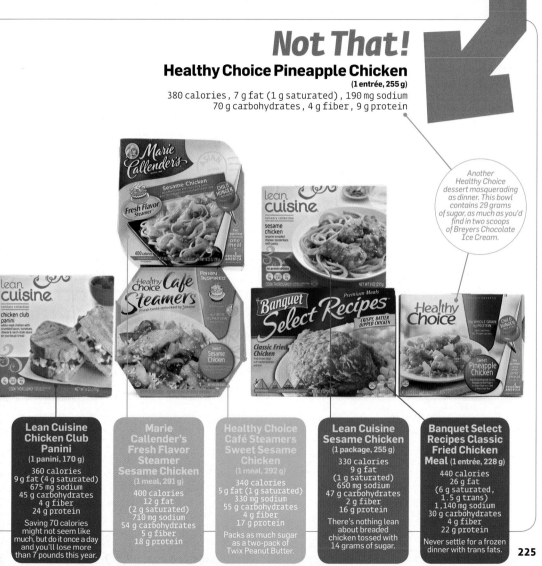

Lean Cuisine Chicken Club Panini
(1 panini, 170 g)

360 calories
9 g fat (4 g saturated)
675 mg sodium
45 g carbohydrates
4 g fiber
24 g protein

Saving 70 calories might not seem like much, but do it once a day and you'll lose more than 7 pounds this year.

Marie Callender's Fresh Flavor Steamer Sesame Chicken
(1 meal, 291 g)

400 calories
12 g fat
(2 g saturated)
710 mg sodium
54 g carbohydrates
5 g fiber
18 g protein

Healthy Choice Café Steamers Sweet Sesame Chicken
(1 meal, 292 g)

340 calories
5 g fat (1 g saturated)
330 mg sodium
55 g carbohydrates
4 g fiber
17 g protein

Packs as much sugar as a two-pack of Twix Peanut Butter.

Lean Cuisine Sesame Chicken
(1 package, 255 g)

330 calories
9 g fat
(1 g saturated)
650 mg sodium
47 g carbohydrates
2 g fiber
16 g protein

There's nothing lean about breaded chicken tossed with 14 grams of sugar.

Banquet Select Recipes Classic Fried Chicken Meal (1 entrée, 228 g)

440 calories
26 g fat
(6 g saturated, 1.5 g trans)
1,140 mg sodium
30 g carbohydrates
4 g fiber
22 g protein

Never settle for a frozen dinner with trans fats.

Frozen Beef Entrées

Eat This

If you'd rather eat a potpie, just pour this into a bowl and eat it with a piece of toasted whole-grain bread. There, all the potpie perks without the fat.

Stouffer's Homestyle Classics Beef Pot Roast

(1 entrée, 251 g)

230 calories, 7 g fat (2 g saturated), 820 mg sodium
26 g carbohydrates, 3 g fiber, 16 g protein

Smart Ones Homestyle Beef Pot Roast
(1 meal, 255 g)

190 calories
6 g fat (2.5 g saturated)
590 mg sodium
18 g carbohydrates
3 g fiber
16 g protein

Most protein bars can't deliver this dose for so few calories. Tack on 3 grams of fiber and you have an amazing 190-calorie package.

Banquet Meat Loaf Meal
(1 meal, 269 g)

280 calories
13 g fat (5 g saturated)
1,000 mg sodium
28 g carbohydrates
4 g fiber
12 g protein

When it comes to delivering comfort dishes for a reasonable number of calories, Banquet's regular line of entrées is among the best in the freezer.

Hot Pockets Sideshots Cheeseburgers
(2 buns, 127 g)

300 calories
10 g fat (3.5 g saturated)
640 mg sodium
40 g carbohydrates
1 g fiber
12 g protein

A fairly innocuous snack to set in front of a group of hungry kids.

Birds Eye Voila! Beef and Broccoli Stir Fry
(1 ¾ cups, 218 g)

230 calories
5 g fat (1.5 g saturated)
690 mg sodium
32 g carbohydrates
2 g fiber
12 g protein

The first ingredient in this bag is broccoli. In the cost-conscious world of processed foods, that's exceedingly rare.

Not That!

Banquet Beef Pot Pie

(1 pie, 198 g)

390 calories, 22 g fat (9 g saturated, 0.5 g trans)
1,010 mg sodium, 36 g carbohydrates, 3 g fiber
12 g protein

A potpie crust is essentially an oversized pastry, which is to say lots of carbohydrates glued together with saturated fat.

P.F. Chang's Home Menu Beef with Broccoli

(½ package, 312 g)

350 calories
17 g fat (3 g saturated)
1,080 mg sodium
26 g carbohydrates
4 g fiber
21 g protein

Chang's bagged meals suffer from the same sodium saturation that plagues its restaurant fare.

Smart Ones Smart Anytime Mini Cheeseburgers

(2 mini-burgers, 140 g)

400 calories
18 g fat (8 g saturated)
720 mg sodium
40 g carbohydrates
6 g fiber
20 g protein

Each burger has 20 percent of your day's saturated fat.

Hungry-Man Home-Style Meatloaf

(1 package, 454 g)

660 calories
35 g fat (12 g saturated)
1,660 mg sodium
61 g carbohydrates
5 g fiber
26 g protein

Word of advice to the calorie conscious: Purge Hungry-Man from your freezer for good. This is consistently the worst brand in the frozen-foods aisle.

Healthy Choice Café Steamers Barbecue Seasoned Steak with Red Potatoes

(1 meal, 269 g)

330 calories
6 g fat (2 g saturated)
550 mg sodium
47 g carbohydrates
4 g fiber
20 g protein

This entrée contains the sugar equivalent of two Rice Krispies Treats bars.

Frozen Sides, Snacks &

Eat This

Ore-Ida Steak Fries

(7 fries, 84 g)

110 calories, 3 g fat (0.5 g saturated)
290 mg sodium, 19 g carbohydrates, 2 g protein

A serving of these hulking spuds contains fewer than half the calories you'd find in the average medium order of fast-food fries.

Cascadian Farm Shoe String French Fries
(3 oz, 85 g)
100 calories
4 g fat (1 g saturated)
10 mg sodium
17 g carbohydrates
2 g protein

Cascadian Farm tosses these fries in apple juice, the sugar from which caramelizes into a crisp, golden crust.

Applegate Organics Organic Chicken Strips
(3 strips, 84 g)
160 calories
7 g fat
(1.5 g saturated)
180 mg sodium
11 g carbohydrates
12 g protein

The relatively light breading makes Applegate's strips less fatty than the competition's.

Foster Farms Mini Corn Dogs Honey Crunchy
(4 dogs, 76 g)
210 calories
12 g fat
(3.5 g saturated)
490 mg sodium
18 g carbohydrates
7 g protein

At only 53 calories per dog, the damage potential here is relatively low.

Hot Pockets Snackers Grilled Italian Style Bites
(4 pieces, 94 g)
210 calories
7 g fat (3 g saturated)
500 mg sodium
28 g carbohydrates
8 g protein

Each Snacker packs in 2 grams of protein. That doesn't make it healthy, but it's not a bad start.

Appetizers

Not That!

Ore-Ida Sweet Potato Straight Fries

(22 fries, 84 g)

160 calories, 8 g fat (0.5 g saturated)
160 mg sodium, 21 g carbohydrates, 1 g protein

A raw sweet potato has more fiber and vitamin A than a raw russet potato, but once the food industry starts mucking with produce, all bets are off.

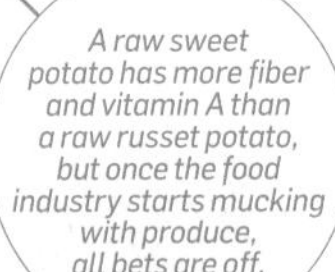

Pillsbury Savorings Cheese & Spinach
(4 pastry bites, 80 g)

260 calories
17 g fat
(8 g saturated)
430 mg sodium
21 g carbohydrates
6 g protein

Fat accounts for nearly 60 percent of the calories in each pastry.

Hebrew National Beef Franks in a Blanket
(5 pieces, 81 g)

300 calories
24 g fat
(8 g saturated, 3 g trans)
680 mg sodium
12 g carbohydrates
8 g protein

You shouldn't consume this much trans fats in an entire day, let alone from a snack.

Tyson Chicken Breast Tenders
(5 pieces, 85 g)

240 calories
14 g fat
(3 g saturated)
460 mg sodium
15 g carbohydrates
12 g protein

The bag says "100 percent all natural," but what's natural about dredging chicken through flour and brown sugar and dropping it in hot oil?

Ore-Ida Onion Ringers
(3 pieces, 76 g)

185 calories
9 g fat
(1.5 g saturated)
450 mg sodium
24 g carbohydrates
3 g protein

Each ring harbors 150 milligrams of sodium and 3 grams of fat. Fries are almost always the better choice.

Ice Creams

Eat This

Breyers Black Raspberry Chocolate

(½ cup, 67 g)

140 calories, 4 g fat (3 g saturated), 16 g sugars

The secret to a low-calorie ice cream is simple: Lead off with something lighter than cream. This one uses regular milk first and cream second. Perfect.

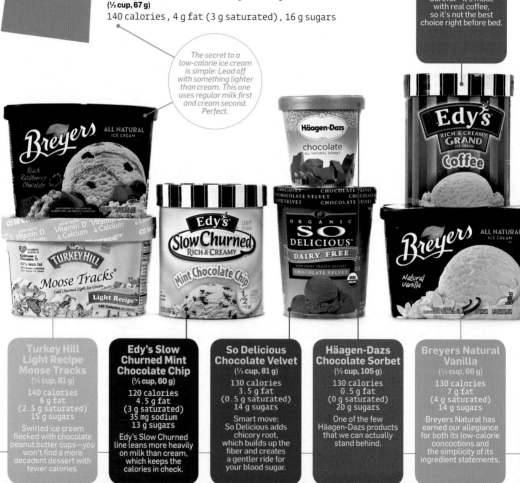

Edy's Rich & Creamy Grand Coffee (½ cup, 65 g)

140 calories
7 g fat
(4 g saturated)
13 g sugars

Careful—it's made with real coffee, so it's not the best choice right before bed.

Turkey Hill Light Recipe Moose Tracks (½ cup, 61 g)

140 calories
6 g fat
(2.5 g saturated)
15 g sugars

Swirled ice cream flecked with chocolate peanut butter cups—you won't find a more decadent dessert with fewer calories.

Edy's Slow Churned Mint Chocolate Chip (½ cup, 60 g)

120 calories
4.5 g fat
(3 g saturated)
35 mg sodium
13 g sugars

Edy's Slow Churned line leans more heavily on milk than cream, which keeps the calories in check.

So Delicious Chocolate Velvet (½ cup, 81 g)

130 calories
3.5 g fat
(0.5 g saturated)
14 g sugars

Smart move: So Delicious adds chicory root, which builds up the fiber and creates a gentler ride for your blood sugar.

Häagen-Dazs Chocolate Sorbet (½ cup, 105 g)

130 calories
0.5 g fat
(0 g saturated)
20 g sugars

One of the few Häagen-Dazs products that we can actually stand behind.

Breyers Natural Vanilla (½ cup, 66 g)

130 calories
7 g fat
(4 g saturated)
14 g sugars

Breyers Natural has earned our allegiance for both its low-calorie concoctions and the simplicity of its ingredient statements.

Not That!

Ben & Jerry's FroYo Cherry Garcia Frozen Yogurt

(½ cup, 108 g)

200 calories, 3 g fat (2 g saturated), 27 g sugars

You buy frozen yogurt thinking you're doing your body a favor, only to find out it's worse than three-quarters of the full-fat ice creams in the freezer. Thanks, Ben & Jerry's.

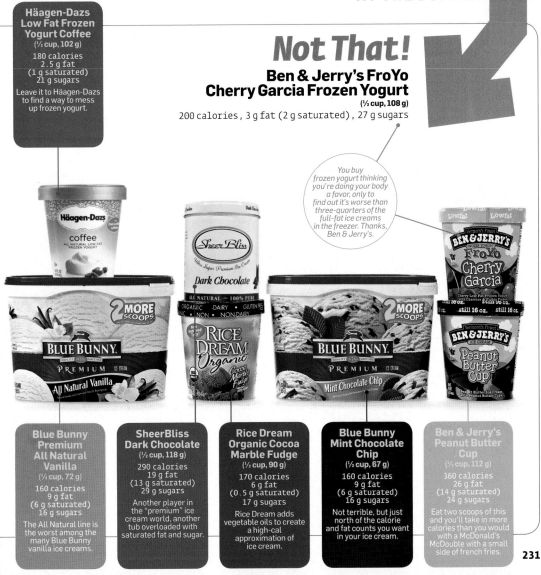

Häagen-Dazs Low Fat Frozen Yogurt Coffee

(½ cup, 102 g)

180 calories
2.5 g fat
(1 g saturated)
21 g sugars

Leave it to Häagen-Dazs to find a way to mess up frozen yogurt.

Blue Bunny Premium All Natural Vanilla

(½ cup, 72 g)

160 calories
9 g fat
(6 g saturated)
16 g sugars

The All Natural line is the worst among the many Blue Bunny vanilla ice creams.

SheerBliss Dark Chocolate

(½ cup, 118 g)

290 calories
19 g fat
(13 g saturated)
29 g sugars

Another player in the "premium" ice cream world, another tub overloaded with saturated fat and sugar.

Rice Dream Organic Cocoa Marble Fudge

(½ cup, 90 g)

170 calories
6 g fat
(0.5 g saturated)
17 g sugars

Rice Dream adds vegetable oils to create a high-cal approximation of ice cream.

Blue Bunny Mint Chocolate Chip

(½ cup, 67 g)

160 calories
9 g fat
(6 g saturated)
16 g sugars

Not terrible, but just north of the calorie and fat counts you want in your ice cream.

Ben & Jerry's Peanut Butter Cup

(½ cup, 112 g)

360 calories
26 g fat
(14 g saturated)
24 g sugars

Eat two scoops of this and you'll take in more calories than you would with a McDonald's McDouble with a small side of french fries.

Frozen Treats

Eat This

Breyers' secret, as with all low-cal ice cream treat makers, lies in keeping cream off the top of the ingredient statement.

Breyers Smooth & Dreamy Triple Chocolate Chip
(1 bar, 49 g)
130 calories, 6 g fat (4 g saturated), 13 g sugars

Nestlé Drumstick Lil' Drums Vanilla with Chocolatey Swirls
(1 bar, 43 g)
110 calories
5 g fat
(3.5 g saturated)
10 g sugars

The perfect portion for an after-dinner indulgence.

Diana's Bananas Banana Babies Dark Chocolate
(1 piece, 60 g)
130 calories
6 g fat
(3.5 g saturated)
14 g sugars

Banana, chocolate, and peanut oil. You don't find a frozen treat with a simpler recipe.

Fudgsicle Original Fudge Pops
(1 pop, 43 g)
60 calories
1.5 g fat
(1 g saturated)
9 g sugars

The classic freezer treat is surprisingly easy on the waistline.

Breyers Pure Fruit Berry Swirls
(1 bar, 51 g)
40 calories
0 g fat
9 g sugars

Much of the sugar comes from the real fruit purees packed into these bars.

So Delicious Minis Vanilla
(1 sandwich, 40 g)
90 calories
2 g fat
(0.5 g saturated)
8 g sugars

This is a good treat to keep in mind even if you're not lactose intolerant. It's low in sugar and laced with 2 grams of slow-digesting fiber.

Not That!

Magnum Double Chocolate

(1 bar, 83 g)

350 calories, 21 g fat (16 g saturated), 30 g sugars

Eat one of these after dinner every night this month and you'll gain 3 pounds.

Tofutti Cuties Vanilla
(1 sandwich, 38 g)

130 calories
6 g fat
(1 g saturated)
17 g carbohydrates
9 g sugars

Made mostly of sugar, corn syrup solids, and vegetable oils. Tofu plays a mere supporting role.

Edy's Fruit Bars Lemonade
(1 bar, 85 g)

70 calories
0 g fat
17 g sugars

Products made with lemon juice require a heavy dose of sugar to balance out the acidity.

Breyers CarbSmart Ice Cream Bar Vanilla
(1 bar, 55 g)

170 calories
15 g fat
(11 g saturated)
5 g sugars

Sure it's low in carbohydrates, but the saturated fat level is unacceptable.

Good Humor Strawberry Shortcake
(1 bar, 83 g)

230 calories
10 g fat
(3.5 g saturated)
17 g sugars

This bar does contain real strawberries, but it contains even more sugar, corn syrup, and high-fructose corn syrup.

Häagen-Dazs Vanilla Milk Chocolate Almond Snack Size
(1 bar, 52 g)

190 calories
14 g fat (8 g saturated)
12 g sugars

Cream is the first ingredient, which is how it packs 40 percent of your day's saturated fat into each bar.

Drink This

Lakewood Organic Lemonade

(8 fl oz)

80 calories, 0 g fat, 16 g sugars

Instead of sugar, this bottle is sweetened with grape juice.

V8 V-Fusion Light Pomegranate Blueberry

(8 fl oz)

50 calories
0 g fat
10 g sugars

Every calorie in this bottle comes from the blend of sweet potatoes, carrots, apples, pomegranates, and blueberries.

R.W. Knudsen Just Blueberry

(8 fl oz)

100 calories
0 g fat
18 g sugars

Blueberries are bursting with brain-boosting antioxidants, and R.W. Knudsen's juice is the only one to give you 100 percent blueberries.

Simply Grapefruit

(8 fl oz)

100 calories
0 g fat
25 g sugars

Grapefruit is the most underrated juice in the cooler. It's delicious, it's naturally low in sugar, and it delivers a dose of cancer-fighting lycopene.

Langers Zero Sugar Added Cranberry

(8 fl oz)

30 calories
0 g fat
8 g sugars

Cranberries make for a tart juice, which is why you routinely see 15 or more grams of sugar added to each serving.

Not That!

Simply Lemonade

(8 fl oz)
120 calories, 0 g fat, 28 g sugars

Contains only 11 percent juice. The rest of the bottle is pure sugar water. Most lemonades follow the same disappointing formula.

Ocean Spray Cran-Apple
(8 fl oz)
130 calories
0 g fat
32 g sugars

This bottle, like so many in Ocean Spray's lineup, contains only 15 percent juice. Water and sugar are the first two ingredients.

Florida's Natural 100% Pure Orange Pineapple
(8 fl oz)
130 calories
0 g fat
30 g sugars

It's hard to find fault with 100 percent juice products, but blends like this tend to pack in too much sugar.

Langers Pomegranate Blueberry Plus
(8 fl oz)
140 calories
0 g fat
32 g sugars

There's more sugar in this bottle than there are blueberries or pomegranates.

V8 Splash Berry Blend
(8 fl oz)
70 calories
0 g fat
18 g sugars

Splash is unfit to carry the V8 brand name. It's made with artificial colors, high-fructose corn syrup, and a pathetic 10 percent juice.

Teas

Drink This

Honest Tea Community Green Tea

(16 fl oz)

34 calories, 0 g fat, 10 g sugars

High in antioxidants and low in sugar, Honest Tea is one of the most reliable brands in any cooler.

AriZona Green Tea with Ginseng and Honey

(6.75 fl oz)

60 calories
0 g fat
16 g sugars

One of the few AriZona drinks worth purchasing. Throw this in your work bag for a little antioxidant boost and a light caffeine kick at lunch.

Lipton Iced Tea Lemon

(8 fl oz)

60 calories
0 g fat
16 g sugars

Consider 16 grams your cutoff for sweetened tea. Any more than that and you're facing a nasty blood sugar surge. Buy this in the smallest serving size you can find.

ITO EN Oi Ocha Unsweetened Green Tea

(16.9 fl oz)

0 calories
0 g fat
0 g sugars

Researchers believe green tea plays a prominent role in the long life spans of the Japanese. ITO EN is the most popular tea in Japan.

Not That!

Lipton Green Tea with Citrus

(20 fl oz)

180 calories, 0 g fat
46 g sugars

We're happy Lipton removed the high-fructose corn syrup from this bottle, but it's going to need to cut the sugar content in half if it wants to compete with the best green teas in the market.

Snapple Green Tea

(16 fl oz)

120 calories
0 g fat
30 g sugars

Catechins found in green tea can boost metabolism, but whatever metabolic boost you find in this bottle is more than offset by the sugar rush.

Nestea Iced Tea with Lemon Flavor

(8 fl oz)

80 calories
0 g fat
22 g sugars

Nearly as sweet as a Coke. If you down this entire bottle, you'll take in 200 calories.

Ssips Green Tea with Honey & Ginseng

(6.75 fl oz)

60 calories
0 g fat
14 g sugars

The honey in the name is just a diversionary tactic. A good part of the sweetness here comes from high-fructose corn syrup. Either way, skip it.

Mixers

Drink This

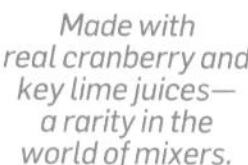

Made with real cranberry and key lime juices—a rarity in the world of mixers.

Stirrings Simple Cosmopolitan Mix
(3 fl oz)
60 calories, 0 g fat, 16 g sugars

JetSet Energy Club Soda Mixer
(10.5 fl oz)
0 calories
0 g fat
0 g sugars

Like Red Bull, JetSet's club soda is loaded with taurine, caffeine, and B vitamins, just without all the sugar.

Reed's Premium Ginger Brew
(8 fl oz)
100 calories
0 g fat
22 g sugars

Ginger beer is made with a larger dose of ginger than ginger ale, which is why we'll cough up the extra 10 calories here.

Pom Wonderful 100% Juice Pomegranate Cherry
(4 fl oz)
75 calories
0 g fat
14.5 g sugars

These are natural sugars, which means you get nutrients, too.

ReaLime 100% Lime Juice
(3 Tbsp)

Madhava Agave Nectar
(1 Tbsp)
50 calories
0 g fat
15 g sugars

This is how real margaritas are made, with fresh lime juice and a hint of sugar.

Not That!

Mr and Mrs T Strawberry Daiquiri-Margarita Mix

(4 fl oz)

190 calories, 0 g fat
44 g sugars

Mostly high-fructose corn syrup and food coloring—enough to spoil any good drink.

Finest Call Premium Margarita Mix
(4 fl oz)
160 calories
0 g fat
38 g sugars

Real margaritas don't contain corn-based sweeteners or artificial colors. Consider this the crutch of the amateur.

Rose's Grenadine
(2 Tbsp)
90 calories
0 g fat
21 g sugars

Looks fruity. Tastes fruity. Yet in truth, there's not a shred of fruit in this syrupy cocktail staple.

Canada Dry Ginger Ale
(8 fl oz)
90 calories
0 g fat
24 g sugars

Better for you than 7Up or Sprite, because Canada Dry also contains real ginger. Still, we prefer the stronger stuff.

Red Bull
(8.4 fl oz)
110 calories
0 g fat
27 g sugars

Be cautious when mixing alcohol with energy drinks. Research has shown people drinking both tend to underestimate their level of intoxication.

Beers

Drink This

Guinness Draught

(12 fl oz)

125 calories, 10 g carbs, 4% alcohol

For our money, Guinness Draught has the best flavor-to-calorie ratio in the cooler.

Keystone Premium

108 calories
6 g carbs
4.4% alcohol

Make this swap with a six pack a week and you'll save more than 3 pounds a year.

Leinenkugel's Honey Weiss

149 calories
12 g carbs
4.9% alcohol

Honey- and fruit-based beers tend to come with high calorie counts, so choose your weapon wisely.

Rolling Rock

120 calories
7 g carbs
4.5% alcohol

A first-rate session beer: crisp, refreshing, and surprisingly gentle in the calorie and carb departments.

Carta Blanca

128 calories
11 g carbs
4% alcohol

Perfect for a Michelada, one of Mexico's most popular drinks: Combine in a glass with a squeeze of lime, a dash of Worcestershire, and a few hits of hot sauce.

Labatt Blue Light

108 calories
8 g carbs
4% alcohol

Both Labatt and Michelob deliver more robustly flavored light beers. Labatt just does so for fewer calories.

Molson Canadian

143 calories
11 g carbs
5% alcohol

In the North American showdown, Canada wins out by a 45-calorie margin.

Beck's Premier Light

64 calories
4 g carbs
3.8% alcohol

Among the lightest beers in the world, Beck's surprises by actually tasting like, well, beer.

Amstel Light

95 calories
6 g carbs
3.5% alcohol

One of our favorite light beers, precisely because it doesn't taste like one.

Michelob Honey Lager

178 calories
19 g carbs
4.9% alcohol

One of the most carb-heavy beers you'll find in the cooler.

Pabst Blue Ribbon

144 calories
13 g carbs
4.7% alcohol

PBR has become a throwback favorite of the hipster crowd in recent year, which doesn't bode well for the bellies of America's young drinkers.

Not That!

Guinness Extra Stout

(12 fl oz)

176 calories, 14 g carbs, 6% alcohol

Mix up these two popular Guinness varieties and it could cost you 10 pounds or more over the course of a year if you drink just one a day.

Bass

156 calories
13 g carbs
5.1% alcohol

English-style ales tend to pack on the calories, and Bass, among the most famous of all ales, is no exception.

Bud Light

110 calories
7 g carbs
4.2% alcohol

In the world of light beers, 110 calories is a bit too much to invest when there are so many other options out there.

Budweiser American Ale

182 calories
18 g carbs
5.3% alcohol

We appreciate Bud's desire to deliver a beer with a more assertive flavor, but this one packs more calories than a Taco Bell Doritos Locos Taco.

Michelob Light

123 calories
9 g carbs
4.3% alcohol

The heaviest light beer in the cooler. A bottle of Guinness Draught has just 2 calories more.

Corona Extra

148 calories
14 g carbs
4.6% alcohol

For a beer that doesn't taste like much, it sure comes with plenty of calories.

Heineken

166 calories
10 g carbs
5.4% alcohol

It's one of the world's best-selling beers, but for 166 calories a can, we'd expect a lot more flavor.

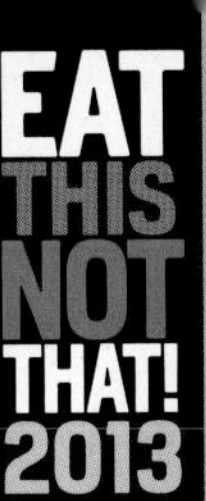

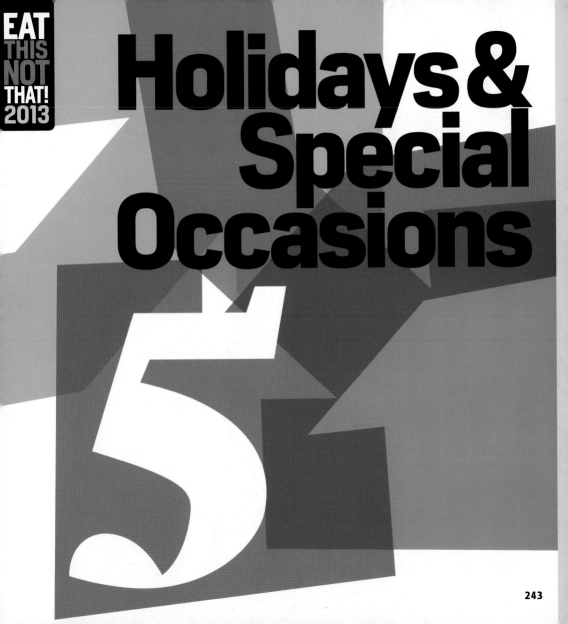

Holidays & Special Occasions

5

Planning a Traditional Thanksgivi Dinner This Year?

OF COURSE YOU ARE! What would this November's family gathering be without a heaping table laden with the very larder that fed the Pilgrims through their long first winter? Delicious! So go ahead—pass the platters of corn, the plates filled with root vegetables, the delightful desserts. And in the middle of it all, a big tray of hot, delicious roasted eels.

Eels? Eww!

Sorry, traditionalists, but if you really want to make like the Pilgrims, you'd better rethink your harvest. Wild turkeys—the kind that roamed the Americas in giant flocks when the first Old Worlders arrived in America—are almost impossible to hunt down with a bow and arrow or a musket. Fast, wily, and ugly as sin, turkeys were a very rare and special meal indeed, but if you lived or died by turkey, well, you died. Not the kind of food you'd try to make a feast out of. Indeed, the naturalist James Prosek claims that eels—abundant, high in fat and protein, and lethargic enough to catch with a spear in cold months—were almost certainly part of the main course at the first Thanksgiving.

Kinda makes you want to not give thanks, doesn't it?

The modern feast we all grew up with is in fact a savvy bit of dietary misdirection, one designed to give today's family table a more palatable protein choice while lining the pockets of the folks at Butterball and providing the nation with its only reason to watch those former college stars whose sad fate it was to be drafted by the Detroit Lions.

And Thanksgiving isn't the only holiday that's been corrupted by food marketers. The children nestled all snug in their beds in "The Night Before Christmas" weren't dreaming of giant chocolate Santas and gummies made of high-fructose corn syrup in the shape of Dora the Explorer. What danced in their heads were sugar-plums—a mixture of dried fruits, nuts, and spices with a light coating of sugar or coconut, and a lot healthier than what will be in your stocking this year. And Halloween? The original treats were roasted nuts, apples, pumpkin seeds, and potatoes.

So this year, don't think you're honoring your ancestors by downing every piece of candy corn, every leftover turkey sandwich, and every red- and green-foil-wrapped Hershey's Kiss. Yes, there are a lot of great holiday options.

But gorging yourself isn't one of them.

THANKSGIVING

BEST ↔ WORST

Protein

Ham
(4 oz bone-in rump)

148 calories
4 g fat (0 g saturated)
948 mg sodium

Ham is one of the leanest hoilday meats, but also one of the saltiest.

White turkey
(4 oz)

176 calories
4 g fat (0 g saturated)
372 mg sodium

A mean, lean, metabolism-boosting protein.

Dark turkey
(4 oz)

208 calories
8 g fat (4 g saturated)
388 mg sodium

The darker the meat, the more fat it harbors.

Fried turkey
(4 oz, white meat)

224 calories
14 g fat (6.8 g saturated)
532 mg sodium

Stick an otherwise healthy bird in a fryer and more than triple your fat intake.

Starchy Sides

Mashed potatoes
(½ cup made with whole milk)

87 calories
0.5 g fat
(0.5 g saturated)
317 mg sodium

To cut calories, prepare these with skim milk.

Roll with butter

130 calories
5 g fat (2 g saturated)
210 mg sodium

The pat of butter lowers this roll's glycemic index, helping to prevent dramatic spikes in blood sugar.

Candied sweet potatoes
(½ cup)

160 calories
4 g fat (0 g saturated)
80 mg sodium

These spuds cede the nutritional high ground when they're covered in sugar.

Stuffing
(½ cup)

175 calories
9 g fat (2 g saturated)
543 mg sodium

An appropriate name for a mash of refined carbohydrates basted with melted butter and turkey fat.

Corn bread
(2" x 2") with butter

190 calories
9 g fat (4 g saturated)
450 mg sodium

More calories, fat, and sodium than a regular roll.

Vegetable Sides

Roasted brussels sprouts
(½ cup)

28 calories
0 g fat
16 mg sodium

Low in calories, high in fiber. Enough said.

Roasted butternut squash
(½ cup, cubes)

40 calories
0 g fat
4 mg sodium

This squash's antioxidant carotenoid may help reduce the risk of lung cancer.

Green bean casserole
(½ cup)

100 calories
6 g fat (1 g saturated)
300 mg sodium

Replace the fried onions with caramelized ones and use fresh green beans.

Creamed spinach
(½ cup)

220 calories
14 g fat (7 g saturated)
440 mg sodium

Better off sautéing this nutritional powerhouse in olive oil and chopped garlic.

Condiments

Turkey gravy
(2 Tbsp)

16 calories
0 g fat
85 mg sodium

Oh so good for so few calories.

Fresh cranberry sauce
(2 Tbsp)

50 calories
0 g fat
11 g sugars

Fresh whole cranberries are some of the richest anticancer fighters.

Canned cranberry sauce
(½-inch slice)

85 calories
0 g fat
20 g sugars

Ban from your plate anything that shimmies like Jell-O.

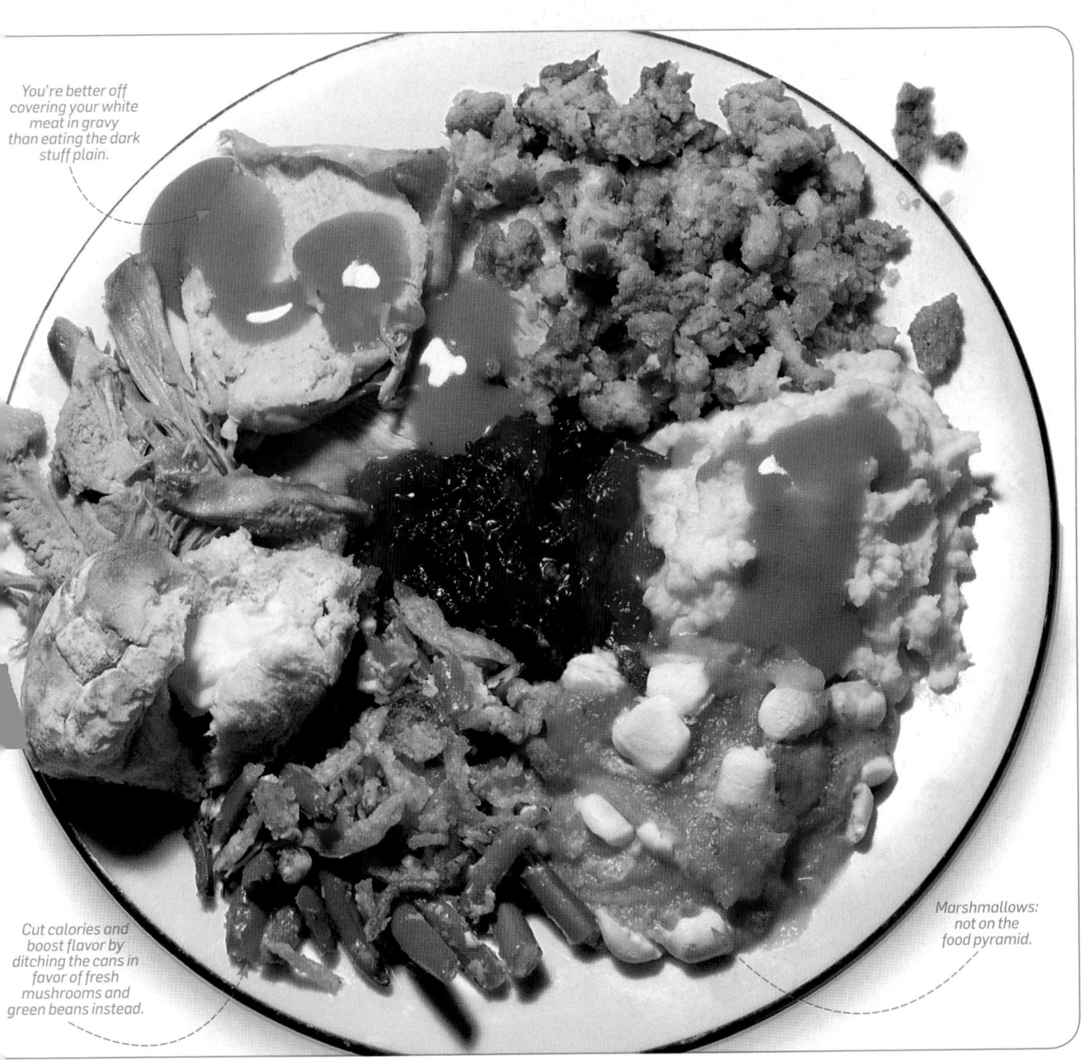
You're better off covering your white meat in gravy than eating the dark stuff plain.
Cut calories and boost flavor by ditching the cans in favor of fresh mushrooms and green beans instead.
Marshmallows: not on the food pyramid.

CHRISTMAS DINNER

BEST ↔ WORST

Protein

Beef tenderloin
(6 oz)
300 calories
15 g fat (6 g saturated)
400 mg sodium
Rubbed with olive oil, garlic, and rosemary, this is a protein powerhouse.

Leg of lamb
(6 oz)
408 calories
24 g fat (12 g saturated)
520 mg sodium
Switch to chops or loin if you want a leaner cut of lamb.

Duck breast
(6 oz)
480 calories
26 g fat (12 g saturated)
620 mg sodium
Peel off the skin and duck's protein-to-fat ratio is surprisingly impressive.

Prime rib
(6 oz)
600 calories
25 g fat (12 g saturated)
870 mg sodium
This cut is spiderwebbed with loads of intramuscular fat.

Vegetable Sides

Steamed green beans
(½ cup)
22 calories
0 g fat
0 mg sodium
These fiber-rich veggies will fend off the food coma.

Roasted red potatoes
(½ cup)
100 calories
5 g fat (1 g saturated)
170 mg sodium
Rule: Roasted over loaded. True always, especially with potatoes.

Salad greens with croutons
(1 oz) and 2 Tbsp Italian dressing
240 calories
12 g fat (4 g saturated)
390 mg sodium
We applaud salad consumption as long as it's sans croutons and light on dressing.

Baked potato
with butter and sour cream (1 Tbsp each)
400 calories
14 g fat (6 g saturated)
500 mg sodium
This tater's only half stuffed and still bloated with calories.

Dessert

Chocolate-covered strawberries
(4)
164 calories
8.5 g fat
(4.5 g saturated)
24 g carbohydrates
Swap milk chocolate for dark to maximize antioxidant intake.

Coconut macaroons
(2)
195 calories
6 g fat (6 g saturated)
34 g sugars
The holiday perennial isn't the worst, but munch within reason.

Chocolate cake
(⅙ cake)
415 calories
13 g fat (5 g saturated)
45 g sugars
Better off eating a few squares of chocolate and calling it a night.

Cheesecake
(⅙ cake)
470 calories
26 g fat (13 g saturated)
39 g sugars
What do you expect from a dessert made almost entirely of cream cheese?

Wine

Sauvignon blanc
(5 fl oz)
119 calories
3 g carbohydrates
Resveratrol level: Very low
The driest white wine is one of the best.

Chardonnay
(5 fl oz)
120 calories
4 g carbohydrates
Resveratrol level: Very low
Though white wines contain heart-strengthening resveratrol, they can't compete with reds on the antioxidant front.

Pinot noir
(5 fl oz)
121 calories
3 g carbohydrates
Resveratrol level: High
This big-bodied vino packs the most resveratrol.

Red zinfandel
(5 fl oz)
129 calories
4 g carbohydrates
Resveratrol level: Medium-high
Not as popular as merlot or cabernet, but it should be.

Dessert wine
(3.5 fl oz)
165 calories
14 g carbohydrates
Resveratrol level: Low
High in sugar, dessert wines always pack more calories than normal table wines.

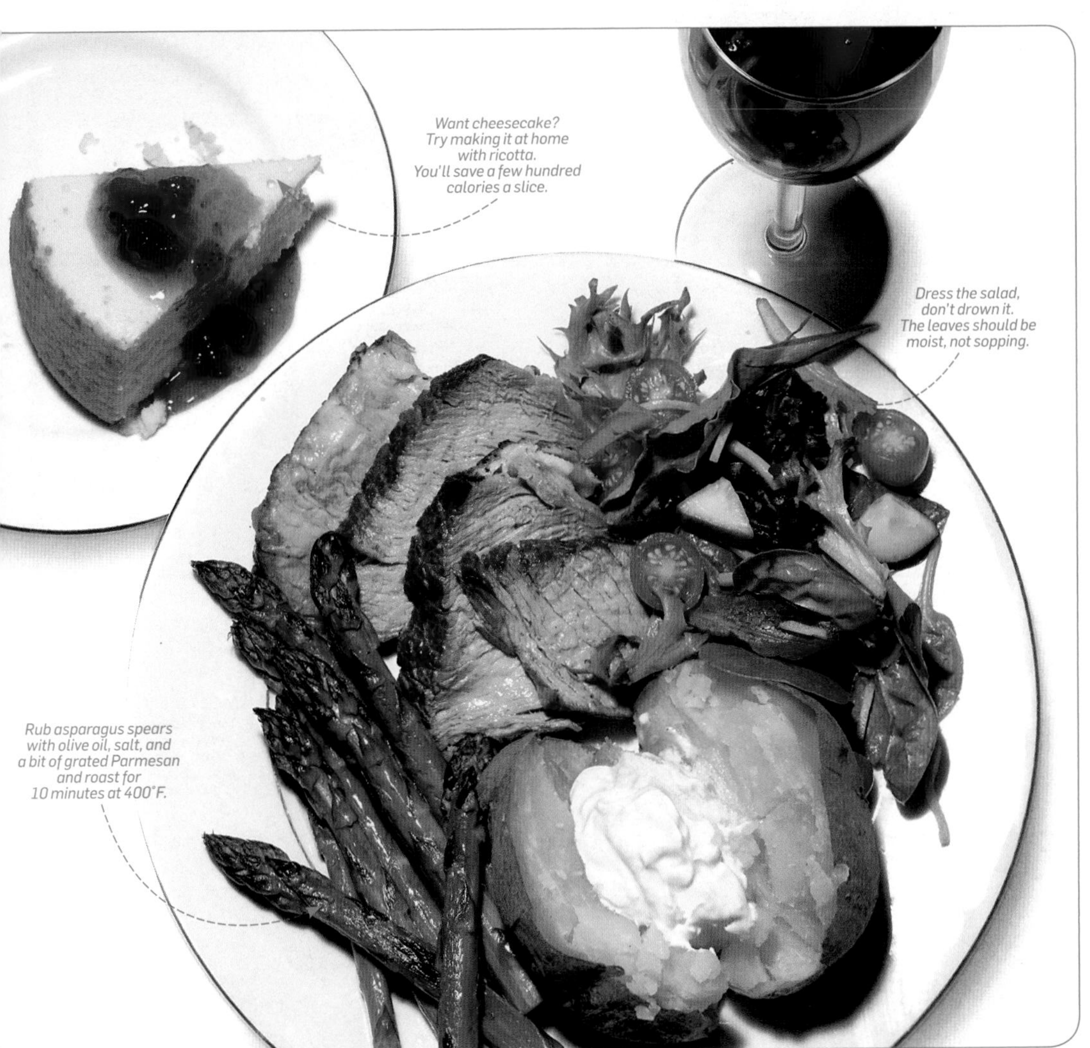
Want cheesecake?
Try making it at home
with ricotta.
You'll save a few hundred
calories a slice.
Dress the salad,
don't drown it.
The leaves should be
moist, not sopping.
Rub asparagus spears
with olive oil, salt, and
a bit of grated Parmesan
and roast for
10 minutes at 400°F.

NEW YEAR'S EVE

BEST

WORST

Hors d'Oeuvres

Jumbo shrimp cocktail
(6) with 2 Tbsp cocktail sauce

60 calories
<1 g fat
470 mg sodium

Indulge in the high-protein, virtually fat-free shrimp. Limit the sodium-rich sauce.

Cheddar cheese
(four ½-inch cubes)

140 calories
12 g fat (8 g saturated)
212 mg sodium

High in fat, but also effective at squashing appetites. If you want cheese, make it the first thing you eat.

Tomato bruschetta
(2 pieces)

200 calories
4 g fat (1 g saturated)
230 mg sodium

Tomatoes, garlic, basil, and olive oil make this a potent party pick.

Crab cake with rémoulade

240 calories
18 g fat (4 g saturated)
600 mg sodium

Bound with mayo and topped with a mayo-based sauce, crab cakes don't offer the biggest bang for your caloric buck.

Pigs in a blanket
(3)

400 calories
25 g fat (9 g saturated)
850 mg sodium

The real danger here is the calorie-dense pastry wrap.

Dips

Salsa
(½ cup and 8 chips)

156 calories
7 g fat (1 g saturated)
300 mg sodium

You can't beat a dip made entirely of produce.

Guacamole
(¼ cup and 8 chips)

260 calories
15 g fat (3 g saturated)
325 mg sodium

High in calories, but filled with fiber and heart-healthy monounsaturated fats.

French onion
(¼ cup and 8 chips)

260 calories
17 g fat (7 g saturated)
440 mg sodium

Nothing but spiked sour cream. Better to spend the calories on guac.

Spinach artichoke
(¼ cup and 8 chips)

325 calories
19 g fat (9 g saturated)
625 mg sodium

Woefully misnamed. This is a cheese and mayonnaise dip with a sprinkling of vegetables.

Booze

Champagne
(5 fl oz)

127 calories
8 g carbohydrates

The standard New Year's drink is also one of the lightest.

Mojito
(8 fl oz)

180 calories
15 g carbohydrates

Based almost entirely on healthy ingredients: lime juice, fresh mint, and sugar-free club soda.

Gin and tonic
(8 fl oz)

240 calories
16 g carbohydrates

Adding tonic to anything is like adding a soda's worth of calories.

Cosmopolitan
(8 fl oz)

300 calories
22 g carbohydrates

Composed of high-sugar additives that will slow you down long before the clock strikes midnight.

Margarita
(8 fl oz)

450 calories
65 g carbohydrates

The worst of all cocktails for one reason: sugar. Margarita mix is nothing but dyed high-fructose corn syrup.

There are no better calories to consume than these ones here.
Your cocktail code: Club soda: Yes! Tonic: No!
The worst option on any party table.

FOURTH OF JULY

BEST ↔ WORST

Off the Grill

Beef kabob

220 calories
9 g fat (4.5 g saturated)
120 mg sodium

Lean protein and fiber-rich veggies mean less need for unhealthy sides.

Hot dog
with relish, ketchup, and mustard

320 calories
18 g fat (8 g saturated)
960 mg sodium

While not the lowest-calorie choice, the frank is a relative winner on the grill.

Hamburger
(4 oz) with ketchup and mustard

462 calories
21.5 g fat (8 g saturated)
700 mg sodium

Cut 150 calories by using ground sirloin and a whole-wheat bun.

Baby back ribs
(½ rack)

490 calories
33 g fat (16 g saturated)
1,650 mg sodium

Universally the worst grill option, regardless of how little sauce has been slathered on top.

Sides

Canned baked beans
(½ cup)

120 calories
1 g fat (0 g saturated)
871 mg sodium

One serving is filled with 5 grams of fiber.

Coleslaw
(½ cup)

150 calories
8 g fat (1 g saturated)
350 mg sodium

Based on a formula similar to that for potato salad, but cabbage is healthier for you than potatoes. This number can climb, though, depending on the mayo application.

Corn on the cob
with butter

170 calories
11 g fat (7 g saturated)
190 mg sodium

Not the healthiest vegetable because most of its calories come from natural sugars, but not a terrible option on a hot summer day.

Homemade potato salad
(½ cup)

190 calories
12 g fat (3 g saturated)
560 mg sodium

Even the words "potato" and "salad" can be ruined by mayonnaise.

Dessert

Grapes
(1 cup)

62 calories
0 g fat
15 g sugar

The phytonutrients in the skin of this fruit protect you against free-radical damage.

Cherry ice pop

50 calories
0 g fat
8 g sugars

A pretty harmless way to end a summer meal.

Ice cream sandwich

160 calories
5 g fat (3 g saturated)
13 g sugars

No matter the brand, this item's size dictates a restrained calorie load.

Chocolate ice cream bar

280 calories
20 g fat (13 g saturated)
20 g sugars

Bars from so-called premium brands like Häagen-Dazs and Dove pack a serious wallop.

Beer

Amstel Light
(12 fl oz)

95 calories
5 g carbohydrates

For when you desire the suds but don't want the heft.

Rolling Rock Premium
(12 fl oz)

132 calories
10 g carbohydrates

One of the lighter regular brews.

Budweiser
(12 fl oz)

145 calories
11 g carbohydrates

The king of beers is not a benevolent ruler.

Corona Extra
(12 fl oz)

148 calories
14 g carbohydrates

Light in flavor, not in calories.

Load up on mustard. That bright yellow color comes from turmeric, a spice with a vast array of health benefits.
Packed with lycopene, the same antioxidant that gives tomatoes their cancer-fighting properties.
At 160 calories, one of summer's great dessert bargains.

HALLOWEEN

Candy

BEST

Sather's SweeTarts
(14 g, 10 pieces)
50 calories
0 g fat
12 g sugars

For tablets of refined sugar, these aren't that bad.

Smarties (14 g, 2 rolls)
50 calories
0 g fat
12 g sugars

Smarties are the intelligent candy choice.

Now and Later
(17 g, 4 pieces)
62 calories
0.5 g fat (0 g saturated)
11.5 g sugars

Opt for these now. Feel good about it later.

3 Musketeers
(15 g, "fun" size bar)
63 calories
2 g fat (1.5 g saturated)
10 g sugars

Compared to its "fun" size brethren, this bar is tame.

Brach's Candy Corn
(20 g, 11 pieces)
70 calories
0 g fat
14 g sugars

The only corn here is of the syrup variety.

Tootsie Roll
(20 g, 3 pieces)
70 calories
1.5 g fat (0.5 g saturated)
9.5 g sugars

Unroll too many of these and you'll add a roll to your midsection.

Snickers
(17 g, "fun" size bar)
80 calories
4 g fat (1.5 g saturated)
8.5 g sugars

Note: Does not actually satisfy.

Starburst (20 g, 4 pieces)
80 calories
2 g fat (1.5 g saturated)
11.5 g sugars

The fat comes from a weird combination of oils.

Skittles
(20 g, "fun" size pack)
80 calories
1 g fat (1 g saturated)
15 g sugars

Sugar, oil, and artificial coloring.

Butterfinger
(21 g, "fun" size bar)
100 calories
4 g fat (2 g saturated)
10 g sugars

Lives up to its name by being one of the fattiest bars out there.

Reese's Peanut Butter Cups
(1 cup)
105 calories
6.5 g fat (2.5 g saturated)
10.5 g sugars

More sugar than peanuts.

M&Ms Milk Chocolate
("fun" size bag)
106 calories
4.5 g fat (2.5 g saturated)
13.5 g sugars

Better off with peanut M&Ms.

WORST

MOVIE THEATER

BEST ↑ … ↓ WORST

Salty Snacks

Homemade trail mix (¼ cup)

150 calories
7 g fat (3 g saturated)
325 mg sodium

Sometimes you need to bend the rules to eat well.

Soft pretzel with mustard

290 calories
0 g fat
850 mg sodium

Skip the sludgy cheese dip to guarantee decent film fare.

Popcorn (medium, 10–12 cups)

600 calories
39 g fat (12 g saturated)
1,120 mg sodium

Though movie theaters have begun to phase out trans fats in their "butter topping," it still packs a wallop.

Nachos (40 chips and 4 oz cheese)

1,101 calories
59 g fat (18.5 g saturated)
1,580 mg sodium

As much sodium as 53 Saltine crackers.

Sweets

Good & Plenty (33 pieces)

140 calories
0 g fat
25 g sugars

Licorice acts as an anti-inflammatory.

Junior Mints (½ large box)

170 calories
3 g fat (2.5 g saturated)
32 g sugars

You can bet on mint candies to be the best chocolate choices.

Milk Duds (½ large box)

230 calories
8 g fat (5 g saturated)
27 g sugars

They're called Duds for a reason.

Twizzlers (½ 6-oz package)

320 calories
1 g fat
38 g sugars

Sure, they're "low fat"—that's because they're pure sugar.

Drinks

Unsweetened iced tea (16 fl oz)

0 calories
0 g fat
0 g sugars

Pack this in your purse for light, antioxidant-rich refreshment.

Cola (20 fl oz)

180 calories
0 g fat
46 g carbohydrates

Nutritionally bankrupt soda is nothing but high-fructose corn syrup.

Slushie (24 fl oz)

335 calories
0 g fat
88 g sugars

More sugar than 13 Double Stuf Oreos.

Pick the wrong popcorn and you could end up with 10 grams or more of trans fat.

Want to eat well and save money? Load up a sandwich bag with trail mix.

AT THE MALL

BEST

WORST

Main dish

Panda Express Potato Chicken

and Mixed Veggies

290 calories
11.5 g fat (2 g saturated)
1,340 mg sodium

You won't find a bowl of such lean proteins and nutrient-packed vegetables anywhere else in malls. Just be sure to skip the rice.

Subway Roast Beef

(6")

320 calories
5 g fat (1.5 g saturated)
700 mg sodium

Subway offers 14 sandwiches with 330 or fewer calories.

Sbarro Pepperoni Pizza

(1 slice)

591 calories
27 g fat (13 g saturated)
1,426 mg sodium

This one piece slices through 25 percent of your day's calories.

Quiznos Tuna Melt

(small)

690 calories
47 g fat (11 g saturated, 0.5 g trans)
840 mg sodium

From such a healthy fish is born a beastly sub.

Snacks

Chick-fil-A Fruit Cup

(medium)

70 calories
0 g fat
0 mg sodium

With this high fiber-to-calorie ratio, you're sure to get full without expanding your waistline.

Taco Bell Fresco Crunchy Taco

150 calories
7 g fat (2.5 g saturated)
350 mg sodium

The reasonable Fresco line includes four items with fewer than 200 calories.

Dairy Queen French Fries

(regular)

310 calories
13 g fat (2 g saturated)
640 mg sodium

You could have two tacos for the dietary cost of these fries.

Dessert

McDonald's Vanilla Reduced Fat Ice Cream Cone

150 calories
3.5 g fat (2 g saturated)
18 g sugars

In an era of colossal cone concoctions, McDonald's gets props for a sensible serving size.

Mrs. Fields Semi-Sweet Chocolate Chip Cookie

210 calories
10 g fat (5 g saturated)
19 g sugars

A step up from the food court's other dessert disasters.

Auntie Anne's Cinnamon Sugar Pretzel

without butter

380 calories
1 g fat (0 g saturated)
29 g sugars

Request your pretzel sans butter and save 90 calories of fat.

Cinnabon Classic Cinnamon Roll

880 calories

36 g fat (17 g saturated)

59 g sugars

A coronary catastrophe with as much fat as three McDonald's cheeseburgers.

Drinks

Orange Julius Raspberry Crush Premium Smoothie

(12 fl oz)

160 calories
0 g fat
32 g sugars

Jamba Juice Orange Dream Machine

(24 fl oz)

470 calories
1.5 g fat (1 g saturated)
97 g sugars

Smoothie King Cranberry Supreme Smoothie

(20 fl oz)

554 calories
1 g fat (0 g saturated)
96 g sugars

Its placement in the "Stay Healthy" section of the menu surely must be a mistake.

Cinnabon may have ditched the trans fats, but its rolls are still explosive calorie bombs.

This old mall classic is still one of the best ways to quench your thirst.

A slice of cheese pizza? Not bad. Pepperoni, though, is another story entirely.

6

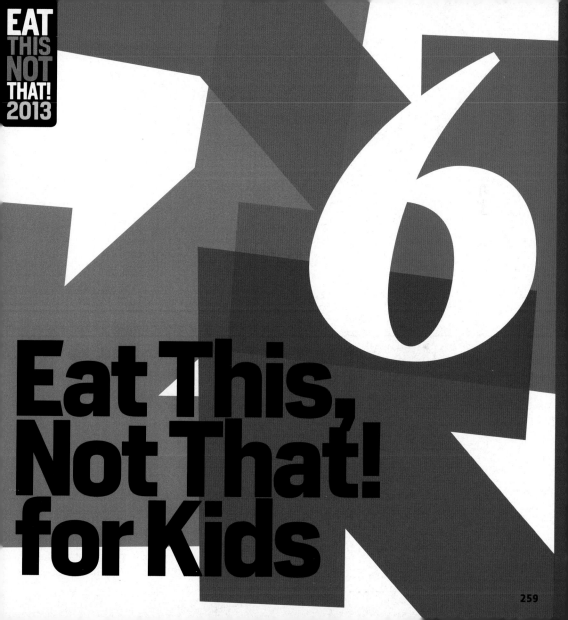

Eat This, Not That! for Kids

Raise an Advent[urous] Little Eater

Let's say a new toy store opened in town, and it had a marvelous array of fascinating gadgets and gizmos that dazzled your eye and that of your towheaded toddler at prices that fit comfortably within your family budget. Sounds great, right?

Now, what if it turned out that more than 1 in every 3 toys you bought there was completely, irrevocably broken? The Rock 'Em Sock 'Em Robots couldn't rock or sock, the Mr. Potato Heads were total lemons, and the Barbies all came with Kirstie Alley's wardrobe. Oh, and there's a no-return policy on everything you buy.

You'd probably never shop at that store again, right?

Well, your local supermarket and fast-food joint have track records that are just as

urous

awful. More than a third of the foods our kids are consuming are utterly broken and useless. But we keep coming back and spending our money, week after week.

A 2010 study published by the American Dietetic Association found that nearly 40 percent of the calories consumed by kids are empty calories. Forty percent of their food is worthless! For a 9-year-old boy consuming 1,400 calories a day, that's equivalent to chewing through 19 Starburst candies every single day of the week.

Now, food isn't exactly the same as toys. Getting kids to eat anything remotely nutritious is often a tug of war to the death. One of you emerges victorious. The other lands facedown in a pile of peas. But what if you just dropped the rope?

See, the food fight is not one you can win through will and force alone. Indeed, the best thing to do is not to fight at all. Do what the smartest parents do: Cheat. Dupe, deceive, dissemble, falsify, beguile, fabricate, prevaricate, exaggerate, and if that doesn't work, then just lie. Trix may be for kids, but tricks are for parents. Use these tactics to fool your kids into eating right, and you'll set them up for a lifetime of health and happiness. Bad daddy! Bad mommy! Lucky kid.

6 WAYS to Encourage a Lifetime of Healthy Eating

Play psychologist with your kid

Nowadays, kids avoid vegetables like they're out-of-style sneakers; only one in five of them actually eats enough plant matter. If you want to reverse that trend, a little scheming can go a long way. Research out of England found that giving children a taste of a new vegetable daily for 2 weeks increased their enjoyment and consumption of that food.

Not all strategies sound as sinister as the exposure therapy. Giving kids ownership over what they eat is also a powerful play. Consider planting a garden. Studies show that kids' acceptance of fruits and vegetables increases after participating in growing them. No time to till? Simply letting your children choose their vegetables can lead to an 80 percent increase in their consumption.

Never skip breakfast. Ever.

"Don't skip breakfast" is the persistent platitude heard 'round the world. Which may explain why so few pay attention—especially children. A 2005 study showed that kids skipped breakfast more than any other meal despite its reign as the king of meals. The effects of this epidemic are by now well known. Test after test shows that breakfast-eating students score higher on short-term memory and verbal fluency, among many other academic benefits.

Maybe breakfast's most important contribution, however, is found not in its own nutritional value, but in its impact on the rest of the day's eating habits. Research says children eating a meal in the morning will themselves choose less soda and fewer fries while opting for more vegetables and milk throughout the rest of the day.

We know time can be an issue in the chaos of the early morning hours. But a nutritious bowl of cereal, cup of yogurt, or even microwaveable breakfast is never more than a few minutes away. Check out dozens of excellent options in Chapter 4.

RULE #3 Forget about force-feeding

Whether it's a Clean Plate Club membership drive or castigations about starving Africans, efforts by parents to get their children to eat healthy foods can backfire. In a 2009 study of 63 children, Cornell researchers found that those whose parents insisted on clean plates ate 35 percent more of a sweetened cereal later in the day. If kids ate 35 percent more than 1 serving of Froot Loops every day for a year, they'd gain 4 pounds.

There is a corollary. A Pennsylvania study indicated that the restriction of specific yummy foods from children's plates actually increased the kids' long-term preference for and consumption of those foods. It's also been found that kids who are barred from having certain indulgences tend to eat more when they're not hungry.

The lesson here is twofold: First, there is a fine line between encouraging your kids to try new foods and forcing them to eat against their will. The negative tone and tenor of all those warnings about not finishing our lima beans when we were kids is probably one of the reasons why most American adults still don't eat enough vegetables.

Set a house rule that your children need to try a new food three times before deciding whether they like it. If they still don't dig it after the third attempt, then Mom and Dad need to let it go. On the flip side, banning foods from your household can backfire, so rather than forbidding certain foods, set up specific parameters for when treats can be enjoyed.

Shrink your silverware

According to another study from Cornell, portion size is the most powerful predictor of how much preschool-age children eat. And with the typical manufacturers' snack package being 2.5 times bigger than the appropriate amount for young kids, health-conscious parents fight an uphill battle.

Control what you can. Keep in mind that restaurant portions—even for kids—are egregiously oversized, so don't force them to wolf down every last tater tot. Splitting a dish with a sibling is never a bad idea (as long as you ask for two toys). At home, use smaller bowls, plates, and utensils. Jedi mind trick or not, there's plenty of evidence that kids will consume fewer calories when you downsize the dishes.

Set an example (especially you, Dad)

The portion of America's food dollars spent on meals out increased from 34 percent to 48 percent between 1974 and 2008. Parents' increasing penchant for restaurant food can translate to nutritionally unsound decisions by kids. One recent study laid the heaviest blame on fathers. Researchers at Texas A&M University say dads carry the most influence largely because when they take their kids to the Mickey D's, it's often as a treat or some sort of celebration. This enforces the idea that unhealthy eating is positive. Mothers, on the other hand, often choose fast food due to time constraints, so the food doesn't hold as much psychological sway.

Turn off the tube

Since 1970, the number of television ads aimed at children has doubled to 40,000 per year, and several studies suggest that the amount of time kids watch television is a strong predictor of how often they request specific foods. This spells big trouble for one reason: Half of all TV ads directed at children promote junk food.

The solution is simple: Shove your kids outside. Surprise them with a bike, a soccer dog, a Chihuahua dog—anything to get them moving. More time spent outdoors means less time being exposed to television marketing. Of course, the larger benefit is that they get more exercise, which decreases the risk of a lot of bad stuff: obesity, diabetes, heart disease, even boredom.

Eat This Plate, Not That One!

SIMPLICITY IS ELEGANT. It's the case in nutrition as it is in design, and the USDA seems to have recognized these truths when it replaced the confusing, data-deluged food pyramid in June 2011. In its place, the government now dishes up a plate-shaped logo cut into smaller and bigger wedges connoting the food groups. Its spare design is meant to illustrate the ideal relative proportions for each category without overloading us with unnecessary details.

The growing need for clear parental guidance is evident: Kids now consume more than a quarter of their daily calories in the form of empty snack calories, the vast majority of which are artery-clogging, blood-pressure-spiking, energy-jolting junk foods. And only one in four of our little ones consumes his or her daily recommended doses of fruits and vegetables. So we applaud the USDA's move. Yet, not all foods within a category are created equal, and plenty of room for error still exists with this stripped-down design. So in the name of true simplicity, we've broken down the best and worst options for each group.

Eat This

79
Pounds of corn the average American eats per year, less than a pound of which is fresh

MEAT, POULTRY, FISH, EGGS, AND BEANS

- **Grilled chicken breast**
- **Sirloin steak**
- **Grilled salmon or tilapia**
- **Deli turkey, ham, or roast beef**
- **Scrambled, poached, or boiled eggs**
- **Stewed black beans**
- **Hummus**
- **Natural, unsweetened peanut butter**

Dietary protein is the body's mechanic, repairing everything from cell walls to cuts to broken bones. It also drives metabolism, meaning that increasing your child's lean protein consumption will make his or her body more efficient at burning calories. For meats, the most important factors are that the cuts and the cooking methods are naturally lean. That means grilling or roasting chicken, pork loin, and less-marbled cuts of beef like sirloin, flank, and fillets.

FRUITS

- **Sliced apples or pears**
- **Berries (straight, or on yogurt or cereal)**
- **Bananas**
- **Grapes**
- **100 percent fruit smoothies**

So much of the fruit consumed by children is heavily processed—either crushed to make juice or smashed into fruit snacks and bars. What you want is whole, unadulterated fruits in their most natural forms—even if that means buying them frozen. Actually, studies show that frozen fruit can be more nutrient packed because it's packaged during peak season.

**Taken together, fruits and vegetables should compose at least half of your child's daily dietary plate.*

DAIRY

- **2% milk**
- **String cheese**
- **Cottage cheese**
- **Plain Greek yogurt with fresh fruit**

Dairy products are great sources of protein and bone-building calcium, but high fat content means they can pack plenty of calories. On the flip side, going fat free means your kid can lose out on some of the nutrients in dairy that your body needs a bit of fat to properly absorb. That's why we like low-fat dairy products like 2% milk and reduced-fat cheese: They have enough fat to make them tasty and nutritious, but not so much that dairy will pack on the pounds.

GRAINS

- **Brown rice**
- **Whole-grain bread**
- **Quinoa**
- **Whole-grain pasta**
- **Oatmeal**

11
Percentage of grain servings eaten by the average American that come from whole grains

Sure, this list's superiority is partially due to its lower glycemic index (meaning that the carbohydrates have less of an impact on the blood sugar level) and the occasional boost in protein provided by some of the foods. But it's the fiber that matters most. Many cram in double or triple what their non-whole-grain counterparts contain. For children, starting this habit now not only helps fend off diabetes, but also helps reduce the risk of cancer and heart disease later in life.

VEGETABLES

- **Steamed broccoli**
- **Mixed salad greens**
- **Sautéed mushrooms**
- **Roasted squash**
- **Grilled sweet peppers and onions**
- **Baby carrots**
- **Sweet potatoes**

Stick with raw vegetables or minimally cooked ones to retain the potent nutrients. And shop the rainbow. By choosing deep green, red, orange, and yellow vegetables, you're guaranteed to consume a balance of vitamins and minerals. One easy-to-make switch is from white potatoes to the sweet version, which lowers the impact on blood sugar levels and makes you feel fuller for longer.

MEAT, POULTRY, FISH, EGGS, AND BEANS

- **Chicken nuggets**
- **Crispy chicken sandwich**
- **Fish sticks**
- **Deli salami, pepperoni, or bologna**
- **Burgers**
- **Fatty cuts of steak**
- **Peanut butter with added sugars and partially hydrogenated fats**

An abnormally large percentage of kids' protein consumption is in the form of chicken nuggets. It doesn't take a genius to know that caked-on crumbs submerged in molten oil are a sure-fire way to jack up a meal's calories and crowd out vital nutrients. So is opting for fatty cuts of beef like ground chuck (used to make burgers) and rib eyes (steaks loaded with intra-muscular fat).

5.5
Pounds gained over a year by eating one Chips Ahoy!'s worth of calories more than you expend every day

40
Percentage of 2- to 5-year-old kids' fruit intake that's in the form of juice

FRUITS

- **More than 8 ounces of juice a day**
- **More than a few tablespoons of dried fruits a day**
- **Smoothies made with sherbet, frozen yogurt, or added sugar**
- **Fruit-flavored yogurt**

These choices might be better than a bag of Skittles, but not by much. Drinking your fruits in the form of juices or non-whole-fruit smoothies makes you miss out on one of fruits' biggest benefits—fiber. And fruit-flavored packaged foods are just that: industrially processed items heavy with sugar and light in actual fruit. On the entire plate, whole foods are better than processed ones.

17
Teaspoons of added sugar most 5-year-olds eat every single day

Not That!

DAIRY

- **Chocolate milk**
- **Ice cream**
- **Queso dip**
- **Yogurt processed with fruit**

Most people think about reducing the fat content of dairy products, and that can be helpful, since many of the listed foods are chock-full of it. But equally as significant nowadays are the spoonfuls of sugar added to so many milk products. One cup of Nesquik Chocolate Lowfat Milk has 28 grams of sugar—almost as much as a Snickers bar.

GRAINS

- **White rice**
- **White bread**
- **Muffins**
- **Pasta**
- **Heavily sweetened cereals**

Quick-burning carbohydrates, the kind found in these refined grains, take a child's blood sugar on a bumpy ride. And that has short-term and long-term consequences. Increased sugar consumption has been linked not just to weight gain and obesity, but also to hyperactivity, ADHD, anxiety, and reduced school performance.

28

Percentage of vegetables consumed by the average American that are french fries

VEGETABLES

- **French fries**
- **Chips**
- **Onion rings**
- **White potatoes**

Don't negate the benefits of vegetables by frying them. The deep-fryer treatment not only zaps vegetables of most of their nutrients, but also subjects them mostly to oils loaded with excess calories and fat.

The 20 WORST Kids' Foods in America

WORST BREAKFAST CEREAL

20 Post Fruity Pebbles (1 cup)

160 calories
1 g fat (1 g saturated)
15 g sugars
0 g fiber

This is Post's rosy appraisal of its flagship kids' cereal: "Fruity Pebbles is a wholesome, sweetened rice cereal. It is low in fat, cholesterol free, and provides 10 essential vitamins and minerals." Here's what it really meant to say: "Fruity Pebbles is a heavily manipulated, egregiously sweetened rice cereal. It is low in nutrients, fiber free, and the second and third ingredients in the cereal are sugar and hydrogenated vegetable oil, respectively." If you plan to feed your kids this stuff when they wake up, you may as well let them keep sleeping.

Eat This Instead!

Kellogg's Froot Loops (1 cup)

110 calories
1 g fat (0.5 g saturated)
12 g sugars
3 g fiber

0
grams
of fiber
Post Fruity Pebbles,
America's
most pathetic
cereal

WORST SIDE DISH

19 Denny's Kids' French Fries

430 calories
23 g fat (5 g saturated)
50 g carbohydrates

As important as it is for your kids to choose healthy entrées, a bad side can bring down even the leanest dinner centerpiece. These fries (disturbingly, the exact same portion as the adult version) alone pack as many calories and grams of fat as a child should consume in an entire meal.

Eat This Instead!

Kids' Apple Dunkers

140 calories
0 g fat
30 g carbohydrates

WORST FROZEN KIDS' MEAL

18 Kid Cuisine All American Fried Chicken (286 g, 1 meal)

540 calories
24 g fat (6 g saturated, 1 g trans)
750 mg sodium

Busy parents understandably need to turn to the freezer section to look for quick dinner solutions when time is tight. Just know that danger lurks in the land of the deep freeze. Despite its cutesy packaging, this Kid Cuisine entrée sports not just excessive amounts of calories and fat, but also a dose of trans fats derived from partially hydrogenated oil—the last thing a growing body needs. While icy blocks of meat and vegetables can never stack up to a fresh, home-cooked meal, there are plenty of solid options out there. Just by switching from Kid Cuisine to Banquet, you'll cut calories and fat nearly in half.

Eat This Instead!

Banquet Chicken Nuggets and Fries (142 g, 1 meal)

290 calories
13 g fat (2.5 g saturated)
520 mg sodium

WORST PB&J

17 Atlanta Bread Company Kids' Peanut Butter & Jelly

550 calories
15 g fat (3.5 g saturated)
89 g carbohydrates

It's hard to lose with the sturdy alliance of peanut butter and jelly—that is, unless you let your kid order it at Atlanta Bread Company. It would be easy to blame it on an excess of peanut butter, but sugary jelly is equally to blame here. Listed first on the sandwich's ingredients list, it accounts for a significant portion of the 89 grams of carbohydrates and helps to make this sandwich more caloric than the chain's grilled cheese.

Eat This Instead!

Kids' Grilled Cheese
390 calories
15 g fat (9 g saturated)
46 g carbohydrates

550 calories
Atlanta Bread Company pushes PB&J to the extreme

WORST CHINESE ENTRÉE

16 P.F. Chang's Kid's Chicken Fried Rice

580 calories
10 fat (2 g saturated)
1,120 mg sodium

Chang's tries to shroud its nutrition numbers by breaking meals into multiple servings. Don't be fooled. The restaurant continues its usual sodium assault on its new kids' menu. There you find a dish whose potential (chicken and rice, what could possibly go wrong?) is outweighed only by the surplus of salt saturating every last greasy grain of rice.

Eat This Instead!

Kid's Stir-Fried Baby Buddha's Feast

60 calories
0 g fat
50 mg sodium

WORST FISH MEAL

15 Long John Silver's Popcorn Shrimp Kid's Meal with Pepsi

710 calories
28.5 g fat (7 g saturated, 8.5 g trans)
1,155 mg sodium

There's plenty to dislike about this meal, but it's the explosive level of trans fats that caught our eye first. In fact, Silver's doesn't offer a single kids' meal with fewer than 5.5 grams of the dangerous fats—that's nearly three times the daily limit for a healthy adult. By simply switching fry oil, like so many other chains have done, LJS can fix that problem. In the meantime, skip the kids' menu entirely and suggest the scampi—one of the few kid-friendly meals not spoiled with heart-threatening fats.

Eat This Instead!

Garlic Shrimp Scampi with Ice Water

200 calories
13 g fat (2.5 g saturated)
650 mg sodium

WORST PIZZA

14 California Pizza Kitchen Kids Honey Chicken Pizza with Tomato Sauce

721 calories
N/A g fat (9 g saturated)
1,583 mg sodium
97 g carbohydrates

The sad truth is that we could have picked any of the kids' pizzas for this list. Even the cheese pizza has 598 calories, and the other four options go up from there. Thank the thick dough and heavy-handed cheese application. The little ones could eat two slices of Original BBQ Chicken pizza from a six-slice adult pie and save more than 300 calories.

Eat This Instead!

Kids Crispy Chicken with Broccoli

366 calories
N/A g fat (3 g saturated)
1,323 mg sodium
32 g carbohydrates

WORST FAST-FOOD CHICKEN MEAL

13 KFC Kids Meal with Popcorn Chicken, Potato Wedges, and Pepsi

730 calories
32 g fat (6 g saturated)
1,535 mg sodium

Fried chicken is almost always trouble, but the Potato Wedges constitute this meal's biggest calorie portion. And its most dangerous. Despite the Colonel's high-profile PR campaign touting its trans-fat-free menu, these wedges are loaded with partially hydrogenated vegetable oils, the precursors to the perilous fats.

Eat This Instead!

Kids Meal with Grilled Chicken Drumstick, Mashed Potatoes (no gravy), and Capri Sun Roarin' Waters Tropical Fruit Juice Drink

210 calories
7 g fat (1.5 g saturated)
625 mg sodium

WORST BURGER

12 Applebee's Kids Mini Cheeseburgers (2)

740 calories
46 g fat (16 g saturated, 2 g trans)
1,130 mg sodium

Just another sad example of Restaurant Law 172A, the Mini-Burger Paradox (MBP). The MBP states that the more diminutive the burger, the more potential it possesses for nutritional mayhem (see: Ruby Tuesday, Chili's, et al.). If restaurants stopped with one mini, you'd be fine, but these baby burgers normally come in groups of two or more—so you end up with two buns, two slices of cheese, two sets of condiments. The end result is a total package with more calories, fat, and sodium than you'd find in one normal-size burger.

Eat This Instead!

Kids Corn Dog

260 calories
14 g fat (4 g saturated)
440 mg sodium

WORST FAST-FOOD BURGER MEAL

11 McDonald's Mighty Kids Meal with Double Cheeseburger, Fries (small), and Fat-Free Chocolate Milk Jug

760 calories
33 g fat
(12 g saturated, 1.5 g trans)
1,315 mg sodium

The Golden Arches should be commended for increasing the number of healthy options in recent years. In particular, its Apple Dippers have inspired other large chains to offer alternatives to fried potatoes. Unfortunately, it's still easier to construct a lousy meal at McDonald's than it is a good one. This combo chews through more than a half day's worth of calories, fat, and sodium. And no toy in the bottom of the box can make that better.

Eat This Instead!

Happy Meal with Hamburger, Apple Dippers with Low-Fat Caramel Dip, and Apple Juice Box

435 calories
9.5 g fat
(3.5 g saturated, 0.5 g trans)
540 mg sodium

WORST BREAKFAST

10 Bob Evans Kids Plenty-o-Pancakes with Chocolate Chips

766 calories
22 g fat (13 g saturated fat)
1,281 mg sodium
137 g carbohydrates

As if five saucer-size pancakes studded with chocolate weren't bad enough, scoops of whip cream top each piece. The result is a load of refined carbohydrates that will have your kid bouncing in the booth (and crashing on the way home). And Bob's nutrition information doesn't even include the sugar dump found in the syrup or the additional fat and calories in the bacon or sausage that comes on the side.

Eat This Instead!

Kids Fruit Dippers

222 calories
1 g fat (0 g saturated)
62 mg sodium
51 g carbohydrates

766 calories
Don't derail your kid's day with this trainwreck of a breakfast from Bob Evans.

WORST NACHOS

9 On the Border Kid's Bean & Cheese Nachos

770 calories
45 g fat (25 g saturated)
1,440 mg sodium

On the Border has scaled back this dish since *Eat This, Not That!* last attacked it, but the changes don't even come close to reining in this time bomb. The only thing worse than the 25 grams of saturated fat—

nearly twice as much as an 8-year-old kid should consume in an entire day—is the fact that these nachos come with a complimentary sundae, pushing the meal total north of 1,100 calories.

Eat This Instead!
Kid's Grilled Chicken with Black Beans
270 calories
4 g fat (1 g saturated)
1,190 mg sodium

WORST DRINK

8 Applebee's Kids Oreo Cookie Shake

780 calories
41 g fat (26 g saturated)
97 g carbohydrates

Though Applebee's doesn't list it in its nutrition guide, we have a sneaking suspicion that nearly all of those 97 grams of carbohydrates are pure sugar. That's an insulin spike that would make diabetes specialists cringe. (Not to mention dentists.) Your child would have to eat 15 Oreos to match this shake's caloric heft. Better off going with chocolate milk—or a scoop of ice cream.

Eat This Instead!
Kids Chocolate Milk
270 calories
6 g fat (3 g saturated)
45 g carbohydrates

WORST GRILLED CHEESE

7 The Cheesecake Factory Kids Grilled Cheese Sandwich

810 calories
N/A g fat (21 g saturated)
1,656 mg sodium

Bread and cheese toasted into a warm, comforting meal. What's simpler than that? Well, the Factory shows it can ruin a simple kid favorite by oversizing every aspect of the sandwich. Its version is built with two thick slices of heavily buttered bread that bookend an even thicker layer of gooey cheese. This is just one of the many reasons the chain has for years resisted releasing comprehensive nutrition guides. The Grilled Chicken is the best alternative, but even that is far from danger free.

Eat This Instead!
Kids Grilled Chicken
510 calories
N/A g fat (16 g saturated)
1,204 mg sodium

WORST CHICKEN MEAL

6 The Cheesecake Factory Kids Southern Fried Chicken Sliders

820 calories
N/A g fat (10 g saturated)
2,049 mg sodium

When the Factory unveiled its kids' menu in 2009, its chief marketing officer said it was an effort to offer meals that fit kids' unique "portion size requirement." On the surface, these sliders fit that bill. But if their size is humble, their nutritional

760 calories
A not-so-happy meal for parents who want to raise healthy kids

numbers are not. These deep-fried slabs of chicken carry more than 2 days' worth of a child's sodium and more calories than a kid would get from eating 17 Chicken McNuggets.

Eat This Instead!

Kids Grilled Chicken

510 calories
N/A g fat (16 g saturated)
1,204 mg sodium

WORST SALAD

5 Friendly's Dippin' Chicken Salad

950 calories
50 g fat (12 g saturated)
1,880 mg sodium

It's an incredible thing to get a child excited about eating a salad. Just not this one. First off, this isn't so much a salad as a fried chicken dish with a few token veggies packed into a cone. Friendly's just doesn't know when to stop. On the side of the deep fried meat are bowls filled with croutons, cheese, and a honey mustard dipping sauce, which itself has 15 grams of fat. You end up with a "salad" that has more fat than three Snickers bars.

Eat This Instead!

Grilled Cheese Sandwich with Mandarin Oranges

430 calories
18 g fat (9 g saturated)
1,050 mg sodium

WORST MACARONI AND CHEESE

4 California Pizza Kitchen Kids Curly Mac n' Cheese with Edamame

989 calories
N/A g fat (34 g saturated)
701 mg sodium

Whereas most kid favorites—chicken fingers, cheeseburgers, even hot dogs—offer some redeeming nutritional value, macaroni and cheese brings nothing but cheese, cream, and refined carbohydrates to the table. CPK appears willing to solve that problem with the inclusion of protein- and fiber-rich edamame in its mac, but instead it stuffs its kiddy bowls to the brim with one of the most calorie-dense pastas we've ever seen. Another good opportunity squandered by the restaurant industry's penchant for excess.

Eat This Instead!

Kids Fusilli with Tomato Sauce

494 calories
N/A g fat (2 g saturated)
719 mg sodium

WORST CHICKEN FINGERS

3 Perkins Kid's Chicken Strips

1,000 calories
68 g fat (13 g saturated)
1,900 mg sodium

These fingers would be criminally caloric even if they were intended for adults. In fact, to match this four-digit calorie count, a kid would need to eat 22 McDonald's Chicken McNuggets. The road to nutritional safety with Perkins' kids menu is pocked with potholes, so either order the mac and cheese or keep on driving.

Eat This Instead!

Kid's Mac & Cheese

310 calories
10 g fat (4 g saturated)
880 mg sodium

WORST MEXICAN MEAL

2 On the Border Kid's Cheese Quesadilla with Mexican Rice

1,120 calories
73 g fat (31 g saturated)
1,690 mg sodium

On the Border's kids' menu mostly offers reasonable Mexican fare, but this cheese quesadilla, along with the nachos, stands out as a disturbing outlier. How the chain veers so far off course with this item, we don't know. Is it overloaded with cheese, or is the chicken poached in butter? Whatever the case, this quesadilla and rice provide more calories than should be in two kids' meals and enough sodium to cure a whole hog.

Eat This Instead!

Kid's Mexican Plate with Crispy Chicken Taco

260 calories
12 g fat (5 g saturated)
540 mg sodium

WORST KIDS' MEAL IN AMERICA

1 The Cheesecake Factory Kids Pasta with Alfredo Sauce

1,810 calories
N/A g fat (89 g saturated)
652 mg sodium

It's no surprise that America's worst restaurant for adult food also offers the Worst Kids' Meal in America. Heck, nine of its children's meals contain more than 800 calories. The Factory's blatant disregard for restraint is evidenced by the fact that this dish contains nearly a full day's calories for a grown adult—and that's not this meal's worst crime. The saturated fat content can only be fully understood by making grotesque comparisons: Taking in the 89 grams of saturated fat clinging to these noodles would require your child to consume nearly 2 pounds of Jimmy Dean Pork Sausage.

Eat This Instead!

Kids Pasta with Marinara Sauce

510 calories
N/A g fat (2 g saturated)
651 mg sodium

1,810 calories

With this Alfredo nightmare, Cheesecake Factory proves once again why it's America's Worst Restaurant.

The Eat This, Not That! No-Diet Cheat Sheets

Find the best and worst versions of all your kid's favorite foods

BURGERS

		CALORIES	FAT (g)	SATURATED (g)	SODIUM (mg)
1.	**Wendy's Kids' Meal Cheeseburger**	260	11	5	570
2.	**Red Robin Kids Rad Robin Burger**	286	12	N/A	380
3.	**Carl's Jr. Kid's Cheeseburger**	290	15	7	790
4.	**McDonald's Happy Meal Cheeseburger** (sandwich only)	300	12	6	750
5.	**Burger King Kids Cheeseburger**	300	14	6	710
6.	**Chili's Pepper Pals Little Mouth Cheeseburger**	400	24	10	950
7.	**Applebee's Kids Mini Cheeseburger**	430	30	9	610
8.	**Outback Steakhouse Joey Boomerang Cheese Burger**	488	21	11	949
9.	**IHOP Just for Kids Cheeseburger**	500	28	13	780
10.	**On the Border Kid's Cheeseburger**	530	42	15	300
11.	**Uno Chicago Grill Kid's Cheeseburger**	700	41	12	1,620
12.	**Ruby Tuesday Kid's Beef Minis**	776	41	N/A	1,559

FRIES

	CALORIES	FAT (g)	SATURATED (g)	SODIUM (mg)
1. **Chili's Pepper Pals Side Homestyle Fries**	190	7	2	600
2. **Red Robin Kids Steak Fries**	217	9	N/A	222
3. **Burger King French Fries** (Value size)	220	11	2.5	340
4. **McDonald's French Fries** (small)	230	11	1.5	160
5. **Carl's Jr. Kids Natural-Cut Fries**	240	12	2	490
6. **Bob Evans Kids' French Fries**	319	13	3	92
7. **Romano's Macaroni Grill Kids Side Fries**	320	14	4	820
8. **Friendly's My Meals Waffle Fries**	390	22	3	950
9. **Applebee's Side Fries**	390	18	3.5	720
10. **Olive Garden Children's Selections Fries**	400	21	2	880
11. **Ruby Tuesday French Fries**	426	18	N/A	1,769
12. **Denny's Kids' Finish Line Fries**	430	23	5	95

CHICKEN FINGER FOODS

		CALORIES	FAT (g)	SATURATED (g)	SODIUM (mg)
1.	**Wendy's Kids' Nuggets** (4)	180	11	2.5	370
2.	**Burger King Chicken Tenders** (4)	190	11	2	310
3.	**McDonald's Chicken McNuggets** (4, Happy Meal)	190	12	2	360
4.	**Carl's Jr. Kid's Hand-Breaded Chicken Tenders** (2)	220	12	2.5	770
5.	**Chick-fil-A Chicken Tenders** (2)	240	11	2	820
6.	**Applebee's Kids Chicken Tenders**	240	14	3	600
7.	**KFC Kids Popcorn Chicken**	260	17	3.5	690
8.	**Olive Garden Children's Selections Chicken Fingers**	330	16	1.5	930
9.	**Chili's Pepper Pals Crispy Chicken Crispers**	380	22	4	630
10.	**Red Lobster Kids' Cove Chicken Fingers**	410	24	2	1,320
11.	**Outback Steakhouse Joey Kookaburra Chicken Fingers**	676	41	12	1,942
12.	**The Cheesecake Factory Kids Fried Chicken Strips**	810	N/A	8	1,306

PASTA

		CALORIES	FAT (g)	SATURATED (g)	SODIUM (mg)
1.	**Olive Garden Children's Selections Spaghetti**	250	3	0.5	370
2.	**Red Lobster Kids' Cove Macaroni & Cheese**	280	7	2	590
3.	**Applebee's Kids' Kraft Macaroni & Cheese**	300	9	2.5	570
4.	**Uno Chicago Grill Kid's Macaroni & Cheese**	440	14	4	820
5.	**Ruby Tuesday Kid's Pasta Marinara**	469	7	N/A	978
6.	**Chili's Pepper Pals Kraft Macaroni & Cheese**	500	18	6	930
7.	**Olive Garden Children's Selections Fettuccine Alfredo**	510	32	19	450
8.	**The Cheesecake Factory Kids Pasta with Meat Sauce**	580	N/A	5	612
9.	**Outback Steakhouse Joey Mac-A-Roo 'N Cheese**	681	32	19	1,257
10.	**Romano's Macaroni Grill Kids Romano's Mac & Cheese**	690	35	21	1,500
11.	**The Cheesecake Factory Kids Macaroni and Cheese**	920	N/A	30	890
12.	**California Pizza Kitchen Kids Curly Mac N' Cheese**	1,041	N/A	33	735

HEALTHY ENTRÉES

		Calories	Fat (g)	Saturated (g)	Sodium (mg)
1.	**Red Lobster Kids' Cove Garlic Grilled Shrimp Skewer**	60	1	0	580
2.	**Subway Kids Black Forest Ham Sub**	180	2.5	0.5	470
3.	**Red Lobster Kids' Cove Grilled Chicken**	210	4	1	710
4.	**Bob Evans Kids Fruit Dippers**	222	1	0	62
5.	**Chili's Pepper Pals Grilled Chicken Sandwich**	230	5	1	230
6.	**Outback Steakhouse Joey Grilled Chicken on the Barbie**	263	14	7	189
7.	**Au Bon Pain Kid's Roasted Turkey Sandwich on Farmhouse Roll**	270	7	2	780
8.	**On the Border Grilled Chicken and Black Beans**	270	4	1	1,190
9.	**Panera Bread Kids Smoked Turkey Deli Sandwich**	290	8	5	1,100
10.	**Ruby Tuesday Kid's Chicken Breast**	294	12	N/A	824
11.	**Olive Garden Children's Selections Grilled Chicken with Pasta**	310	5	1	680
12.	**Uno Chicago Grill Kid's Chicken Caesar Salad**	320	20	4	840

PIZZAS

		CALORIES	FAT (g)	SATURATED (g)	SODIUM (mg)
1.	**Romano's Macaroni Grill Kids Pepperoni Pizza**	440	18	10	1,190
2.	**Olive Garden Children's Selections Italian Cheese Pizza** (no toppings)	470	14	6	1,170
3.	**Applebee's Kids' Cheese Pizza**	550	31	13	1,280
4.	**Chili's Pepper Pals Cheese Pizza**	570	24	9	1,120
5.	**Red Robin Red's Cheese Pizza**	605	27	N/A	1,465
6.	**California Pizza Kitchen Kids Traditional Cheese Pizza**	637	N/A	8	1,337
7.	**Uno Chicago Grill Kid's Deep Dish Cheese Pizza**	820	56	16	1,160
8.	**The Cheesecake Factory Kids Cheese Pizza**	840	N/A	14	1,504

DESSERTS

		CALORIES	FAT (g)	SATURATED (g)	CARBS (g)
1.	**Red Lobster Kids' Cove Surf's Up Sundae**	170	9	6	20
2.	**Olive Garden Children's Selections Sundae**	180	9	6	21
3.	**Applebee's Kids' Vanilla Sundae with Hershey's Syrup**	330	14	9	49
4.	**On the Border Kiddie Sundae with Chocolate Syrup**	370	18	13	51
5.	**Uno Chicago Grill Kid's Sundae**	430	19	10	58
6.	**Chili's Pepper Pals Choc-A-Lot Shake**	460	22	14	61
7.	**California Pizza Kitchen Kids M&Ms Sundae**	509	N/A	21	43
8.	**Ruby Tuesday Kid Sundae**	574	29	N/A	71
9.	**TGI Friday's Kid's Sundae**	640	N/A	N/A	N/A
10.	**Denny's Kids' Oreo Blender Blaster**	690	33	17	88
11.	**Outback Steakhouse Joey Spotted Dog Sundae**	1,216	94	59	89

7

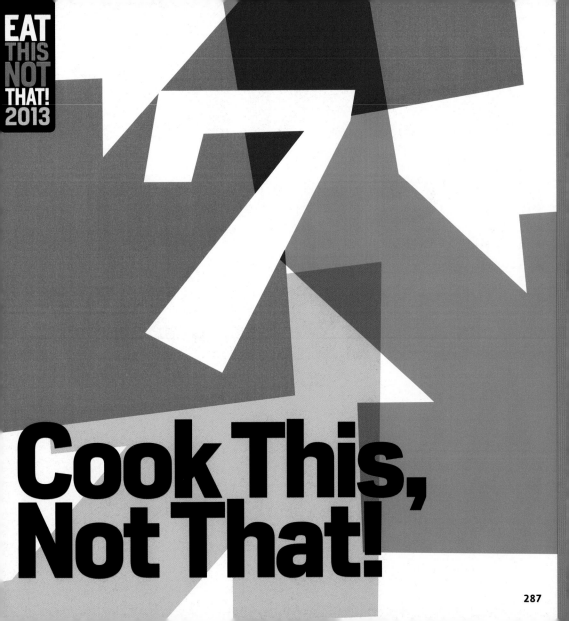

Cook This, Not That!

We Know It's Been a Long Day. A Long Week.

We Understand That You're Tired.

BUT SINCE WHEN is going out to eat any easier than cooking at home? By the time you've loaded up the family or coordinated with friends, you've already lost 30 minutes. You wait a few minutes or more for a table, another 10 to order, 20 minutes or more for your food. When all is said and done, you've invested 2 hours and about $25 dollars per person in a meal you could have bettered at home for a fraction of the cost, time, and effort. To wit: The average meal in this chapter takes approximately 17 minutes to prepare and costs $2.82 per serving.

On the flip side, the restaurant meals we replace average $10.75 (and that's without tax, tip, dessert, or drinks) and pack an astounding 1,087 calories per plate. That's three times more calories than you'll find in the average home-cooked meal in the pages to come. Fire up the stovetop just one more time a week and you and everyone at the table will drop nearly 11 pounds this year. Not bad.

But if shedding pounds and saving time and pocketing hard-earned cash aren't really your thing, we offer one last piece of motivation for experimenting with a few of these recipes: Every last morsel is downright delicious. Good luck finding that at your neighborhood Applebee's.

Eat This!

Mushroom-Sausage-Caramelized Onion Pizza

In an ideal world, every pizza would start out as a fresh mound of homemade dough and end up in a raging hot wood-burning oven, but few of us have the time or the equipment to pull it off. The good news is that even shortcut pizza can be hugely satisfying and, when done right, healthy enough to become a weekday staple. Here we split a baguette, line it with sauce, then top the entire thing with a sweet-savory mixture of caramelized onions, turkey sausage, cremini mushrooms, and smoked mozzarella. Add a light salad and ring the dinner bell.

You'll Need:

1½ Tbsp olive oil

2 links fresh Italian-style chicken or turkey sausage

1 medium onion, sliced

½ lb cremini mushrooms, stemmed and sliced

¼ lb shiitake mushrooms, stemmed and sliced

Salt and ground black pepper to taste

1 can (14 oz) whole peeled tomatoes

1 baguette or ciabatta, split in half lengthwise

1¼ cups grated smoked mozzarella or fontina

A few pinches of dried thyme or herbes de Provence

How to Make It:

- Heat ½ tablespoon of the olive oil in a medium sauté pan set over medium heat. Remove the sausage from the casing, breaking up the meat into bite-size pieces, and sauté until just cooked through, about 4 minutes. Remove the sausage from the pan. Add more oil if needed, then add the onions and mushrooms to the same pan. Sauté until nicely browned and softened, about 10 minutes. Season with salt and pepper to taste.
- Preheat the oven to 375°F. Combine the tomatoes with the remaining olive oil and season with salt to taste. Spread the tomato sauce evenly over both halves of the baguette, then top with the cheese, sausage, mushrooms, and onions, plus a bit of thyme.
- Place the pizzas directly on the center rack of the oven and cook until the cheese is lightly browned and bubbling, 15 to 20 minutes. Cut into wedges and serve (with a salad, preferably).

Makes 4 servings

Per Serving: $3.12

420 calories
18 g fat (6 g saturated)
920 mg sodium

MEAL MULTIPLIER

Low-calorie pizzas can be formed with any number of basic supermarket staples. Try one of these combinations baked in a 375°F oven for 15 minutes.

- English muffins topped with pesto, roasted red peppers, chopped olives, and feta cheese
- Whole-wheat pitas topped with barbecue sauce, shredded chicken, smoked Gouda, red onion, pineapple, and jalapeño chili peppers
- Ciabatta split widthwise, covered with cherry tomatoes, and topped with fresh mozzarella before baking and then with arugula and prosciutto before eating

Eat This!

Grilled Vietnamese Steak

Few cuisines pack more flavor into fewer calories than Vietnamese. Citrus, chili peppers, fresh herbs—all of these add huge flavor and big doses of antioxidants to almost any classic Vietnamese recipe you'll find. And all of these are at the heart of this dish. It looks like a lot of ingredients, but the recipe itself couldn't be simpler: a grilled steak salad with vermicelli noodles standing in for lettuce, plus a few high-impact garnishes. Try it with pork tenderloin or chicken breast, if you prefer.

You'll Need:

- ¼ cup fish sauce or soy sauce
- 2 Tbsp honey
- ½ tsp ground black pepper
- 1 lb flank, skirt, or hanger steak
- 2 medium carrots, cut into matchsticks
- 1 large cucumber, peeled, seeded, and cut into matchsticks
- ¼ cup rice wine vinegar
- 1 tsp salt
- ½ Tbsp sugar
- ¼ cup water
- 4 oz rice noodles (preferably vermicelli)
- Juice of 2 limes
- 1 Tbsp chili garlic sauce
- 1 Tbsp canola or peanut oil
- ¼ cup peanuts, chopped
- ¼ cup chopped mint
- ¼ cup chopped fresh cilantro

How to Make It:

- Combine the fish sauce, 1 tablespoon of the honey, and the pepper in a flat baking dish or sealable plastic bag. Add the steak and marinate in the refrigerator for at least 30 minutes (and up to 4 hours) before cooking.
- Combine the carrots and cucumber in a mixing bowl. Add the vinegar, salt, sugar, and water. Stir until the salt and sugar are evenly mixed, then let the vegetables pickle in the vinegar mixture for at least 30 minutes before eating.
- Preheat a grill over medium heat. While the grill is warming up, cook the noodles according to package directions. Reserve.
- Grill the steak for 3 to 4 minutes per side (depending on thickness), until nicely charred on the surface and firm but yielding to the touch. Let the steak rest for 5 minutes before slicing.
- While the steak rests, combine the lime juice, chili garlic sauce, remaining 1 tablespoon of honey, and oil in a mixing bowl. Whisk until evenly blended.
- Divide the noodles among four bowls. Top with the vegetables, peanuts, mint, cilantro, and steak and pour a bit of the lime-chili sauce over the top.

Makes 4 servings

Per Serving: **$3.62**

400 calories
14 g fat (3 g saturated)
730 mg sodium

Balsamic Chicken Breasts

The best thing that can be said about a chicken breast—apart from the fact that it's a lean, powerful source of protein—is that it takes well to outside flavors. This balsamic barbecue sauce is pretty amazing stuff: Six ingredients that everyone has in their pantry come together to make a complex, deeply satisfying sauce that elevates the prosaic chicken breast to delicious new heights. It tastes every bit as good when painted onto pork chops, duck breasts, or flank steak.

You'll Need:

- 1 cup ketchup
- 1 cup balsamic vinegar
- 1 Tbsp brown sugar
- 1 Tbsp Dijon mustard
- 1 Tbsp Worcestershire sauce
- 1 clove garlic, minced
- 4 small chicken breasts (about 6 oz each)
- Salt and black pepper to taste

How to Make It:

- Bring the ketchup, vinegar, brown sugar, mustard, Worcestershire, and garlic to a simmer in a saucepan set over medium heat. Simmer for about 5 minutes, until the liquid has reduced by half and the sauce is thick like a bottled barbecue sauce. Allow the sauce to cool, then set aside half of the sauce to serve with the chicken.
- Preheat a grill over medium heat. Season the chicken with salt and pepper. Paint the chicken all over with a thin layer of sauce from the saucepan and place on the grill. Cook for 2 minutes, turn the breasts 45 degrees, and cook for another 2 minutes, until nice diamond-shaped grill marks have developed. Flip, brush one more time with the sauce, and grill for another 3 minutes, until the chicken is firm to the touch and an instant-read thermometer inserted into the thickest part of the chicken registers 160°F. Brush the chicken with the reserved barbecue sauce before serving.

Makes 4 servings

Per Serving: $1.97

270 calories
4.5 g fat (1 g saturated)
610 mg sodium

Eat This!

Roasted Halibut
with Spring Gazpacho

This is the type of dish you pay $29 for at a fancy downtown restaurant, yet even a novice cook can produce it at home in 30 minutes. The key is to get excellent, fresh fish; halibut is a favorite, but freshness trumps variety, so feel free to try it with cod, salmon, or even ahi tuna. If cash is a factor, look beyond halibut to more affordable alternatives like flounder, mahi mahi, or red snapper. As the name of the dish implies, this works best in the spring months, when asparagus and peas are sweet and tender and in thick supply, but you can pull it off any time of year.

You'll Need:

- 12 spears asparagus, woody ends removed, cut into 1-inch pieces
- 1 cup green peas
- 4 halibut fillets (6 oz each)
- 1 Tbsp olive oil + more for rubbing
- Salt and ground black pepper to taste
- ½ clove garlic
- 8 leaves mint
- Juice of 1 lemon
- ¼ cup Greek yogurt
- 2 Tbsp water

How to Make It:

- Preheat the oven to 325°F.
- Bring a small pot of water to a boil. When it is fully boiling, add a few pinches of salt. Add the asparagus and cook for 90 seconds. Add the peas and cook for 1 minute more, then drain and run cold water over the vegetables for 30 seconds.
- Rub the halibut with olive oil and season all over with salt and pepper. Place the fillets in a roasting pan and cook until the fish flakes with gentle pressure from your finger, 12 to 15 minutes.
- While the halibut cooks, combine half of the peas, half of the asparagus, the garlic, mint, the tablespoon of olive oil, lemon juice, yogurt, and 2 tablespoons water in a blender. Blend on high until you have a smooth puree. Season it to taste with salt.
- Divide the remaining asparagus and peas among four wide, shallow bowls. Pour the asparagus-pea puree over them. Place a halibut fillet on top of each.

Makes 4 servings

Per Serving: $5.67

270 calories
8 g fat (1.5 g saturated)
250 mg sodium

Eat This!

Cowboy Burgers

We're not afraid to admit when a fast-food joint has a good idea. The inspiration for this burger comes from a Carl's Jr. classic, the Western Bacon Cheeseburger, a how-can-it-not-be-delicious comingling of beef, barbecue sauce, and fried onions. Problem is, the small version of Carl's burger packs 740 calories and a full day's worth of saturated fat. This version uses naturally lean bison and replaces the breaded onion rings with sweet grilled ones.

You'll Need:

- 1 lb ground bison or beef sirloin
- 1 medium red onion, sliced into ¼"-thick rings and skewered with toothpicks
- ½ Tbsp finely ground coffee
- 1 tsp chipotle or ancho chile powder
- Salt and black pepper to taste
- 4 slices sharp Cheddar
- 4 sesame seed buns, lightly toasted
- 6 strips bacon, cooked until crisp and halved
- 4 Tbsp barbeque sauce

How to Make It:

- Gently form the meat into 4 patties, being careful not to overwork the meat. Let the patties rest for 15 minutes.
- Preheat the grill or grill pan over medium heat. Grill the onion slices, turning, for about 10 minutes, until soft and lightly charred. Just before cooking the patties, season them on both sides with the coffee, chile powder, and salt and pepper. Grill the patties alongside the onions for about 4 minutes, until nicely browned. Flip, top with the cheese, and continue grilling for 3 to 4 minutes longer, until the centers of the patties are firm but gently yielding to the touch and an instant-read thermometer inserted into the thickest part of a burger registers 135°F.
- Place the burgers on the bun bottoms, and top with onions, bacon, and barbecue sauce.

Makes 4 servings

We have no idea if cowboys actually eat burgers, but if they did, they would taste an awful lot like this one.

Normally we're not huge fans of heavily spiced burgers, but the coffee here adds a roasted depth to the burger that pairs beautifully with the barbecue sauce and bacon.

Per Serving: $2.62

460 calories
22 g fat (11 g saturated)
850 mg sodium

Eat This!

Roasted Butternut Squash Salad

Butternut squash is an *ETNT* Hall of Fame vegetable, delicious enough to crave year-round and nutritionally powerful enough to fight off a multitude of maladies, from cancer to vision problems to inflammation. So when fall rolls around, we try to find as many ways as possible to work it into meals: stuffed into raviolis, pureed into soup, and, as seen here, playing the base of a seriously tasty salad. Roasted until soft and sweet, it anchors a salad that is at turns creamy, tart, sweet, and spicy. Add a cup of soup for one of the healthiest autumn meals imaginable.

You'll Need:

- 1 butternut (or other firm winter) squash, peeled, seeded, and cut into ¼-inch-thick crescents
- 3 Tbsp olive oil + additional for coating
- Salt and ground black pepper to taste
- 2 Tbsp balsamic vinegar
- 1 small red onion, thinly sliced
- ¼ cup chopped pecans
- 8 cups arugula or mixed greens
- ½ cup crumbled goat cheese
- Seeds of 1 pomegranate

How to Make It:

- Preheat the oven to 400°F. Toss the squash with just enough oil to coat it and season it with salt and pepper. Arrange the crescents on a baking tray, making sure the pieces don't overlap. Roast until the squash is lightly caramelized on the outside and tender throughout, about 20 minutes. Set the tray on the stovetop to cool for 5 minutes.
- While the squash cools, combine the vinegar and onions in a large mixing bowl with goodly pinches of salt and black pepper. Let it sit for 5 minutes, then stir in the olive oil. Add the squash, pecans, greens, cheese, and seeds to the bowl and mix thoroughly, until all of the ingredients are lightly coated.

Makes 4 servings

Per Serving: $2.90

360 calories
23 g fat (7 g saturated)
290 mg sodium

Prepping Squash

A butternut squash's size and shape make it an awkward vegetable to cut, but do it once and it's yours for life. Separate the squash into two manageable parts by cutting across the long neck right where it meets the bulbous bottom. Use a very sharp vegetable peeler or a chef's knife to peel the squash, then halve each part vertically. Remove the seeds from the base (save those for toasting, if you like) and cut all four pieces into wedges or cubes, depending on what the recipe calls for.

Chipotle Turkey Meatballs

Anyone who has read our recipes before will know that we're unabashed fans of chipotle peppers. It's not just because they're spicy; it's because these tricked-out jalapeños carry a huge smoky punch and a subtle sweetness that adds instant depth and deliciousness to sauces, stews, and condiments. It's the secret weapon in these meatballs, the single ingredient that takes them from standard to superb.

You'll Need:

- ½ Tbsp oil
- 1 small yellow onion, finely chopped
- 3 cloves garlic, minced
- 1 lb ground turkey
- 2 eggs
- ½ cup bread crumbs
- ½ cup chopped cilantro or parsley + additional for garnish (optional)
- 2 pinches of ground cinnamon
- Pinch of nutmeg
- Salt and ground black pepper to taste
- 1 can (32 oz) crushed tomatoes
- 1 canned chipotle pepper + 1 Tbsp marinade
- ½ cup chicken stock

How to Make It:

- Heat the oil in a saucepan over medium heat. Sauté the onion and garlic until they're soft and translucent, about 5 minutes.
- Preheat the oven to 400°F. Combine the turkey, eggs, bread crumbs, cilantro or parsley, a pinch of cinnamon, the nutmeg, and a few generous pinches of salt and black pepper. Fold in half of the onion-garlic mixture, reserving the rest. Gently mix the ingredients until blended. Form golf-ball-size meatballs and arrange them in a baking dish. Bake until they're browned on the outside, about 15 minutes.
- Return the pan with the remaining onion mixture to the stove over medium heat. Add the tomatoes, chipotle and marinade, and chicken stock, plus a pinch of cinnamon and salt and black pepper to taste. Simmer while the meatballs cook.
- When the meatballs are browned, remove the baking dish from the oven, pour the sauce over them, and return the dish to the oven. Cook for another 15 minutes. Serve the meatballs by themselves or over brown rice, polenta, or sautéed spinach.

Makes 4 servings

Per Serving: $2.30

380 calories
16 g fat (4 g saturated)
800 mg sodium

LEFTOVER♥LOVE

Surplus meatballs are one of the great scores of the leftovers world. Here are just a few of the many glorious ways to bring them back to life.

- Chop into rough pieces, stuff into warm corn tortillas, and top with onions, cilantro, and chunks of avocado
- Tuck into a hoagie or soft roll, top with Jack cheese, and place under the broiler until the cheese is melted
- Chop into rough pieces and use to top homemade pizza

Eat This!

Pork Tonkatsu

Leave it to Japanese cooks to find a way to turn a breaded and fried piece of pork into something light and refreshing. The secret is in the panko bread crumbs, which are flatter and lighter than normal bread crumbs, so they crisp up into a beautiful crust without much effort (or oil). The tonkatsu sauce—a dead-simple mixture of common pantry ingredients—is the type of delicious condiment you'll want to slather on everything.

You'll Need:

- 4 pork cutlets, pounded to a uniform ¼-inch thickness
- ¾ tsp salt
- ½ cup ketchup
- 1 tsp Dijon mustard
- 2 Tbsp soy sauce
- 2 Tbsp Worcestershire sauce
- 3 Tbsp canola or peanut oil
- 2 eggs
- 1 ½ cups panko bread crumbs
- Steamed brown rice (optional)
- 4 cups finely shredded cabbage

How to Make It:

- Two hours before cooking, salt the cutlets generously on both sides. Return them to the refrigerator until you're ready to cook.
- In a mixing bowl, combine the ketchup, mustard, soy sauce, and Worcestershire sauce. Whisk until evenly blended. Reserve.
- Heat the oil in a large, shallow sauté pan over medium heat. Crack the eggs into a bowl and beat. Place the bread crumbs on a large plate or shallow baking dish. Working with one cutlet at a time, dredge it in the egg, then cover it thoroughly with bread crumbs (using your fingers to press in the bread crumbs if necessary). Cook for 2 to 3 minutes per side, until crispy and golden brown.
- Serve over steamed brown rice, if you like, with the shredded cabbage and the sauce for spooning over it on the side.

Makes 4 servings

Per Serving: **$2.62**

310 calories
10 g fat (2 g saturated)
840 mg sodium

Though this dish comes out surprisingly lean, you can trim another 50 calories per serving from the total by turning this into baked pork tonkatsu. Follow the same instructions, but instead of frying them, place the breaded cutlets on a lightly oiled baking sheet and cook in a 400°F preheated oven until the bread crumbs are golden brown, about 15 minutes. Want to take it down even lower? Try the same dish, but with boneless skinless chicken breasts, or even fish fillets.

Eat This!

Moroccan Braised Chicken

North African cuisine relies heavily on the spice cabinet, which is why we love turning to places like Morocco when looking for ways to transform chicken into something special without elevating calorie or fat counts. The potent blend of cumin, cayenne, and cinnamon does just that, infusing the slow-cooked chicken with a sweet, smoky, spicy flavor while improving the overall nutritional profile of the dish (remember: dried spices = powerful antioxidants). Add in vegetables, fiber-rich garbanzos, and a bed of fluffy couscous and you have a meal long on nutrition and flavor, and short on calories and fat.

You'll Need:

- ½ Tbsp olive oil
- 1 lb boneless, skinless chicken thighs
- Salt and ground black pepper to taste
- 1 large zucchini, chopped
- 1 can (12 oz) garbanzo beans
- 1 can (12 oz) diced tomatoes
- ¼ cup golden raisins or chopped dried apricots
- 1 cup chicken stock or water
- ½ tsp cayenne
- ½ tsp cinnamon
- 1 tsp cumin
- 1 cup couscous
- Chopped fresh cilantro for garnish

How to Make It:

- Heat the oil in a large sauté pan or wide pot over medium-high heat. Season the chicken to taste with salt and black pepper and add it to the pan. Brown thoroughly on both sides. Add the zucchini and continue cooking.
- When the zucchini is lightly browned, add the garbanzos, tomatoes, raisins, and chicken stock and season with the cayenne, cinnamon, and cumin. Turn the heat down to low and simmer for 15 to 20 minutes, until the chicken is tender and cooked through. Season with salt and black pepper. Prepare the couscous according to package directions.
- Serve each portion with a scoop of the couscous and garnish with cilantro.

Makes 4 servings

Per Serving: **$2.17**

440 calories
11 g fat (2 g saturated)
790 mg sodium

S'mores

Chocolate–Peanut Butter & Chocolate-Caramel

In the 80-odd years since the first known recipe for s'mores surfaced in an obscure Girl Scout publication, very little has changed with the campfire classic; it had the same three ingredients back then as it does now: graham crackers, chocolate, marshmallow. Admittedly, it's tough to improve upon the time-tested formula, but having used the original as our inspiration and the grill as our muse, we think these two new iterations would do the Girl Scouts proud.

You'll Need:

- 8 large marshmallows
- 8 metal skewers, or wooden skewers soaked in water for 30 minutes
- 2 Tbsp dulce de leche
- 16 chocolate wafer cookies (like Nabisco Famous Chocolate Wafers)
- 2 Tbsp smooth peanut butter

Dulce de leche is a special type of caramel popular in Latin America. It's now widely available in the States, but if you can't find it, standard caramel sauce will do.

How to Make It:

- Preheat a grill over medium heat. Place a marshmallow at the end of each skewer. (If everyone wants to toast their own marshmallows, pass them around to guests.) Grill the marshmallows, turning, for about 3 minutes, until lightly brown and toasted all over. If using a charcoal grill, remove the grate and roast the marshmallows close to the coals; if using a gas grill, you can place directly on the hot grate.
- Spread ½ tablespoon of dulce de leche on each of 4 cookies and spread ½ tablespoon of peanut butter on each of another 4 cookies. Top each with a toasted marshmallow and another cookie. If you like, place the s'mores directly on the grill just long enough to warm, 1 to 2 minutes.

Makes 4 servings

Per Serving: $1.02

330 calories
13 g fat (3 g saturated)
29 g sugars

While swapping in peanut butter for chocolate in this recipe constitutes a step up in the nutrition status of the s'more, there are even greater strides that can be made while not sacrificing the overall feeling of decadence. Try pairing slices of banana with the peanut butter, slices of apple or pear with dulce de leche, or, in a riff on the classic s'mores construction, thick slices of strawberry with antioxidant-rich dark chocolate.

Index

Boldface page references indicate photographs. Underscored references indicate boxed text.

C

D

E

F

L

M

N